中国文化释疑

A HUNDRED QUESTIONS ON THE CHINESE CULTURE

主　编: 金乃逯

编　者: 金乃逯　　马衍森
　　　　李　瑜　　郑　欣

翻　译: 吕新莉　　刘　昕
　　　　李　瑜　　马衍森

北京语言文化大学出版社

BEIJING LANGUAGE AND CULTURE UNIVERSITY PRESS

1999

▲北京北海九龙壁
The 9-Dragon Screen at Beihai Park in Beijing

▲北京孔庙
The Confucious Temple in Beijing

▲天安门前的华表
The Ornamental Pillar in Front of Tian'anmen

▼ 云南大理县崇圣寺三塔
The Three Pagodas in Saint Temple in Dali County, Yunnan Province

▲北京十三陵牌楼
The Memorial Archway at the Ming Tombs in Beijing

▲北京真觉寺塔
The Pagoda in Zhenjue Temple in Beijing

前　言

在对外汉语教学中，外国人常常向老师提出一些有关中国传统文化的问题。这一方面说明外国人越来越对灿烂的中国文化感兴趣；另一方面也说明对外汉语教学中文化导入是不可缺少的部分。本书正是为了弘扬中华文化，为对外汉语教学的文化导入提供一些有用的材料而编写的。中国文化博大精深，要在一本小册子中全面介绍是很困难的。本书仅就一些在教学中常常涉及到的问题，做简明扼要的解释。为了便于外国朋友直接阅读，采取汉英对照的方式。本书也可供对中国文化有兴趣的中外朋友参考。

本书中文部分承程裕祯先生审阅校正，特表示感谢！

本书英译部分承高福圣、陈坤如、程绍富三位先生审阅，并提出宝贵意见。在全书编辑中，北京语言文化大学出版社王素云女士做了艰苦细致的工作。谨此一并致谢。

在编写中，我们参阅了大量文献、著作，篇幅所限，不能一一列举，谨向前辈专家、学者致谢！

由于编译人员水平所限，错误疏漏之处定有不少，尚希广大读者指正。

编　者
1999 年

PREFACE

When teaching foreigners Chinese, teachers often meet many questions about Chinese culture put forward by their students. This indicates that foreigners are becoming more and more interested in the glorious Chinese culture; and on the other hand, it also indicates that cultural introduction in teaching Chinese as a foreign language is a part that can not be ignored. The compilation of this book is to supply some useful materials for Chinese teaching with a view to spread Chinese culture. Since Chinese culture is so rich and colorful, it is surely impossible to give an overall introduction in such a small book. In this book, we will give very brief explanations to those questions frequently popping up in our teaching. To make it easier for foreigners to read, we also provide English translations. However, we should specify that not every article in this book has been translated word by word.

Hereby we would like to acknowledge Mr. Cheng Yuzhen for his revising the Chinese part of the articles in the book, and Professor Wang Yuju for his proof-reading a number of our English translations.

Special thanks go to Messes. Gao Fusheng, Chen Kunru and Cheng Shaofu, who share the work of examining the English version and making a great deal of valuable comments. We would also like to express our thanks to Ms. Wang Suyun from Beijing Language and Culture University Press, whose conscientious and detailed editorial work is a big contribution to the final publication of this book.

We would also like to acknowledge many authors because we have taken their works as reference in compiling our book. Their names will not be listed here because of a big number of them.

authors
1999

目　录

语言文字

古代思想家

宗　教

戏曲与音乐

绘画、书法和艺术

中医中药

民间传说

民俗

国名、制度

古代书籍

古代建筑

古代称谓

古代科技

其　　他

CONTENTS

Language and Characters

Ancient Thinkers

Religion

Drama and Music

Painting, Calligraphy and Art

Chinese Medicine

Folk Legend

Folk Customs

Names and Systems

Ancient Books

Ancient Architecture

Ancient Forms of Address

Ancient Technology

Miscellaneous

1. 甲骨文是什么文字?

中国古代曾流行过用龟甲和兽骨占卜的习俗,就是把龟甲或兽骨加以烧灼,观察烧灼后形成的裂纹的形状并据以判断吉凶。在许多新石器时代晚期的遗址里,都曾发现有卜骨。80年代在河南舞阳县贾湖新石器时代遗址曾发现距今约8000年的带有契刻符号的甲骨。但人们通常所说的甲骨文是指商代(约公元前1600~约前1100年)的今人可以释读的卜骨上的契刻文字。

甲骨文代表商代的文字,距今已有3000多年的历史了,但是直到上个世纪末本世纪初才被发现并确认为是商代的文字。甲骨的最早发掘者是河南安阳县小屯村附近的农民。那里是中国古代商朝国都的遗址,农民在田地里耕作时常常掘出一些龟甲和兽骨。然而他们只是把捡拾到的甲骨作为药材卖给药店并名之曰"龙骨"。1899年,北京著名的金石学家王懿荣有一次患病,从中药店购得的药材里偶然发现龙骨上刻有"文字"。王以其深厚的古文字知识对龙骨上的文字进行了鉴定,认为是商代的文字。从此,甲骨文才为人们所知。

王懿荣死后,他所藏甲骨为刘鹗所得。刘鹗又经多方收集,到1903年已获甲骨5000余片。他从中选出1058片进行拓印,并于当年出版了第一部甲骨文著录《铁云藏龟》。第二年,著名学者孙诒让根据《铁云藏龟》撰写的《契文举例》问世。这是第一部研究甲骨文的专著。

甲骨文从发现至今已有近100年的历史了。据专家统计,近100年来从安阳小屯及其附近出土甲骨共计10万片左右。这10万片甲骨是属于商代盘庚迁殷以后从武丁到帝乙时期,前后约200多年。甲骨主要出自殷墟,但其他地方也有发现。70年代在陕西原西周遗址曾两次出土甲骨,也包括有字甲骨。这说明甲骨不是殷墟所独有,也不仅仅限于商王朝。

殷墟出土的甲骨文代表商代文字。从已出土的甲骨文中发现的字数已超过5000,其中经过考释已经能释读的有1700多个。但这5000多甲骨文字并不是甲骨文的全部,除尚未出土的之外,还有相当数量的甲骨在当时或后来被毁坏了,包括一部分被人们当做药材服用了。

甲骨文字的结构是颇为复杂的,"六书"均可在甲骨文字中找到实例。因此,从甲骨文字的数量和字的结构,可以看出甲骨文已经是相当发展和成熟的文字体系。这说明甲骨文虽然是距今有3000多年历史的古老的文字,但它还不是中国最古老的文字,距文字的源头还有着一段相当长的时间。

甲骨文也称作卜辞,因为它是用来占卜的。而当时的文字也正是依靠甲骨这种特殊的材料才得以保存下来。甲骨上的文字绝大多数是用刀刻上去的,也有少部分是写上去的。由于商代统治者十分迷信,无论做什么事都要进行占卜,所以甲骨文的内容可以说是无所不包,是商代社会生活的真实记录,对研究商代的历史和社会有着非常重要的价值。

1. What Is *Jiaguwen*?

Divination with tortoise shells and animal bones was in vogue in ancient China. When a piece of shell or bone was burnt, fortune or luck could be told by studying how it cracked. Such shells and bones have been found in many sites of the Neolithic Age. In the 1980s, 8000-year-old inscribed shells and bones were unearthed in Jiahu, Wuyang County, Henan Province, one of the Neolithic Age sites. However, the term *jiaguwen* (oracle bone inscriptions) refers to the writing of the Shang Dynasty (c.1600—c.1100 B.C.) deciphered by modern Chinese scholars.

Jiaguwen, the Shang Dynasty writing, has a history of more than three thousand years. However, it was not discovered and identified as such until the threshold of the twentieth century. The first excavators of the oracle bones were farmers near Xiaotun Village of Anyang County, Henan Province. The place is the old site of the capital of the Shang Dynasty. The villagers often found pieces of tortoise shells and animal bones while working in the fields. They collected and sold them to the pharmacy as traditional Chinese medicine called "dragon bones". In 1899, Wang Yirong, a well-known paleographer in Beijing, was ill and bought some Chinese medicine in which he accidentally and surprisedly discovered that some "dragon bones" bore inscriptions. With his profound knowledge in paleography, he determined and established that they were the Shang Dynasty writing. Since then *jiaguwen* has become widely known.

After the death of Wang Yirong, his collection of oracle bones came into the possession of Liu E. Liu made further efforts to enlarge his collection and by 1903 he had obtained as many as over 5000 pieces. In the same year he picked out 1058 pieces from his entire collection to make rubbings, with which he published the first selection of *jiaguwen* entitled *Tie Yun Cang Gui* (*A Collection of Oracle Bones by Liu E*). The next year, Sun Yirang, a then noted scholar, completed his *Qiwen Juli* (*Decipherment of Some Inscribed Characters*), which was the result of his research work on *Tie Yun Cang*

Gui. This book is the first monograph on *jiaguwen*.

About a hundred years have passed since *jiaguwen* was discovered. According to statistics, oracle bones unearthed from Xiaotun Village and the nearby area over the past century amount to approximately 100000 pieces. These bones came from a period of more than two hundred years starting from the reign of Wuding to that of Diyi after Pangeng moved the capital of the Shang Dynasty to Yin. The oracle bones were mainly from the remains of Yin although they were also found in other places. In the 1970s, oracle bones, including the inscribed ones, were found twice in Shaanxi Province in the old site of the Western Zhou Dynasty. It proves that oracle bones do not belong to the remains of Yin and the Shang Dynasty only.

Jiaguwen represents the Shang Dynasty writing. The number of characters so far discovered has exceeded 5000 and over 1700 of them have been deciphered. However, these 5000 characters are of course not the entirety of *jiaguwen*. Apart from those that remain underground, there are a considerable number of bones which were either damaged in the Shang Dynasty or in later times, or taken by people as medicine.

The structure of *jiaguwen* as a written script is rather complicated and the *liu shu* (the six categories of Chinese characters) principles can all be applied in analyzing *jiaguwen*. Considering this and the number of characters in *jiaguwen*, we believe *jiaguwen* is surely not the oldest Chinese writing although it has a history of over three thousand years, and there is a fairly long period of time between *jiaguwen* and its fountainhead.

Jiaguwen is also known as *buci* (divination script) because they were used for divination. The durability of the shells and bones has made it possible for *jiaguwen* to be preserved till today. Most of the *jiaguwen* characters were engraved on the bones and shells with a few of them written. The rulers of the Shang Dynasty were all very superstitious, and whatever they did, they divined. As a result, *jiaguwen* covers a lot of ground and is the truthful record of the social life of the Shang Dynasty. It is of great value to the study of the history and society of the Shang Dynasty.

2. 什么是石鼓文？它是怎样被发现的？

石鼓文是秦刻石。它上边的文字是战国时期所使用的大篆。这些刻有文字的石头，因为样子像鼓，所以就叫石鼓文。

石鼓共有10个，是凿工比较粗糙的圆形石柱。他们的高低不尽相同，从46厘米到1米左右不等，其周长大约为2.3米。石鼓文是唐朝初年在陕西省凤翔府（今陕西宝鸡）被发现的，其内容是记述游猎，因此，石鼓文的另一个名字又叫"猎碣"。一般认为，它所记录的是周宣王（姬静）年间（公元前827～前782年）的事。

石鼓文到底有多少个字？历来说法不一。因为石鼓文被发现时，有一块石鼓上的字已完全不能辨认了，由于长期风吹日晒，大部分石鼓上的字已残缺不全，只有一块石鼓上的字比较清楚，容易辨认。据说，在秦代（公元前221～前206年）时，石鼓文一共有700个字。但宋代（公元960～1279年）的人说石鼓文有465个字，元代（公元1271～1368年）的人说有386个字，到了乾隆（公元1737～1796年）时期，石鼓文就只有310个字了。幸运的是，在宋代就有了石鼓文的拓片，这些拓片一直较好地保存了下来，到了明代嘉靖（公元1522～1567年）年间，人们又按照拓片上的字，重新刻在石头上。当时，石鼓文的字共有462个。

石鼓文被发现以来，经历了不少的磨难。在公元9世纪初，石鼓被安置在凤翔府的孔庙里，但在五代大动乱的年代里，石鼓失踪，再也见不到了。到了宋代才又把这些石鼓收集到了一起。后来，北宋和辽交战，北宋大败，皇朝南逃，把石鼓带到了当时的新京汴京（今开封），这是公元1108年的事。到了公元1126年金兵攻占汴京，石鼓落入金人手中，他们把石鼓运到了北京。但金代统治者并不重视这些艺术珍品，没有把石鼓放在孔庙或皇宫里。1307年，石鼓才被摆在孔庙的门口。从此以后，石鼓就一直放在那儿，现存故宫博物院。

2. What Is *Shiguwen*? How Was It Discovered?

Shiguwen refers to the stone inscriptions of the State of Qin. The characters on the stones were in *dazhuan* (greater seal script) style of the Warring States Period. Because these stones were drum-shaped, the characters on them got the name *shiguwen* (characters engraved on drum-shaped stones).

There were ten pieces of stones in roughly round shape. The heights of these stones varied from 46cm to 1m, and their girth was about 2.3m. *Shiguwen* was found in Fengxiang Prefecture (present Baoji), Shaanxi Province in the early Tang Dynasty. It carried narrations of hunting. Therefore, it got another name *liejie* (hunting stone tablet). It was usually believed that events described in these narrations happened in the reign of King Xuan of the Zhou Dynasty(827—782 B.C.).

How many characters were included in *shiguwen*? There were various sayings for this question. When *shiguwen* was found, characters on one of the stones were totally illegible because long time exposure in the open air had made many characters incomplete. There was only one piece of stone with fairly clear and legible characters. It was said that there were altogether 700 characters of *shiguwen* in the Qin Dynasty(221—206 B.C.); but record in the Song Dynasty(960—1279 A.D.) said there were 465 characters; record in the Yuan Dynasty(1271—1368 A.D.) said there were 386 characters; and record in the reign of Emperor Qianlong (1737—1796 A.D.) of the Qing Dynasty said there were only 310 characters. Fortunately, there were already rubbings from the stones in the Song Dynasty, and all these rubbings have been well preserved. In the reign of Emperor Jiajing(1522—1567 A.D.) of the Ming Dynasty, characters of the rubbings were re-inscribed on stones. At that time, there were about 462 characters.

Shiguwen has undergone quite a few hardships since it was found. In the early ninth century, the stones were kept in the Confucius temple of Fengxiang Prefecture. They were lost in the years of upheaval of the Five Dynasties. It was not until the Song Dynasty that these stones were gathered together again. When the Northern Song was defeated in the war against the State of Liao in 1108 A.D., the royal family fled to the new capital Bianjing(present Kaifeng) in south China. The stones were also carried down there. In 1126 A.D., when the soldiers of the State of Jin occupied Bianjing and got the stones, they took them back to Beijing. Unfortunately, the rulers of the Jin Dynasty did not treasure these relics very much. They did not keep the stones in the Confucius temple or in the imperial palace. It was not until 1307 A.D., were the stones placed at the gate of the Confucius temple. They are now preserved in the Palace Museum.

3. 中国第一部语法专著是哪本书？

中国第一部有完整体系的汉语语法专著是《马氏文通》，出版于1898年，作者是马建忠。

马建忠，字眉叔，生于1845年，江苏丹徒（现镇江市）人，是中国近代一位著名的语言学家。他31岁时曾被派往法国留学，后毕业于巴黎大学。在留学期间他曾兼任中国驻法国公使的翻译。他通晓拉丁文、希腊文、英文和法文，在国学和西文上均有很高的造诣。

中国传统的语言学是以对训诂、文字和音韵的研究为主，对虚词、语序、句读等的研究虽有涉及，但只是零散和片断的，并主要附属于传统的训诂学。由于汉语本身的结构特点及中国封建社会长期的封闭状态，对汉语语法的研究一直没有形成独立的科学的体系。到19世纪后半叶，随着中国逐步沦为半封建半殖民地社会，不少有志之士为拯救中华开始学习西方先进的科学技术。马建忠即是其中之一。在中西文化的对比中，他认识到要学习西方先进的科学技术，首先需要缩短学习本国文化的时间。而对照西文把隐寓在华文中的规律揭示出来，创建汉语的语法，就可以使孩童们通过语法规则较快地掌握中国的文化。为此，马建忠经过十余年的艰苦努力，完成了中国第一部系统的语法学专著《马氏文通》。

《马氏文通》是用文言写成的。这一巨著是马建忠在继承中国传统语言学成就的基础上，对先秦两汉的语言材料进行了深入的分析，并仿照拉丁文文法才完成的。全书共分十卷。第一卷是"正名"，作者通过23个"界说"就词法和句法阐述了自己的见解，是全书的总纲。第二卷至第九卷是"字类"，其中第二卷至第六卷讲述"实字"，第七卷至第九卷讲述"虚字"。第十卷是"句读"，是对句子各种成分的分析。词类的区分是中西语法比较研究的一大成果。马建忠把汉语的词分为两大类，即"实字"和"虚字"。实字又分为名字、代字、动字、静字和状字。虚字又分为介字、连字、助字和叹字。这种对汉语词的分类是十分严整和完备的。时至今日，汉语词的分类仍以此为基础，只不过从名字中独立出一类量词，从静字中独立出一类数词而已。马建忠把句子的成分分为起词、语词、止词、表词、司词、转词和加词七大类。起词相当于主语；语词相当于谓语；止词相当于宾语；表词相当于形容词谓语句中的谓语；司词指介词的宾语；转词较为复杂，一般指及物动词所带双宾语中的间接宾语，或指表示不及物动词的动作处所的成分；加词有两种，一种相当于介词短语，一种相当于同位语。

《马氏文通》的问世标志着汉语语法学已经从中国传统的小学中独立出来，标志着中国语法学的创立，是中国传统小学向现代语言学转变的起点，在中国语言学发展史上树立了一座里程碑。从此，语法的研究逐渐成为中国语言学中的一个重要门类。《马氏文通》

之后，不少语法书相继问世，使汉语语法的研究获得了较快的发展。

3. What Is the First Monograph on Chinese Grammar?

The first monograph on Chinese grammar is *Mashi Wentong* (*Master Ma's Introduction to Grammar*), a book of an integrated system. The book, written by Ma Jianzhong, was published in 1898.

Ma Jianzhong, also known as Ma Meishu, was born in Dantu (present Zhenjiang), Jiangsu Province in 1845. He was a celebrated philologist of modern China. Ma was sent to study in France at the age of thirty-one and graduated later from the University of Paris. While studying in France, he was concurrently the interpreter for Chinese counselor to France. Ma was not only of great attainments in Chinese studies, but also proficient in Latin, Greek, English and French.

Chinese traditional linguistics focused its studies on *xungu* (the study of classics, concerned with the ancient meaning of words), *wenzi* (the study of ancient forms of the written characters) and *yinyun* (phonology). Although the study of form words, word order, syntax, etc. was not excluded, it was fragmentary and mainly attached to *xungu*. Due to the special morphological features of the Chinese language and the isolationism of China's feudal society, the study of Chinese grammar had never developed into an independent and scientific system. Seeing China degrade step by step to a semi-feudal and semi-colonial society, many people with lofty ideals started to learn the advanced science and technology from the West for national salvation from the second half of the 19th century. Ma Jianzhong was among those people. Having compared the Chinese culture with the Western culture, he came to know that in order to learn the advanced Western science and technology it was of prime necessity to shorten the period of time devoted to learning to read and write in Chinese. He also realized that through comparison between Chinese and Western languages it would be possible to bring to light the rules hidden in the Chinese language and establish a set of Chinese grammar with which we could facilitate a quicker command of Chinese culture by children.

Mashi Wentong was written in classical Chinese. This great work was not just an adoption of Latin grammar. The author also inherited much from the achievement of the

Chinese traditional philology and made a profound analysis of the language materials of the Pre-Qin Period and the Han Dynasty. The book is divided into ten chapters. The first chapter is entitled *Zheng Ming*, in which the author sets forth his views on morphology and syntax in twenty-three *jieshuo* (definition), which constitute the general outline of the book. From the second to the ninth chapter the book deals with *zilei* (parts of speech), in which the first five chapters are devoted to *shizi* (notional words) and the rest three chapters to *xuzi* (form words). In the tenth chapter *Judou*, analysis is made on the different components of sentences. The classification of Chinese words was a great accomplishment resulting from comparison between Chinese grammar and the grammar of the Western languages. In this book, words are divided into two categories, *shizi* and *xuzi*. *Shizi* is further divided into *mingzi* (analogy to noun), *daizi* (analogy to pronoun), *dongzi* (analogy to verb), *jingzi*, and *zhuangzi*. *Xuzi* is subdivided into *jiezi* (analogy to preposition), *lianzi* (analogy to conjunction), *zhuzi* (structural particle) and *tanzi* (interjection). This classification was fairly rigorous and integrated. The current classification of Chinese words is still based on it except that *liangci* (measure word) has been separated from *mingzi* and *shuci* (numeral) from *jingzi*. The different elements in sentences are classified in this book as *qici*, *yuci*, *zhici*, *biaoci*, *sici*, *zhuanci* and *jiaci*. *Qici* is analogy to subject. *Yuci* is analogy to predicate. *Zhici* is analogy to object. *Biaoci* is analogy to the predicate of a sentence with an adjectival predicate. *Sici* stands for prepositional object. *Zhuanci*, a bit more complicated, usually refers to either the indirect object of a transitive verb or the sentence element which shows the place of an action indicated by an intransitive verb. *Jiaci* is divided into two kinds, one functions like a prepositional phrase and the other appositive.

The publication of *Mashi Wentong* is a milestone in the development of Chinese philology, which marks the separation of Chinese grammar from *xiaoxue* (traditional Chinese philology), the establishment of Chinese grammar and the starting point of the transition from traditional Chinese philology to modern philology. From then on, the study of Chinese grammar has become an independent part in Chinese philology and a great many books on grammar have come out, resulting in a quick development in the study of Chinese grammar.

4. 普通话就是官话吗?

一个统一的社会的全体成员所共同使用的语言,即在这一社会中操不同方言的人彼此交际时所使用的语言称为共同语。中国最早的汉民族共同语称为"雅言"。公元前11世纪,西周建都镐京(今陕西长安县),因此以秦语为雅言。这一标准至东周未变,孔子讲学也用雅言。秦变法之后日渐强大并统一了中原,使得秦语和晋语相互融合。秦统一中国后,书同文、言必雅,并以国都咸阳(今陕西咸阳市东北)的语音为标准音。

汉民族共同语在不同的时期有不同的名称。周秦时称为"雅言",汉代则称为"通语",元代称为"天下通语",明、清则称为"官话",民国时期称为"国语"。"国语"一词目前仍在台湾及其他一些地区使用。现在汉民族共同语的正式名称则是"普通话"。

在封建社会,统治阶级往往利用皇权推行王都之音。中国历代王朝建都大多在北方城市,并有着从西向东迁移的趋势。虽然有的朝代也曾在南方建都,也出现过如南北朝时期南北语音平分秋色的局面,但从历史上看,以北方方言为基础、以北京语音为标准音是汉民族共同语的发展趋势。

普通话形成的源头可以上溯至元代。共同语有两种形式:一种是口头形式,一种是书面形式。在口头形式方面,北京是辽、金、元、明、清五代的都城,既是政治中心,北京话也就自然成为各级官府的交际语言,并随着政治影响传播到全国各地。在书面语方面,中国长期用"文言"作为书面语的局面自元代发生了变化,用"白话"写的作品日渐丰富。元曲基本是白话文作品。《水浒传》、《红楼梦》、《儒林外史》等文学巨著也以基本上属于北方话的白话写成。特别是到了本世纪,五四运动及新文化运动的开展彻底动摇了文言文的地位。白话文代替文言文取得了文学语言的地位。这两方面的结合为作为汉民族共同语的普通话的形成奠定了基础。1955年的全国文字改革会议及现代汉语规范问题学术会议最终为汉民族共同语作了规定,即是以北京语音为标准音、以北方方言为基础方言、以典范的现代白话文著作为语法规范的普通话。1982年,"推广全国通用的普通话"作为一项条款被列入了《中华人民共和国宪法》。

4. Is *Putonghua* an Equivalent of *Guanhua*?

Common speech is the language spoken by all members of the society and used when people of different dialect regions communicate. The earliest common speech for the Han nationality was *Yayan* (elegant speech). In the 11th century B.C. when the Western Zhou Dynasty established its capital at Haojing (present Chang'an County, Shaanxi Province), the Qin (Shaanxi) dialect was taken as *Yayan*, or the standard speech. Later, in the Eastern Zhou Dynasty(770—256 B.C.) the Qin dialect was still regarded as the standard speech. Confucius spoke this dialect as well when he travelled and gave lectures in different states. Following the political reform, the State of Qin became increasingly strong and finally unified China. As a result, the Qin dialect and the Jin (Shanxi) dialect were merged. With the founding of the Qin Dynasty(221—206 B.C.), standardization of writing and speech was carried out on imperial decree. The common speech then took Xianyang (capital of Qin, northeast of present Xianyang) pronunciation as the standard.

There have been different names for the common speech of the Han nationality in different times. In the Zhou and Qin dynasties(c.1100—206 B.C.), it was called *Yayan*; in the Han Dynasty(206 B.C.—220 A.D.), *Tongyu* (popular speech); in the Yuan Dynasty(1271—1368 A.D.), *Tianxia Tongyu* (popular speech under heaven); in the Ming and Qing dynasties(1368—1911A.D.), *Guanhua* (speech of the officials, or Mandarin); and during the time of the Republic of China(1911—1949 A.D.), *Guoyu* (the national language). The term *Guoyu* is still used in Taiwan and some other regions. Presently the official term for the standard common speech of the Han nationality is *Putonghua*.

In the feudal society like old China, the ruling class always tried to push forward the speech of the capital. Most of the capitals of the ancient dynasties were founded in the northern part of China with a tendency of moving eastward. Although some dynasties did make their capitals in south China and there were times when northern and southern speeches had equai shares of prevalence as in the Northern and Southern Dynasties(420—581 A.D.), it had been the general historical trend that the common speech for the Han nationality was based on the northern dialect with Beijing speech pronunciation as the standard.

The origination of *Putonghua* dated back to the Yuan Dynasty (1271—1368 A.D.). The common speech took two different forms, the spoken language and the written language. In terms of the spoken language, as the capital for the Liao, Jin,

Yuan, Ming and Qing dynasties, Beijing expectedly became the political centre, and Beijing dialect was thus taken as the commonly-accepted language for officials of various administrative levels and was spread throughout the country with the political influence of the capital. In terms of the written language, changes took place in the Yuan Dynasty to the fact that only classical Chinese had been used in writing, and works written in the vernacular gradually increased. The Yuan Dynasty drama were basically vernacular works. *Shuihu Zhuan* (*The Water Margin*), *Honglou Meng*(*The Dream of the Red Mansions*) *Rulin Waishi*(*The Scholars*) and some other masterpieces of literature were all written in the northern vernacular. At the beginning of the 20th century, the May 4th Movement completely shattered the dominating position of classical language and replaced it with the modern vernacular language. The changes in the above two aspects combined to lay a solid foundation for *Putonghua*, the standard common speech for the Han nationality. In 1955 at the national conference on reforming the written language and at the symposeum on the standardization of modern Chinese language, *Putonghua* was defined as the standard Chinese language with Beijing speech sounds as its standard sounds, with the northern dialect as the basic dialect and with modern classic works written in the vernacular as its grammatical models. In 1982, it was written into the Constitution of the People's Republic of China that *Putonghua* be popularized throughout China.

5. 历史上汉字有哪些注音方法?

汉字是属于表意系统的文字。汉字不同于拼音文字,人们不能根据某字的字形直接读出该字的音。因此,给汉字注音就成为必不可少的手段了。从古至今,为汉字注音大体有三种方法:用一个汉字为另一个汉字注音、反切法和使用拼音文字。

在古代中国曾采用“直音法”和“读若法”(也有称为“读作”或“读如”)为汉字注音。这两种方法都是用一个汉字为另一个汉字注音。“直音法”是用一个汉字为另一个同音字注音的方法。如“诞,音但”。“读若法”是用一个汉字为另一个读音相近的汉字注音的方法。如“闯,读若郴”,“娓,读若媚”。东汉许慎的《说文解字》就常采用读若法。以上两种方法虽然简便,但如果不认识用作注音的字,也就无法知道被注汉字的读音了。还有一种方法叫作“譬况”,就是通过描写某个汉字的发音情况和发音方法来指示该字的读音。这种方法在指示发音上虽往往使人困惑,但却有助于人们对汉字字音结构的分析和研究。

“反切法”是用两个汉字为另一个汉字注音的方法。反切的前一个字称为反切上字,后一个字称为反切下字。反切上字与被切字的声母相同,反切下字则代表被切字的韵母及声调。其形式如“同,徒红切”。用汉语拼音表示就是 tóng = t [u + h] óng。反切法产生于东汉末年,它的发明与佛教传入中国有着密切的关系。在翻译佛经的过程中,中国学者从梵文中的元音和辅音相拼成音节的原理得到了启示。他们结合汉字的实际,在原有二合音、双反语的基础上发明了这种反切法。这种方法与直音法、读若法相比,无疑是进了一大步。反切法一直沿用了 1000 多年。直至清代的《康熙字典》和 1919 年出版的《中华大字典》,这种方法仍被采用。当然反切法也有不便和局限。使用反切法首先要熟记 1000 多个反切用字,这当然不是一件易事;另外,随着古今汉字读音的演变,在使用过去的工具书时,用反切法往往不能得到正确的读音。

用拼音字母为汉字注音是明、清才开始的,是与中西文化交流分不开的。1605 年来中国的意大利传教士利玛窦最初用拉丁字母给汉字注音,距今已有将近 400 年了。后来又有多种或由中国人或由外国人创制的用拼音字母给汉字注音的方案。这些方案主要有国语罗马字、威妥玛氏音标、注音字母以及现行的汉语拼音方案。

国语罗马字全称是《国语罗马字拼音法氏》,是 1928 年公布施行的。该方案的特点是用字母表示声调。

威妥玛氏音标是曾任英国驻华公使威妥玛设计的。过去在英语中用这种拼法拼写中国的人名和地名。

注音字母又称注音符号,是 1918 年公布施行的。这一方案共计有 39 个由汉字的笔画偏旁演化来的字母。1920年又增加一个字母，变成40个。这一方案一直使用到50年代。

现行的为汉字注音和拼写普通话语言的方案是《汉语拼音方案》。此方案于1958年2月11日由第一届全国人民代表大会第五次会议批准推行。此方案共分五部分，即字母表、声母表、韵母表、声调符号和隔音符号。在韵母表部分还规定了拼法规则。1977年在联合国第三届地名标准化会议上，通过了按照《汉语拼音方案》拼写中国地名的决议。

5. What Methods Have Been Used in History to Mark the Pronunciation of a Chinese Character?

Chinese characters, different from the alphabetic writing, are ideographs. As the character itself does not give a clue to its pronunciation, it becomes absolutely necessary to mark a character with phonetic symbols. Since ancient times there have been basically three different ways to do this: using one character to show the pronunciation of another, the application of *fanqiefa* and the adoption of the Romanized letters.

In ancient China, *zhiyinfa* and *duruofa* were used to note the sound of a character. They were basically the same in using one character to indicate the sound of another. *Zhiyinfa* was to note a character's pronunciation with another homonymic character. For example, "诞(*dan*) is pronounced as 但(*dan*)." To indicate a character's pronunciation with a character of similar sound was known as *duruofa*. For example, "闯(*chuang*) is pronounced similarly to 郴(*chen*)", and "娓(*wei*) is read similarly to 媚(*mei*)". This method was adopted in *Shuo Wen Jie Zi*, a dictionary of the Eastern Han Dynasty (25—220 A.D.) compiled by Xu Shen. One would not be able to know the pronunciation of a new character unless he knew that of the character used to indicate the sound. There was still another method of marking a character's pronunciation known as *pikuang*, which was characterized by way of describing the sound of the said character. Although it was sometimes puzzling, it helped deepen the analysis and study of the phonetic system of the Chinese language.

Fanqiefa is a method which marks the sound of a Chinese character with two other characters. The consonant of the first character and the vowel and tone of the second combine to represent the pronunciation of a new character. For example, the pronunciation of the character 同(tóng) is co-indicated by the two characters 徒(tu) and 红(hóng) with 徒 representing the consonant and 红 the vowel and tone. *Fanqiefa* came out in the late years of the Eastern Han Dynasty and was associated with the introduction of Budhism into China. In translating Budhist classics, Chinese scholars drew much inspiration from Sanscrit, which used a vowel and a consonant to form a syllable. Compared with *zhiyinfa* and *duruofa*, *fanqiefa* was surely a great progress. This method was used for more than one thousand years. In *Kangxi Zidian* (a dictionary compiled in the Qing Dynasty (1644—1911 A.D.) under the instruction of Emperor Kangxi) and *Zhonghua Da Zidian* (a comprehensive dictionary published in 1919), *fanqiefa* was still used. *Fanqiefa*, good as it is, has its inconveniences and limitations. One has to memorize more than one thousand characters to be able to use this method, which proved to be by no means easy. Further more, with constant changes in the pronunciation, one often finds it hard to obtain the correct sound of a character.

It was not until the Ming and Qing dynasties (1368—1911 A.D.) were Romanized letters taken to mark the pronunciation of Chinese characters. The adoption of Romanized letters was related to the exchanges between the Western and Chinese cultures. In 1605, Ricci Matteo, an Italian missionary, became the first to use Latin alphabet to mark the pronunciation of Chinese characters. Since then a variety of schemes have been devised either by Chinese or by foreign scholars. They are mainly *Guoyu Luomazi* (the National Language Romanization), the Wade System, *Zhuyin Zimu* (the Sound-Notating Alphabet) and the current *Hanyu Pinyin Fang'an* (the Scheme for the Chinese Phonetic Alphabet).

Guoyu Luomazi was promulgated in 1928. Its distinguishing feature is that the tone of each character is indicated in the spelling. The Wade System was designed by Thomas Francis Wade, a British diplomat to China. His scheme had been used to spell names of Chinese persons and places in English.

Zhuyin Zimu was promulgated in 1918 and had been in use until the early fifties. This scheme had a total number of 39 symbols derived from the strokes and radicals of Chinese characters. Another symbol was added in 1920, thus making a total of 40 symbols.

Hanyu Pinyin Fang'an is the current scheme of phonetic script to mark the pronunciation of Chinese characters and transliterate *Putonghua* (the standard common speech of the Han nationality). It was approved and put into force on February 11, 1958 at the Fifth Session of the First National People's Congress. The scheme includes five parts: the alphabets, the table of initials, the table of finals, tone marks and the syllable-dividing mark. The rules for spelling is stipulated in the table of finals. In 1977, a resolution was adopted by the Third United Nations Conference on the Standardization of Geographical Names to accept *Hanyu Pinyin Fang'an* as the international standard for Romanization of Chinese geographical names.

6. 中国古代使用标点符号吗?

中国古代的书籍一般都没有标点符号。最早在书中表示断句的方法是在两句之间空一两个字的位置以表示停顿。到了汉代才开始有了“句读”符号。所谓“句读”,即文辞语意已尽处为“句”,语意未尽而须停顿处则为“读”。使用的符号有“、”和“ˇ”。到了宋代开始采用在字旁加圈表示句读的方法。也有的在两字之间加圈表示读,在字旁加圈表示句。这种表示句读的方法在当时一般只用于经书,普通的书籍仍没有任何标点。这种情况一直延续到近代。19 世纪末,随着大量外国书籍被译成中文,在西文中使用的标点符号也被吸收过来。1897 年王炳耀根据中国原有断句方法,吸收西文的标点,首次拟订了 10 种标点符号。本世纪初胡适等人提出了《请颁行新式标点符号议案(修正案)》,以后由北洋政府教育部于 1920 年通令全国采用施行。这一方案一直沿用到中华人民共和国成立后。

1951 年 9 月中央人民政府出版总署公布了《标点符号用法》。这一方案包括有 14 种标点符号。从那时起,这一方案施行了将近 40 年。在此期间,文字的书写排印已由竖行改为横行,标点符号的用法也有某些发展变化,因此需要修订。1990 年 3 月国家语言文字工作委员会和新闻出版署公布了重新修订的《标点符号用法》。修订本增加了连接号和间隔号,共有标点符号 16 种,它们是:

1. 句号(。):表示陈述句末尾的停顿。
2. 问号(?):表示疑问句末尾的停顿。
3. 叹号(!):表示感叹句末尾的停顿。
4. 逗号(,):表示句子内部的一般性停顿。
5. 顿号(、):表示句子内部并列词语之间的停顿。
6. 分号(;):表示复句内部并列分句之间的停顿。
7. 冒号(:):表示提示性话语之后的停顿,用来提起下文。
8. 引号(“”):标明行文中直接引用的话。
9. 括号(()):标明行文中注释性的话。
10. 破折号(——):标明行文中解释说明的语句。
11. 省略号(…… ……):标明行文中省略了的话。
12. 着重号(.):标明要求读者特别注意的字、词、句。
13. 连接号(—):把意义密切相关的词语连成一个整体。
14. 间隔号(·):表示外国人或某些少数民族人名内各部分的分界。
15. 书名号(《》):标明书名、篇名、报刊名等。

16. 专名号(__)：表示人名、地名、朝代名等。

6. Were There Any Forms of Punctuation in Ancient China?

No punctuation was used in ancient Chinese writings. The earliest form of punctuation was to leave a space of one or two characters in the text where a pause was needed. In the Han Dynasty (206 B.C.—220 A.D.) *judou*, a simple form of punctuation, was first applied in writing. *Ju* indicated the place where a complete sense was shown and *dou* indicated the place where a slight pause was needed although the sentence was yet to be completed. To show *ju* and *dou*, two marks, the dot "、" and the tick "ˇ", were used. In the Song Dynasty (960—1279 A.D.), another method was taken by way of putting a small circle beside a character as the mark of *ju* or *dou*. Sometimes *dou* was indicated by the circle inserted tetween two characters and *ju* was marked with the circle beside a character (In ancient China the text was written in vertical lines.). However, such forms of punctuation were only employed in the classics and not in ordinary books. That had been the case until modern time. At the end of the 19th century, as more and more foreign books were translated into Chinese, the punctuations used in the Western languages were also introduced into China. In 1897, Wang Bingyao devised ten different punctuations on the bases of combining the old Chinese methods with the Western punctuations. In the beginning of the 20th century, Hu Shi, a famous modern Chinese scholar, and others submitted an amendment of a motion pleading for the promulgation of a new form of punctuations, which was later put into force throughout the country in 1920 under the order from the Ministry of Education of the Beiyang Government.

In September 1951, the Central Publishing House under the Central People's Government published *Biaodian Fuhao Yongfa* (*Directions for the Use of Punctuations*), which had been used for nearly forty years. In the meantime, the typesetting and printing of Chinese changed from vertical lines to horizontal, and changes also took place in the usage of punctuations, thus revising became necessary. In March, 1990, the State Language Work Committee and the Press and Publications Administration of the People's Republic of China promulgated the revised edition of *Biaodian Fuhao*

Yongfa, in which two more punctuation marks were added. There are now a total number of sixteen punctuation marks shown as follows.

1. *juhao* (。)——full stop, indicating stop at the end of a declarative sentence.
2. *wenhao* (?)——question mark, indicating stop at the end of an interrogative sentence.
3. *tanhao* (!)——exclamation mark, indicating stop at the end of an exclamatory sentence.
4. *douhao* (,)——comma, indicating a pause within a sentence.
5. *dunhao* (、)——a slight pause mark, indicating a slight pause between parallel parts of a sentence.
6. *fenhao* (;)——semicolon, indicating a pause between clauses of a compound sentence.
7. *maohao* (:)——colon, indicating a pause following the reminding words and introducing the following passage.
8. *yinhao* (“”)——quotation mark, enclosing the words quoted.
9. *kuohao* (())——brackets, enclosing the explanatory words.
10. *pozhehao* (——)——dash, preceding the explanatory words.
11. *shengluehao* (… …)——ellipsis, indicating omission of words from a sentence.
12. *zhuozhonghao* (.)——mark of emphasis, indicating emphasis on special characters, words or sentences.
13. *lianjiehao* (—)——hyphen, joining together words that are closely related in meaning.
14. *jiangehao* (·)——separation dot, separating the parts of a name of a foreigner or of a person of the minority nationality.
15. *shuminghao* (《》)——book mark, enclosing the title of a book, an article, a newspaper or a periodical.
16. *zhuanminghao* (__)——mark for a proper noun, underlining the name of a person, a place, a dynasty, etc.

7."小学"研究什么学问?

"小学"是中国封建时代传统的语言文字学。它包括文字学、训诂学和音韵学三个门类。"小学"一词始于周代,但在不同的历史时期有着不同的内容。在周代"小学"指为贵族子弟设立的初级学校,相当于现代的小学校。用"小学"指文字学始于西汉。后来"小学"又增加了训诂和音韵学的内容。到宋代"小学"才用来明确地指文字学、训诂学和音韵学。中国传统的"小学"萌芽于先秦,创立于西汉,在以后的朝代里又得到了发展。清代是"小学"研究获得辉煌成就的时代,出现了众多的"小学"大家。但是由于西方文化传入中国,并在此影响下产生了现代语言学,清代也是"小学"终结的时代。

文字学是以文字为对象,研究文字的起源、演变、性质、体系以及文字的形、音、义关系的学问。中国对文字的研究有着悠久的历史。作为"小学"的文字学早在西汉(公元前206~公元24年)已经创立。秦(公元前221~前206年)统一文字是中国文字发展史上的一次大转折。经过这一转折,汉代的文字和先秦的文字有了很大的差异,以致汉代人已很难读懂先秦的文字。另外,一些以古文字书写的在秦代属于禁书的典籍在汉代重现于世,带有古文字的青铜器和竹简也不断被发现。这就产生了对古文字进行研究的客观需要,同时也造就了一批对古文字作专门研究的学者,如孔安国、张敞、扬雄和许慎等。他们的研究工作为文字学的发展打下了基础。东汉(公元25~220年)许慎所著的《说文解字》一书是文字学上最有影响的一部著作。直到清末发现甲骨文之前,此书一直是文字学研究的中心。

训诂学是从词义和语义的角度研究古代文献的一门学科。早在春秋时代,训诂已有萌芽。由于语言是不断发展的,文字也处在不断的演变之中,后代人读前代人撰写的文献典籍就会遇到困难。为了扫清语言和文字的障碍,就要对前人的著作进行注解,这就产生了训诂。最初的训诂只是一种附属于某一典籍的随文释义的工作,还不是一门独立的学问。后来在此基础上产生了训诂的另一种形式,就是把训诂的资料从它们所附的典籍中抽出来,进行分类、整理和加工,编纂成类似字典的训诂专著。这就使训诂从古文献中独立了出来,并逐渐发展为一门独立的学科。《说文解字》不仅是一部文字学著作,也是一部影响极大的训诂学著作。而早于此书的《尔雅》则是在汉武帝时代就已广泛流行的训诂专著,被称为中国和世界上第一部百科辞典。

音韵学是研究汉语语言在各个历史阶段其声、韵、调系统及其发展变化规律的一门学科。音韵学包括古音学、今音学和等韵学三个门类。古音学是研究周、秦时期的汉语语音系统;今音学是研究魏、晋至唐时期的汉语语音面貌;等韵学是制成若干图表,着重分析汉语语音的声、韵、调的结构，阐述汉语发音的原理和方法。对音韵的研究始自东汉。这一研究是随着印度文化，包括古印度语音学传入中国而开始的。在两种语言和文字的对比中，中国学者在东汉末年发明了为汉字注音的反切法。反切法的发明为音韵学的创立作了开端。南北朝的沈约发明了“四声”之说。隋朝颜之推等人作《切韵》以统一南北的读音。唐、宋时期又产生了字母和韵图。这样就从不同角度揭示了汉语字音结构在声调、韵母、声母上的特征，形成了有中国特色的音韵学。

在“小学”里，文字学、训诂学和音韵学分属三个不同门类。文字的研究偏重于形；训诂的研究偏重于义；音韵的研究偏重于音。但这三者之间又有着有机的联系，相互贯通，不能分开，统一于“小学”这一汉语传统语言文字学之中。

7. What Is the Study of *Xiaoxue*？

Xiaoxue was the traditional Chinese philology in feudal times. It included *wenzixue* (the study of ancient forms of the written characters), *xunguxue* (the study of classics, concerned with the ancient meaning of words) and *yinyunxue* (phonology). The term *xiaoxue* was first used in the Zhou Dynasty(c.1100—221 B.C.) and its contents varied at different historical periods. In the Zhou Dynasty, *xiaoxue* was primary school for children from the noble families. In the Western Han Dynasty(206 B.C.—24 A.D.) *xiaoxue* included only the study of the ancient forms of Chinese characters. Later, it covered as well the ground of *xunguxue* and *yinyunxue*. However, it was not until the Song Dynasty(960—1279 A.D.) that the term *xiaoxue* clearly stood for all the above three subjects of learning. Chinese traditional *xiaoxue* was in the bud during the Pre-Qin Period(before 221 B.C.), founded in the Western Han Dynasty and gradually developed in the successive dynasties. Brilliant achievements were secured in the study of *xiaoxue* in the Qing Dynasty(1644—1911 A.D.), which saw many *xiaoxue* masters. However, *xiaoxue* also came to the end in the Qing Dynasty, with the founding of modern philology following the introduction of Western culture nto China.

Wenzixue, taking the written script as its subject of study, focuses on the origin, development, nature and system of the written script as well as the relationship between the form, pronunciation and meaning of the character. Founded as early as in the Western Han Dynasty, *wenzixue* boasted a very long history. The standardization of the written language in the Qin Dynasty(221—206 B.C.) marked a great turning point in the development of Chinese written script. As a result, the written characters of the Han Dynasty (206 B.C.—220 A.D.) differed so greatly from that of the Pre-Qin Period that the Han people could hardly understand the previous language. Besides, some ancient books that were banned in the Qin Dynasty reappeared in the Han Dynasty. Bronze wares as well as bamboo slips bearing ancient inscriptions were discovered. All these called for the study of ancient-form characters and created a good number of scholars specializing in ancient written script, such as Kong Anguo, Zhang Chang, Yang Xiong, Xu Shen, etc. Their research laid a good foundation for the development of *wenzixue*.

Shuo Wen Jie Zi, the first Chinese dictionary written by Xu Shen of the Eastern Han Dynasty(25—220 A.D.), is deemed to be the most invaluable of books on *wen-zixue*. The study of *wen-zixue* had all along been based on this book up to the end of the Qing Dynasty when *jiaguwen* (oracle bone inscriptions) was discovered.

Xunguxue is a branch of philology which is concerned with the changes in the meaning of words in classical Chinese works. As early as in the Spring and Autumn Period(770—476 B.C.), *xunguxue* was already in the embryonic stage. Because of constant changes and development of the language, people found it hard to understand the classics written by people from the previous times. To remove the language barriers, explanations of the ancient meaning of words became necessary and this gave birth to *xunguxue*. In the initial stage, *xunguxue* was not an independent branch of learning but was attached to a specific book as a kind of explanatory notes. Out of this, another form of *xunguxue* developed later. *Xunguxue* monographs in a form similar to dictionaries were compiled on the basis of classification, systematization and treatment of the explanatory notes attached to various classics. This not only provided reference books one could consult when reading ancient classics, but also led to the separation of *xunguxue* from the classics and to the gradual establishment of a new branch of learning. *Shuo Wen Jie Zi*, apart from being a great work on *wenzixue*, is equally famous as a work on *xunguxue*. *Erya*, known as the first encyclopaedia in the world, is a *xunguxue* monograph prior to *Shuo Wen Jie Zi* and was widespread as early as in the reign of Emperor Wu of the Han Dynasty.

Yinyunxue is a branch of learning which studies the consonants, vowels and tones of the Chinese language at different historical periods and the laws governing their development. *Yinyunxue* is subdivided into *guyinxue*, *jinyinxue* and *dengyunxue*. *Guyinxue* concerns the phonetic system of the Chinese language of the ancient periods of the Zhou and Qin dynasties, while *jinyinxue* concerns that of the periods from the Wei and Jin dynasties (220—420 A.D.) to the Tang Dynasty (618—907 A.D.). *Dengyunxue* is devoted to the analysis of the structures of the consonants, vowels and tones as well as to the description of principles and methods of pronunciation of the Chinese language by way of phonetic diagrams. The study of phonetics of the Chinese language started in the Eastern Han Dynasty, following the introduction into China of Indian culture including ancient Indian phonology. Drawing much from the comparison between the Indian and Chinese languages, Chinese scholars created in the late Eastern Han Dynasty *fanqiefa*, an old method of marking the pronunciations of Chinese characters. This method marked the beginning of the founding of *yinyunxue*. During the Northern and Southern Dynasties (420—581 A.D.), Shen Yue put forward the theory of the "four tones". Yan Zhitui and other scholars of the Sui Dynasty (581—618 A.D.) came up with *Qieyun* (a rhyme dictionary), which served to standardize the different accents. During the Tang and Song dynasties (618—1279 A.D.), alphabets and finals were devised. By then the special features of the Chinese characters manifested in consonants, vowels and tones had been brought to light from different aspects, and phonology with Chinese characteristics finally took shape.

Within the range of *xiaoxue*, *wenzixue*, *xunguxue* and *yinyunxue* are three different subjects with their emphases respectively on the forms of characters, the meanings of words and the speech sounds. However, no hard and fast lines can be drawn between the three. They merge into an organic whole—the traditional Chinese philology *xiaoxue*.

8. 汉字什么时候由竖写改为横写？最先是由谁提出来的？

几千年来，中国的汉字书写方式都是按自上而下、自右向左竖写。但是到了近代，随着中西文化的交流，在用汉字写成的文章及各类文件中，经常要引用外文原文，书写阿拉伯数字、外文字母，使用新标点。这样，原来的书写形式就成为应用中的障碍，需要进行改革。提出汉字由竖写改为横写的第一个人，是中国新文化运动的先驱者、《新青年》杂志编辑之一的钱玄同。

钱玄同(1887～1939)，字德潜，号疑古，自称"疑古玄同"，浙江省吴兴县人。1906 年他 19 岁时赴日本留学。留日期间，他与鲁迅等人一起向章太炎学习文字学，研究音韵训诂。在学习中，他逐渐感到汉字由竖写引起的麻烦和不便，立志改革，产生了把汉字由竖写改为横写的念头。1917 年，钱玄同在《新青年》杂志第 3 卷第 3 期上发表了致陈独秀的公开信，首次提出了汉字"竖改横"的见解，并陈述理由说明这种改革的好处。此后，钱玄同又在《新青年》杂志上连续发表了 10 封公开信，积极倡导"竖改横"的主张。陈独秀、陈望道等学者也表示赞同，并准备从《新青年》第 4 卷第 1 期起由竖写改为横写。但是由于印刷和经费方面的困难，加上当时很多人反对，没有成功。

解放以后，由于人民政府大力支持和提倡这种改革，中国大陆从 1956 年 1 月起，全国的报纸、杂志一律由竖写改为横写，这给人们的工作、学习和生活都带来了极大的方便。

8. When Did Chinese Characters Begin to Be Written Horizontally Instead of Vertically? Who Was the First One to Put Forward This Idea?

Over thousands of years, Chinese characters had been written in vertical lines form right to left. However, along with the cultural exchanges between China and the West in modern times, quoting of original foreign texts, writing Arabic numbers and letters of foreign languages, and the using of new punctuation marks appeared more and more frequently in articles and various documents written in Chinese. Thus, the old way of writing became a barrier in usage and a reform was needed. The first man to put forward the idea of writing characters sideways was Qian Xuantong, a pioneer of the New Culture Movement in China and one of the editors of *Xin Qingnian* (*The New*

Youth).

Qian Xuantong (1887—1939), also Known as Deqian, and nicknamed Yigu, called himself "Yigu Xuantong". His hometown is in Wuxing County, Zhejiang Province. In 1906, he went to study in Japan at the age of nineteen. During that period, together with Lu Xun, he studied philology from Zhang Taiyan and researched into phonetics and the critical interpretation of ancient texts. In the process of studying, he began to realize the inconvenience and trouble caused by writing characters vertically and was determined to reform it, and the idea of "changing vertical ways to sideways" was born. In 1917, for the first time his idea was put forward in an open letter to Chen Duxiu, which was published in the third journal of Volume 3 of *Xin Qingnian* together with a statement of the advantages of the new idea. (At that time, Chen Duxiu was the editor-in-chief of the journal.) After that, he published a series of ten open letters in *Xin Qingnian*, advocating for his idea, which met with approval from Chen Duxiu and Chen Wangdao, who were prepared to adopt the new way in the first journal of Volume 4 of *Xin Qingnian*. However, due to difficulties in printing and lack of funds as well as objections, the new idea fell flat.

After the founding of the People's Rublic of China, with the support and advocation of the reform from the government, ever since January 1956, all the newspapers and magazines published on the mainland of China have adopted the new way of writing, which has brought great convenience to people in their work and study.

9."五花八门"、"三教九流"等词是怎么来的?

据《古书典故辞典》的释义,"五花八门"本来是指古代兵法中的阵名。"五花"即五行阵,"八门"即八门阵。后来人们以此来比喻事物花样繁多、变化莫测。另据史书记载:古代帝王封赠的诏书,用五色金花绫纸,故名"五花官诰"。另外,旧时僧侣出家的书面凭证,因为由官府签发,并且有多种画押,因此,这种凭证称为"五花度牒"。在宋代,中书省的官员,凡是有重要文书上奏,根据规定,必须在文书上方签署具体意见和名字,称作"五花判事"。

后来,人们用"五花八门"比喻各种行业。"五花"中,金菊花喻卖茶女;木棉花喻沿街行医的郎中;水仙花喻酒楼歌女;火辣花喻杂耍者;土牛花喻挑夫。八门中,一门巾,隐喻占卜算命者;二门皮,喻卖草药者;三门彩,喻变戏法者;四门挂,喻江湖卖艺者;五门平,喻说书、评弹者;六门团,喻街头卖唱者;七门调,喻搭棚扎彩者;八门柳,喻高台唱戏者。从以上五花及八门所代表的行业看,都属下层劳动者行业。

人们常用"三教九流"一语来泛指社会上形形色色、五花八门的各式人物或学说。那么,何谓"三教九流"呢?

"三教"最早出于《翻译名义集》:"吴主问三教",尚书令阚泽答曰:"孔、老设教,法天制用,不敢违天,佛之设教,诸天奉行。"所以,"三教"即指儒教、道教和佛教。

所谓"九流",就是指九派学说。据《汉书·艺文志》记载:九流,即儒家者流、道家者流、法家者流、名家者流、墨家者流、阴阳家者流、纵横家者流、杂家者流、农家者流。

"三教"和"九流"之称,在汉时并无贬义。后来到了唐代,唐代撰《春秋谷梁传·序》,才把"九流"与"异端"并列,加之佛教、道教迷信日盛,"三教九流"便渐渐含有贬义了。

9. What Are the Origins of the Expressions *Wu Hua Ba Men* and *San Jiao Jiu Liu*?

According to the explanation in *Gu Shu Diangu Cidian* (*A Dictionary of Allusions in Ancient Books*), at the very beginning, *wu hua ba men* referred to names for battle formations in ancient times. *Wu hua* referred to a five-row battle formation and *ba men* an eight-gate battle formation. Then it was used to stand for variety and changeability of things. According to other historic records, the ancient imperial edicts granting titles or giving gifts, which were usually decorated with a kind of five-coloured silk paper, were called *wu hua guangao*. The certificate conferred to a monk was called *wu hua dudie* because it was usually issued by a government organ and there were many stamps of official seals to make it colourful. In the Song Dynasty (960—1279), high ranking officials are required to write their own remarks and names on the top when they submitted important reports to the emperors. This kind of reports were called *wu hua panshi*.

Later on, *wu hua ba men* was used to refer to various trades. Of *wu hua*, *jinjuhua* referred to tea girls; *mumianhua*, traditional Chinese medicine doctors; *shuixianhua*, female singers; *huolahua*, acrobats; and *tuniuhua*, bearers. Of *ba men*, the first, *jin*, referred to fortune-tellers; the second, *pi*, herbal medicine salesmen; the third, *cai*, magicians; the fourth, *gua*, itinerant entertainers; the fifth, *ping*, story tellers; the sixth, *tuan*, street singers; the seventh, *diao*, hut binders; the eighth, *liu*, stage performers. All the trades above were those engaged by laborers of low social status.

San jiao jiu liu is used to refer to all kinds of people and schools of theories in the society. But, what is *san jiao jiu liu*?

The term *san jiao* can be seen first in *Fanyi Mingyi Ji* (a translation collection): The king of the State of Wu (770—221 B.C.) inquired about *san jiao*. His Prime Minister Gan Ze replied that the doctrines created by Confucianists and Taoists were based on the law of the nature which they had the slightest intention to go against, while Buddhists advocating to it surpassed the nature. Therefore *san jiao* referred to Confucianism, Taoism and Buddhism.

Jiu liu used to refer to the nine schools of theories. According to *Han Shu* (*History of the Han Dynasty*), *jiu liu* included *Rujia* (Confucianism), *Daojia* (Taoism), *Fajia* (Legalism), *Mingjia* (the School of Logicians), *Mojia* (Mohist School), *Yinyangjia* (the School of the Positive and Negative Forces), *Zonghengjia* (Political Strategists), *Zajia* (the Eclectic) and *Nongjia* (Agrarians).

San jiao and *jiu liu* were not derogatory in the Han Dynasty. It was not until the Tang Dynasty that *jiu liu* and *yiduan* (heresy) were put together in *Chunqiu Guliang Zhuan*: *Xu* (the preface for *The Biography of Guliang in the Spring and Autumn Period*). In addition, Buddhism and Taoism became more and more rampant during that period. Gradually, *san jiao jiu liu* transformed into a derogatory term.

10. 为什么常用“五”和“十”来表示圆满？

我们人人都有一双手，每只手有五根手指，当屈指计数时，到五、十就终止了。中国古代以东、西、南、北、中五个方位表示全部地域；以五色代表全部颜色。古人认为金、木、水、火、土五行构成了天地万物；五谷则泛指全部供人食用的谷物；五味包括了人的全部味觉。人脸上有五官，内脏统称五脏、五内；人际关系统称五伦；道德修养要坚持五常；各种礼仪统称五礼；拜佛要求“五体投地”，表示全身心的敬奉；人的全部亲属按丧服分为“五服”；一夜划分为五更；天下名山有五岳；传说中的帝王有“五帝”；刑罚统称五刑；审讯的方法为“五听”；武器的统称是“五刃”；等等，这种以五为圆满之数的习俗处处可见。

除了五以外，还常常用十来表示圆满。圆满无缺就叫十全十美；杂取各种不同事物、不同样式配合的整体，称之为“十(什)锦”，如什锦菜；中医有十问、十剂、十全大补药；民间乐器叫“十番锣鼓”；甚至法律规定的最重的罪名也叫“十恶不赦”；形形色色各种现象总称“五光十色”。

在世界其他民族中也往往有类似的习俗。如犹太教、基督教对其信徒的要求也都称“十戒”。佛教中冠以“十”的教义要求很多，如十力、十戒、十因、十地、十事、十善等等。

在中国古代，五与十表示圆满的习俗还受到儒家思想和文字书写本身含义的影响。中国古代字书《说文解字》中，对十的解释是：“数之具也，一为东西，丨为南北，则四方中央备矣。”即认为一横代表东西，一竖代表南北，四面八方全部具备于此，故称十为数字的全体之具备。而五字又具有神秘性，“五，五行也，二从阴阳，在天地间交午也”。把五字的上下两横看作是天与地的象征，中间的竖、横折表示天地阴阳的交配繁衍万物。近代有人认为，五与鱼音近，在甲骨文中写作 ㄨ或 㐅形，与鱼形类似。古代华夏族有以鱼为图腾崇拜物的部落，如仰韶文化中的半坡遗址就是以鱼为图腾崇拜物的。五从图腾崇拜的鱼转化而来，因此一直被视为神圣。所以中国文化中有以五与十为圆满的习俗。

10. Why Are *Wu* (Five) and *Shi* (Ten) Often Used to Signify Perfection?

Everyone of us has two hands and each hand has five fingers. When we try to do the counting with our fingers, it always ends at the numbers *wu* and *shi*. In ancient times, the five directions of east, west, south, north and center were used to represent all the areas. All the colors are represented by *wuse*. All creations on the earth and in the heaven are made from *wuxing* (the five elements: metal, wood, water, fire and earth). Food stuffs are called *wugu*, and all sorts of flavors are *wuwei*. Everyone has five sense organs, *wuguan*, and five internal organs, *wuzang*. Human relations are concluded as *wulun*. To accomplish good morality and virtue, you have to insist on *wuchang*. All kinds of etiquette are summed up as *wuli*. Prostrating before the Buddha requires you to *wu ti tou di* (throw your five parts of the body to the ground) to express your whole-hearted worship. All mourning relatives are divided into *wufu* according to their mourning apparel. The night is divided into *wugeng*. There are altogether five great sacred mountains (*Wu Yue*) in China. There are also *wu di* (five emperors) in Chinese legends, *wuxing* in punishment, *wuting* in interrogating a case in a court, and *wuren* for all kinds of weapons, etc. The custom of using *wu* to signify perfection can be seen everywhere.

Apart from *wu*, *shi* is also used to express perfection. *Shi quan shi mei* is used to mean flawless. Assortment made from various things is called *shijin*. The Chinese medicine has *shi wen* (inquiries), *shi ji* (dosages) and *shiquan dabu yao* (tonic). The folk musical instrument is called *shifan luogu*. Even the charge of the most heinous crimes stipulated by law is *shi e bu she*. Various phenomena are described as *wu guang shi se* (five lights and ten colors).

Similar customs can be found in other nations of the world. For example, both Judaism and Christianity have the ten commandments (*shi jie*) for their believers. There are many doctrines in Buddhism that are preceded by *shi*: *shi li* (ten forces), *shi jie* (ten commandments), *shi yin* (ten causes), *shi di* (ten places), *shi shi* (ten things) and *shi shan* (ten virtues), etc.

The custom of using *wu* and *shi* for perfection in ancient China was also influenced by Confucianism and the meanings of the written characters themselves. The ancient book *Shuo Wen Jie Zi* explained the character "十" (*shi*) as the complement of all numbers—the horizontal stroke stands for east to west. and the vertical one north to south. So the four directions and the center are all included here. "五" (*wu*) is also a mystical number. The upper and lower horizontal strokes are regarded as the heaven and the earth, while the vertical stroke and the horizontal stroke with a downward turning stand for the mingling of *yin* and *yang* that creates everything in the world. Someone stated recently that *wu* is very similar to *yu* (fish) both in pronunciation and in shape in the oracle bone inscriptions. There were tribes in ancient China who regarded fish as their totem. Such examples can be found from the relics of the Banpo village of the Yangshao culture. Evolving from the totem of fish, *wu* was thus regarded as holy. Hence comes the custom in Chinese culture of making *wu* and *shi* symbols of perfection.

11. 孔子在思想与教育方面有哪些重要贡献？“仁”是孔子的中心思想吗？“仁”是什么意思？

孔子(公元前551~前479年)名丘，字仲尼，是中国春秋时代的思想家、政治家、教育家。他的祖先曾为宋宗室，在孔子上几代时，迁往鲁国。孔子小时候，家中贫穷。年轻时曾经做过“委吏”(司会计)和“乘田”(司畜牧)，在50岁的时候，任鲁国司寇(主管刑法狱讼)。后来周游过宋、卫、陈、蔡、齐、楚等诸侯国，都没有受到重用。孔子从青年时就教过一些弟子，晚年除整理《诗》、《书》，编定《春秋》外，致力于教育弟子。传说他的弟子有3000人，其中“通六艺”者72人。

“仁”是孔子学说的中心思想。关于仁，在《论语》中有几种不同的说法。孔子说过：“吾道一以贯之。”(我的学说贯穿着一个基本观念。)这个基本观念据孔子的学生曾参解释，就是忠和恕。“忠”的意思按照一些人的解释是：“己欲立而立人，己欲达而达人。”(自己要站得住，同时也使别人站得住；自己要事事行得通，同时也使别人事事行得通。)而“恕”，可以解释为：“己所不欲，勿施于人。”(自己所不喜欢的事物，就不强加于别人。)忠、恕合起来也就是仁的主要意思。关于仁，孔子还说过：“克己复礼为仁。”(抑制自己，使言语和行动都合乎礼，就是仁。)在同学生子张的一次谈话中，孔子说：能实行恭(庄重)、宽(宽厚)、信(诚实)、敏(勤敏)、惠(慈惠)的，可以算作仁了。学生樊迟问孔子什么是仁，他回答说：“爱人。”综合以上的内容，可以大致了解孔子所说的仁的意思。当时，孔子认为能够算得上仁的人并不多，在他的学生当中，孔子只说过颜回是：“回也，其心三月不违仁。”(回呀，他的心长久地不离开仁德。)春秋时期政治家管仲辅佐齐桓公使齐国有一个长期安定的局面，尽管孔子认为管仲有许多错处，他仍然说：“桓公九合诸侯，不以兵车，管仲之力也！如其仁！如其仁！”意思是：齐桓公多次主持诸侯间的盟会，停止了战争，都是管仲的力量所致，这就是管仲的仁！孔子认为“博施民而能济众”(广泛地给人民以好处，又能使大家生活得好)，那就是比仁更高的圣了。但是即使古代尧舜那样贤明的先王也难做到圣。

除了上述仁的观念外，孔子主张人们遵守礼制行事，对于古时的礼制，他也认为应该在继承中有所改变。他提倡多学多问，说：“三人行，必有我师焉。择其善者而从之，其不善者而改之。”孔子虽然也提到天命，但不妄谈鬼神。他主张为人忠诚信实，有“自古皆有死，民无信不立”的名言。

在教育上，孔子突破了以前只有贵族子弟才能受教育的传统做法，主张并实行“有教无类”,不分贫富和地区,对各类学生都采取“诲人不倦”的态度。对其中安于贫困而勤于学习的,如颜回,孔子倍加称赞。他主张既要读书又要思考,说:“学而不思则罔,思而不学则殆。”(只是读书却不思考,就会受骗;只是空想却不读书,就会失去信心。)并且认为,面临仁德的问题,即使是老师,也不谦让。他说:“当仁,不让于师。”

两千年来,孔子的思想对中国人民起了极大的影响,在相当长的时间里,也被统治者当做维护封建秩序的工具。到今天,对孔子各方面的观念,仍有深入研究的必要。

11. What Are the Significant Contributions Made by Kongzi (Confucius) to the Chinese Thought and Education? Is *Ren* His Main Idea? What Does *Ren* Mean?

Kongzi (551—479 B.C.) was a great thinker, politician and educationist during the Spring and Autumn Period (770—475 B.C.). His ancestors were of the royal clan of the State of Song and later moved to the State of Lu. He was poor in his childhood. When he was young, he was at one time an official in charge of accounting and animal husbandry. At the age of fifty, he was appointed attorney general of the State of Lu. Afterwards, he travelled to many states, including Song, Wei, Chen, Cai, Qi, Chu, etc., never attaining a high office in these states. He was once engaged in teaching in his early years. In his late years, beside sorting out *Shi* (*The Book of Songs*) and *Shu* (*The Book of History*) and compiling *Chun Qiu* (*The Spring and Autumn Annals*), he mainly devoted himself to teaching. It is generally known that he had a total of some three thousand disciples, and seventy-two out of them mastered *liu yi* (six skills, namely rites, music, shooting, driving, books and mathematics.)

Ren is the main idea of Confucianism. In *Lunyu* (*The Analects of Confucius*), there are different interpretations on the meaning of *ren*. Kongzi once stated that there was always a basic idea running through his thought, which, according to Zeng Can, one of his disciples, was *zhong* (loyalty) and *shu* (forgiveness). As for *zhong*, some people interpreted that when you want to stand your ground, let others do the same; when you want to go far in every business, allow others to do the same. As for *shu*, the interpretation was: do not do to others what you do not want others to do to you.

The combination of *zhong* and *shu* is the main idea of *ren*. Kongzi once explained that *ren* meant that one should constrain himself and conform his speech and conduct to rites. In a talk with Zizhang, one of his disciples, Kongzi said that those who were serious, generous, honest, diligent and kind could be considered *ren*. Asked by Fan Chi, another of his disciples, about what *ren* meant, he answered: "To love." Summing up all the above ideas, we can get to know the main meanings of *ren*. In the opinion of Kongzi, not many people could be considered as *ren*. Among his disciples, Yan Hui was the only one who had been thought to be *ren* by Confucius. Guan Zhong was a politician in the Spring and Autumn Period who helped the head of the State of Qi, Huangong, to maintain a long-time stability in the state. Kongzi thought that he could be considered as *ren*. Kongzi thought that if one could do things to benefit the people in many ways and let them lead a good life, he would be considered a saint, which is even higher than *ren*. However, even those ancient sagacious emperors such as Yao and Shun had not reached the degree of being saints.

Apart from the above ideas, Kongzi maintained that people should follow the ancient rites which should be inherited while some changes should also be made. He advocated studying extensively and asking questions with an inquiring mind. He said that even when only three persons were together, there was always one among them who could be learned from. One should learn his strong points and learn a lesson from his weak points. Though Kongzi believed in fate, he did not make improper comments on ghosts and deities. He maintained that people should be loyal and honest.

As for education, Kongzi broke the traditional practice that only children from noble families were entitled to education. He maintained that education should be no respecter of social status. He thought highly of those who were poor but studied hard, such as Yan Hui. He also advocated the integration of thinking with reading. He said that one would be misled if he just read without thinking; and one would have no confidence if he just fancied without reading. Kongzi also said that in terms of *ren* and *de* (morality), one should never give them up, even to one's teacher.

Confucianism has strongly and deeply influenced the Chinese people's minds for the past two thousand years. It also served as a tool to protect the feudal order. Even up to now, it is still worthwhile to study the various aspects of Confucianism.

12. 老子的《道德经》是一部什么书？它对“道”及“无为”是如何阐述的？

老子是中国古代伟大的思想家和哲学家。

据《史记》记载：老子姓李，名耳，字伯阳，生于周定王 53 年，即公元前 604 年。他继承了前人形而上学思想的遗产并大胆地对其进行改造，从而产生了不朽的名著《道德经》，这是道家哲学的经典著作，它奠定了道家的基础。

《道德经》分两部分，即道经和德经。道和德是什么关系呢？道是老子哲学最基本的原则，而德则是对道的解释。老子的《道德经》分为两卷，81 章，5000 余言。别看就这么一本薄书，它对人类思想的影响却是不可低估的。《道德经》的思想体系可分为三个部分，即老子的宇宙观、人生观和政治观。这三部分内容相互交织在一起，表达一种虚无缥缈的神奇的理想主义的思想。

老子的宇宙观集中表现在他对道的阐述上。老子称宇宙本体为道，道广大无边，为生天地之母。道是永恒的而又运行不息。正如老子在《道德经》中对“道”所阐述的那样。老子说：“有物混成，先天地生，寂兮寥兮，独立而不改，周行而不殆，可以为天地母。吾不知其名，强字之曰‘道’。”老子对道又进一步加以说明，他说：道是不可以讲说的，它是永远存在的“常道”。不可以命名，而称它为道，则是永远存在的“常名”。这就是人们所熟知的老子的一句名言：“道可道，非常‘道’；名可名，非常‘名’。”老子不仅对于“道”下了定义，而且阐述了“道”对治国安邦的影响和作用。按老子的观点，有道的侯王掌握着大道的规律，那么天下的人都去归附他，正因为天下的人都去归附他，侯王不对他们进行伤害，所以国家方能平安通顺。

老子的人生观和政治观集中反映在他的“无为”思想上。历代的统治者都标榜自己的统治是“无为而治”，在故宫的养心殿里悬挂的大匾上就书写着醒目的“无为”两个大字。那么，“无为”是什么意思呢？按照老子的观点，道是永远不做作的，却能养天地万物，而又无所不能作为。这就是老子的“道常无为而无不为”的“无为”思想。这个哲理的意思就是说：道家圣贤的行动是出自他的直觉的智慧，是自发的并与其周围的环境相协调，他不需要强迫自己或自己周围的事物，而只是使自己的行动适应道的运动。这种行为方式，就是道家哲学的“无为”。从字面上来看，“无为”就是不采取什么行动的意思。李约瑟认为：“‘无为’是指抑制违反自然的行动。”而庄子则认为：“‘无为’并不是什么事也不做而持寂静，而是让每一种东西都按其本性去做，使它的本性得到满足。按照李约瑟的说法，如果抑制了违反自然的行为，也就避免了与事物格格不入，这样的人就和“道”能够协调起来，他的行为也就会获得成功。这也就是老子那句让人费解的话“道常无为而无不为”的含义。

12. What Kind of Book Is *Dao De Jing* Written by Laozi? How Does it Interpret *Dao* and *Wuwei*?

Laozi was a great thinker and philosopher in ancient China.

According to *Shi Ji* (*Records of the Historian*), Laozi's first name was Er and his family name was Li. He was born in the 53rd year of King Ding's reign of the Zhou Dynasty, i.e. 604 B.C. Carrying on the ideology of metaphysics from the older generations and remolded it boldly, he came out with the great book *Dao De Jing* (*The Scripture of Ethics*), which was the scripture of Taoism and laid the foundation for Taoists.

Dao De Jing is composed of two parts: *Dao Jing* and *De Jing*. What is the relationship between *dao* and *de*? *Dao* is the most basic principle in the philosophy of Laozi; and *de* is the interpretation for this principle. *Dao De Jing* has two volumes with over 5000 words in 81 chapters. Do not look down upon such a thin book because its influence on the ideology of human beings has been very deep. The ideological system of *Dao De Jing* can be classified into three segments: his universal view, life view and political view. These segments are interwoven with one another and show a theory of imaginary magical idealism.

Laozi's universal view is mainly embodied in his interpretation of *dao*. Laozi believed that the universe itself was vast and boundless, and was the mother of all things. *Dao* was eternal and moved without stop. This point of view was clearly reflected in his interpretation for *dao* in *Dao De Jing*. Laozi said that there was something formless yet complete, that existed before heaven and earth, without sound or substance, independent, unchanging, all pervading, unfailing. One may think of it as the mother of all things under heaven. Its true name we do not know, so *dao* (way) is the by-name that we give it. Laozi then gave a deeper interpretation for *dao*. He said that *dao* was an unvarying way that could not be explained but existed eternally. Since it could not be named, it was called *dao*, which was an eternal unvarying name for it. The following is one of the most well-known words of Laozi: "The way (*dao*) that can be told of is not an unvarying way; the names that can be named are not unvarying names." Laozi did not just define the term *dao*, but also expounded its influences and functions on governing a state. According to Laozi, the king with *dao* knew the law of great *dao*, and then people would submit to his authority. It was because people submitted to him and he did not hurt them that the state could be stable and peaceful.

Laozi's life view and political view are mainly embodied in his thought *wuwei* (non-action). All the rulers in China boasted of their rule with *wuwei*. The characters hung in the hall of the Forbidden City were no other than *wuwei*. Then, what is the exact meaning of *wuwei*? In the opinion of Laozi, *dao* was real for ever and could support all the things under the heaven and on the earth, and meanwhile could do anything. This was Laozi's thought of *wuwei*: "Dao never does , yet through it all things are done." The thought of this philosophy was that the action of all the sages of Taoism came from their intuitive wisdom so that they were spontaneous actions and were in harmony with the surroundings. They did not need to force themselves or the things around them, but just adapted their actions to the laws of *dao*. This is the real meaning of the thought *wuwei* of Taoism. Literally, *wuwei* means non-action. Joseph Needham believed that *wuwei* meant to curb actions that were against nature. Zhuangzi stated that *wuwei* did not mean doing nothing and keeping quiet, instead, it let everything develop to the full satisfaction of its nature in its own way. According to Joseph Needham, if actions that went against nature could be curbed, disharmony could be avoided. Thus, human beings could be in harmony with *dao*, and their actions could achieve success. This is the real meaning of the hard-to-understand words of Laozi: "*Dao* never does, yet through it all things are done."

13. 常与老子并称“老庄”的庄子有哪些主要思想主张？

庄子是继老子之后的道家，是战国时期的哲学家。庄子名周，宋国蒙（今河南商丘东北）人，他的生卒时间约为公元前 369 年至前 286 年。史书记载，他曾经做过蒙地方的漆园吏，楚威王派人带大量金钱礼聘他，被他拒绝。

庄子继承和发展了老子关于“道法自然”的观点，认为世界上万物都是变化的，有生于无，经过发展变化又归于死灭。并且进一步认为，有与无、大与小、贵与贱、美与丑都是相对的，无差别的。他说：“天下莫大于秋毫之末，而泰山为小。”从这一点出发，认识与现实之间也是无差别的。有名的“庄周梦蝶”的故事就是一例，庄子说，有一次他做梦觉得自己变成蝴蝶，而醒来又觉得自己成为庄周，究竟是庄周梦见蝴蝶，还是蝴蝶梦见庄周？在庄子看来，二者都是“道”的“物化”。

庄子认为，既然人在“道”的面前不能有所作为，所以应该“无为”。他说：“知其不可奈何而安之者命，德之至也。”他主张通过“坐忘”达到“天地与我并生，万物与我为一”的精神境界。从认识的角度说，认识的主体与认识对象之间存在着有限与无限的矛盾。庄子说：“吾生也有涯，而知也无涯。”

现存《庄子》33 篇。其中内篇 7 篇，外篇 15 篇，杂篇 11 篇。一般认为内篇为庄子著，外篇及杂篇里，可能有他的门人和后来道家的著作搀杂其中。《庄子》在哲学和文学上都有很高价值。其特色是想像丰富、气势雄奇，很多寓言与比喻十分生动感人。如《庖丁解牛》，把一个熟练的宰牛工人分解牛肉的劳动，形容成一次合于音律的艺术表演，使人读来印象至深。

13. What Are the Main Thoughts of Zhuangzi, Who Is Usually Placed on the Same Par as Laozi?

Zhuangzi, a Taoist who came after Laozi, was a philosopher of the Warring States Period(475—221B.C.). Zhuangzi, named Zhou, was from Meng in the State of Song (northeast of present Shangqiu, Henan Province). He lived in the period from about 369 to 286 B.C. It was recorded that he was once an official in charge of gardens in Meng. He declined a large sum of money from the king of Chu who sent for him.

Zhuangzi carried on the ideas put forward by Laozi and maintained that everything in the world kept changing, and that existence came out of nonexistence and would end up in nonexistence after having undergone many changes. He further stated that existence and nonexistence, bigness and smallness, nobleness and humbleness, prettiness and ugliness were all relative to one another, with no difference in nature. He said that everything in the world was no bigger than minute particles, and even something as big as Mount Tai was made up of particles. From this point of view, he insisted that there was no difference between knowledge and reality. He had a famous story entitled *Zhuang Zhou Dreamed of a Butterfly*. He said that once in a dream, he felt himself turning into a butterfly. But when he woke up, he felt he was still Zhuang Zhou. Did Zhuang Zhou dream of a butterfly, or did the butterfly dream of Zhuang Zhou? According to Zhuangzi, both were materialized *dao*.

Zhuangzi thought that since human beings could not affect *dao*, they ought to do *wuwei* (non-action). He advocated that people should make efforts to reach this spiritual status: nature and people coexist and material and people be blended in one. From the aspect of knowledge, he thought that between the subject of knowledge and the object of knowledge, there were contradictions of definiteness and indefiniteness. He said that our life was limited, but knowledge was unlimited.

The present book *Zhuangzi* contains 33 chapters. Among them, there are 7 internal papers, 15 external papers and 11 comprehensive papers. It is generally agreed that those internal papers were written by Zhuangzi himself, while the external and comprehensive papers were probably written by his disciples and other Taoists. *Zhuangzi* stood high both philosophically and literarily. Rich imagination, imposing style, active and moving fables and metaphors feature this book.

14. 墨子是哪个时期的人？他有哪些主张？

墨子名翟，是墨家的创始人。他的生卒年代已经不能确切知道，约生于公元前 468 年，死于公元前 376 年，鲁国（现山东西南部）人（一说宋国）人。是春秋、战国时期的思想家、政治家。墨子曾经学习儒学，因为对“礼”不满，而自己创立新的学派，就是墨家。据说墨子和门徒过着俭朴刻苦的生活，有极其严格的纪律。

墨子反对儒家所强调的等级尊卑，认为“官无常贵而民无常贱”。主张“选择天下贤可者，立以为天子”。天子以下，也要选能人担任官长，不论出身的贵贱。针对儒家提出的“仁”，墨子主张“义”。所谓“义”，就是要“兴天下之利，除天下之害”，使“饥者得食，寒者得衣，劳者得息”。墨子主张兼爱，也就是社会上的人要互爱互助，对待别人就像对待自己一样，这样才够得上称为“义”。当时正是战国时期，诸侯之间战乱不已。墨子认为祸根就在于“不相爱”。他主张“非攻”，也就是要求好战的大国停止攻伐无罪之国。墨子把禹征有苗、汤伐桀、武王伐纣这一类征伐叫作“诛”，认为这一类征伐是顺应天意和民心的。

在名（概念）与实（具体事物）的关系上，墨子主张名从属于实。他认为天下所以认为有的，必然是大家耳闻目睹的，反之，则认为无。他举例说，盲人所以不知道黑白，不是他讲不出黑白的名称，而是因为他看不到黑白的实物。墨子提倡以“三表”作为判断是非真假的标准。三表就是本、原、用，也就是上面“本之于”古代圣明君王的行事，下面“原之于”百姓的耳闻目见的经验，“用”就是检验它实践的效果是不是符合国家百姓的利益。

墨子主张人们通过努力来改变自己的命运。他说：“强必贵，不强必贱”；“强必富，不强必贫”；“强必饱，不强必饥”；“强必暖，不强必寒”。这里的强是指人们的主观努力，所谓“赖其力者生，不赖其力者不生”。

墨子还提出，天的意志是衡量人们行为的准则，要求人们言行要“取法于天”，认为天子如果行善，天能赏他；天子为恶，天能罚他。要求人们尊天地，敬鬼神。

现在流传下来的《墨子》53 篇，大部分是墨子的弟子或再传弟子记述墨子言行的集录。有人指出，其中《亲士》、《修身》、《所染》几篇是后人伪作，不能代表墨家思想。

墨子的学说对当时思想界影响很大，曾与儒家并称“显学”。

14. When Did Mozi Live? What Are His Thoughts?

Mozi, named Zhai, was the founder of Mohism. It is estimated that he was born in about 468 B.C. and died in 376 B.C. He came from the State of Lu (southeast of Shandong province) and was a thinker and politician during the Spring and Autumn and the Warring States periods. He once studied Confucianism. Since he was not satisfied with its idea of *li* (rites) he founded his own doctrine—Mohism. It is said that Mozi and his disciples lived a simple and hard life and followed strict disciplines.

While opposing the idea of social superiority and inferiority stressed by Confucians, he maintained that officials would not always be superior and ordinary people would not always be inferior and advocated selecting the most sagacious person in the whole state to be the king and selecting competent persons to be officials, regardless of their origins. Against *ren* (benevolence) advocated by Confucians, he put forward *yi* (justice). The so-called *yi* means to make sure that the starving are fed, cold sufferers are clothed and workers get proper rest by promoting things beneficial to all and eliminating things harmful to all. Mozi advocated universal love, namely, everyone should love and help each other and treat others the way he would treat himself. During the Warring States Period, wars among different states broke out frequently. Mozi attributed all these to lack of mutual love. He also advocated *feigong* (no attack). He requested the warlike states to stop attacking the innocent states. He thought the war led by Dayu against Youmiao, the war led by King Tang against King Jie and the war led by King Wu against Zhou were all just and conformed to the will of both the heaven and the people.

Concerning the relationship between *ming* (concepts) and *shi* (concrete materials), Mozi maintained that *ming* is subordinate to *shi*. He thought that things that were considered to be existent in the world were those that could be seen and heard by people, otherwise, they were considered as nonexistence. He said that the fact that a blind man could not tell white from black was not because he did not know the concepts of white and black, but because he had never seen the two colours. Mozi put forward three principles to judge the truth. They are: *ben* (in administering the state, the conduct of the previous sagacious kings should be referred to); *yuan* (decisions should be based on the experiences which people gained from what they had seen and heard); and *yong* (the effect of policies should be examined to see whether it served the interest of the state and the people).

Mozi maintained that people should make efforts to change their own fate. He said, "Strive hard, and you will become noble, otherwise, you will be humble forever; strive hard, and you will be rich, otherwise, you will be poor; strive hard, and you will have enough to eat, otherwise, you will suffer starvation." In this way, he stressed the role of subjective will.

Mozi also pointed out that the will of heaven was the criteria to judge the conduct of people. People were requested to act in accordance with the law of heaven. He thought that if a king did good deeds, heaven would reward him, otherwise, he would be punished. So people were requested to pay respect to heaven and to ghosts and deities.

Most of the 53 chapters of *Mozi* still available today were recorded by his disciples or the disciples of his disciples. It was pointed out that some papers in *Mozi* were written by others later and did not reflect the thought of Mozi.

Mohism had significant influence on the ideology and was placed on the same par with Confucianism.

15."民贵君轻"是孟子的观点吗?孟子还有哪些主要观点?

孟子(约公元前372~前289年),名轲,字子舆,邹(今山东邹县东南)人。曾受业于孔子之孙子思的门人。孟子是战国时期的思想家、政治家和教育家。在总的思想体系上,他继承了孔子的儒家思想。孟子曾周游齐、魏、滕等诸侯国,但是他的政治主张没有受到重视。晚年与弟子公孙丑、万章等著述《孟子》7篇。《孟子》书中有很多生动的比喻和雄辩的记述。孟子是继孔子之后儒家的代表人物。

孟子把孔子主张的"仁"发展成"仁政",提倡省刑薄赋,以使"黎民不饥不寒",提出"民为贵,社稷次之,君为轻"的观点。在君臣关系上,他说:"君之视臣如手足,则臣视君如腹心;君之视臣如犬马,则臣视君如路人;君之视臣如草芥,则臣视君如寇雠。"如果统治者十分残暴,则可以把他看作"独夫",起来推翻他。孟子主张统治者"法先王"。认为"不嗜杀人者"才可以统一天下。

在个人修养方面,孟子认为,人"性无有不善"。人生来就有同情、怜悯、羞恶之心,这就是仁、义、礼、智四种天赋道德的萌芽。关于如何做到修养的完善,孟子说:"我善养吾浩然之气。"所谓"浩然之气",后人有的解释为"正气"。孟子认为,只要存心正直,不为邪恶侵害,正气就能发扬光大,"充塞于天地之间",达到"万物皆备于我"的境地。他认为,一个正人君子应该做到"富贵不能淫,贫贱不能移,威武不能屈"。

除此以外,孟子还提出了"天时不如地利,地利不如人和"及"得道者多助,失道者寡助"等著名观点。

孟子的很多主张对后世影响很大。人们常以孔、孟来称呼儒家。

15. Is It Mengzi's Idea that Subjects Are More Valuable than Rulers? What Are His Other Main Points of View?

Mengzi (Mencius) (c.372—289 B.C.), who had once received education from a disciple of Confucius' grandson, was a thinker, politician, and educationist in the Warring states Period (475—221 B.C.). Ideologically, he carried forward Confucianism. He once travelled to the states of Qi, Wei, Teng and so on, where his political views were not accepted. In his late years, together with his disciples such as Gongsun Chou and Wan Zhang, he composed *Mengzi* (*Mencius*), which contained a great number of vivid metaphors and convincing records. Mengzi is the representative figure of Confucianism after Confucius.

Mengzi developed Confucius' main idea *ren* into *renzheng* (benevolent ruling). He advocated less penalty and fewer levies so that the subjects would not suffer from hunger and cold. He also said that the subjects should be most valued, the country lesser valued and the rulers least valued. As to the relationship between the rulers and their subjects, Mengzi said, "If the ruler treats his subjects like brothers, they will take him as an intimate friend in return; if he treats them like horses and cattle, they will regard him as a stranger in return; and if he treats them like wild grass, they will look upon him as foe in return." If a ruler is cruel, he could be seen as an "autocrat" and should be overthrown by his subjects. Mengzi said that rulers should learn from the previous rulers, and those who took a fancy to killing could not be rulers.

As for individual cultivation, Mengzi said that nobody was born evil by nature, and the sense of sympathy, leniency and shame were innate characters of man. This was the bud of the morality of *ren* (benevolence), *yi* (justice), *li* (rites) and *zhi* (wisdom). In practising individual cultivation, Mengzi said that one should develop his sense of justice. He believed that if one was upright and not affected by evilness, his sense of justice would expand so greatly that it will find itself everywhere and in everything. He also stated that a true gentleman would not be corrupted either by wealth or by honours, nor would he swerve from his principles when in poverty or in humble positions, or bend under threats or force.

Apart from the above ideas, Mengzi also put forth the following important ideas: Opportunity is less important than favorable geographical position which is less important than subjective initiatives; a just cause enjoys abundant support while an unjust one finds little support.

Mengzi's ideas have imposed such a great influence on later generations that Confucianism is also referred to as the doctrine of Confucius and Mencius.

16. 继孔、孟之后的著名儒家荀子有什么主要思想主张?

荀子(约公元前313～前238年)名况,赵国(现河北、山西、陕西三省各一部分)人。是战国时期的思想家、教育家。据史书记载,他曾经到齐国游学,后来又到了楚国,由春申君任他为兰陵(现山东苍山县兰陵镇)令。后来留在兰陵著书。战国末期思想家韩非和后来担任秦朝丞相的李斯都是荀子的学生。

荀子批判地继承了孔、孟的儒家思想。他认为天是列星、日月、四时、风雨、寒暑、阴阳等自然界变化的现象,有自己的规律。"天行有常,不为尧存,不为桀亡。"就是说,贤明的尧和残暴的桀,都不能改变自然的规律。同时,荀子进一步提出了"制天而用之"的"人定胜天"的思想,也就是在顺应自然规律的基础上,发挥主观作用,利用自然规律。

荀子认为,人生下来就有各种物质欲望,"饥而欲食,寒而欲暖,劳而欲息,好利而恶害"。所以人生本来性恶,而善是后天学来的。由于人的物质欲望得不到满足,便产生争夺,争夺导致社会秩序混乱,然后有"礼义之道",使社会得到治理。所以,如果坚持不断地学礼义,可以由愚变智,由士、君子学以后成为圣人。

荀子认为,治理国家应该礼、法并用,"由士以上,则以礼乐节之,众庶百姓,则以法数制之"。说到法治,他认为还是离不开人的作用。"法不能独立,令不能自行,得其人则存,失其人则亡。"所以,统治者必须拥有强制权力,用重刑来治理混乱。荀子认为,战国时期之所以那样混乱,原因之一是"百家异说",应该做到"天下无二道,圣人无二心",才能使社会达到安定。他主张"法后王",说:"天地始者,今日是也。"这并不是说今天与开天辟地时一样,而是荀子认为古代帝王的统治术到当时已不能完全适用了。

后世流传的《荀子》共32篇,大部分为荀子所著,《大略》、《宥坐》等后6篇可能是荀子的学生所记。荀子的著作长于说理,分析透辟,组织严密,而且文笔气魄雄浑,说理性很强。其中的《赋篇》开创了以赋为名的文学体制。《成相》篇采用了当时的民歌体,也是诸子散文中少见的。《荀子》诸篇对后世有一定影响。

16. What Are the Main Thoughts of Xunzi, One of the Most Eminent Confucians after Confucius and Mencius?

Xunzi, whose first name was Kuang, lived from about 313 to 238 B.C. in the State of Zhao (a place on the border of present Hebei, Shanxi and Shaanxi provinces).

He was a great thinker and educator during the Warring States Period (475—221 B.C.). It was recorded that he once travelled to the State of Qi on a lecture tour, and then to the State of Chu where he was appointed magistrate of Lanling by the head of Chu, Chunshen. Later on, He stayed there to write books. Both Hanfeizi, a thinker in the late Warring States Period, and Li Si, who was once the prime minister of the State of Qin, were his disciples.

Xunzi inherited the thought of Confucius and Mencius critically. He held that *tian* (heaven) is the phenomenon of the changes of nature, including the various stars, the sun and the moon, the four seasons, wind and rain, coldness and hotness, and *yin* and *yang*. It has its own law, which is influenced neither by Emperor Yao nor by Emperor Jie. This means that neither the sage emperors such as Emperor Yao nor the cruel emperors such as Emperor Jie could change the law of nature. In the meantime, he also put forward the idea that man would triumph over *tian*, if man could apply his subjective initiatives and conform to and take advantage of the natural laws.

According to Xunzi, man has material lusts of all kinds from the date of his birth: feeling hungry, he will have the desire to eat; feeling cold, he will have the desire to keep himself warm; and feeling tired, he will desire to have a rest. Every man prefers advantages to disadvantages. Thus the nature of man is evil, while the virtue of man comes from learning. Failure to satisfy all the material lusts of man results in fights and social turmoil. Following this, the idea of *li* (rites) and *yi* (justice) will come out to bring the society to order. For this reason, if one can persist in learning *li* and *yi*, he will turn wise from stupid and become a saint from a scholar and a gentleman.

According to his thinking, *li* and *fa* (laws) should go together in administering the state. To the literati and officialdom, *li* should be applied, while the ordinary people should be restricted by *fa*. He also insisted that *fa* would not work without man. *Fa* could not stand independently or come to force by itself. With right persons in charge, *fa* would work, while with wrong persons in charge, it would perish. Thus, governors should have coercive power to suppress chaos by severe punishment. Xunzi concluded that one of the causes of the chaotic situation in the Warring States Period was the spread of the unorthodox schools of thought. Only when there was only one school and a unique theory in a society, could the society be stable. He thought that the way to govern should be adjusted in the light of the changing situation, for the ways adopted by previous rulers might have already been out of date.

The book *Xunzi* handed down to this generation contains a total of 32 articles. Most of these articles were written by Xunzi himself. The rest might have been recorded by his disciples. His works feature good reasoning, clear analysis, strictly-organized structure and a touching and lofty style of writing. His *Fupian*, a descriptive prose interspersed with verse, started another literary style. His *Chengxiang* adopted the popular folk song style of that time, which was also rarely seen among the proses written by the famous thinkers during the Warring States Period. The book *Xunzi* had strong influences on the later generations.

17. 先秦诸子之一的韩非子有什么主要思想主张?

韩非(约公元前280~前233年),韩国(现山西一部分及河南一部分)人,战国时期思想家,法家代表人物。他和李斯同是荀子的学生,李斯自以为不如韩非。韩非曾把自己的革新政治的主张几次向韩王提出,都没有被采纳。他的一些著作传到秦国后,得到秦王(即后来的秦始皇)的重视。他应邀到秦国后,引起李斯等人的嫉妒,被谋害(一说自杀)在狱中。所著《韩非子》55篇,大部分为韩非所写,有些篇章可能是后人补充的。

韩非对荀子的思想有所继承和发展,并且部分吸收了老子、商鞅等人的思想,形成了自己的法家思想。韩非认为,历史是进化的。上古时期人们穴居野处,茹毛饮血。有人教给大家构木为巢,以火烹食,这就是圣人。但是如果到大禹治水的时代,还来讲构木为巢,钻木取火,一定会遭到耻笑。同样,到商、周时期,如果有人主张像禹那样,把治理洪水当做迫切任务,也会被耻笑。因此,治理国家不能拘泥于古代圣贤的主张,而应该用法治。韩非继承了商鞅的"法"治,申不害的"术"治,慎到的"势"治,提出了一套法、术、势结合统治的主张。法是君主制定的成文法,术是君主驾驭臣民的手段,势是君主至高无上的权势。韩非认为,对于统治者来说,这三者缺一不可。韩非主张"刑过不避大臣,赏善不遗匹夫"。从现实是在不断变化的这一观点出发,主张用"参验"的办法来认识现实,现实变化了,认识也应该随着变化。他认为,人生来是自私的,如有的父母生了男孩就高兴,生了女孩就杀死,对亲生子女尚且如此,对其他人就更从自己的功利出发了。只有用法来规范人们的行为,调整人们的关系,才能使国家安定。

《韩非子》中的文章说理精密,文笔犀利,有些寓言故事流传到今天,如楚人卖矛与盾的故事,今天我们所用矛盾一词,就是从这儿来的。

17. What Are the Main Thoughts of Hanfeizi, One of the Important Thinkers in the Pre-Qin Period?

Hanfeizi, who lived between about 280 and 233 B.C. in the State of Han (a place on the border of present Shanxi and Henan provinces), was a thinker and a representative of *Fajia* (the Legalists) in the Warring States Period (475—221 B.C.). Although he and Li Si were both disciples of Xunzi, Li Si believed that Hanfeizi was better in many ways. Hanfeizi presented to the ruler of the State of Han his ideas of reform several times, but they were not accepted. Unexpectedly, some of his papers that had spread intc the State of Qin aroused the interest of the ruler there. So he was invited to the State of Qin, where his achievements became the envy of Li Si and others who later on plotted against him. He died in prison in the State of Qin. Most of the 55 papers contained in the book *Hanfeizi* were written by Hanfeizi himself but some might be supplements from others.

By carrying forward and developing the thoughts of Xunzi and also absorbing some of the thoughts of Laozi, Shang Yang (a reformer) and other thinkers, Hanfeizi developed his own *Fajia* doctrine. He thought that history was in evolution. In the far ancient past, people lived in caves and wilderness and ate birds and animals raw. Those who taught people to build shelters with wood and cook food with fire were respected as saints. But when history developed to the time when Dayu harnessed floods, those who still preached about building shelters with wood and making fire by drilling wood would surely be a butt of jokes. If someone took the harnessing of floods as his pressing task during the Shang and Zhou dynasties (c.1600—221.B.C.), he would also be laughed at. This was because that the administration of a state should depend on *fa* rather than on the thoughts of previous sages. By inheriting *fa*, *shu* and *shi* of other thinkers, Hanfeizi came out with his own thought, which combined all the three thoughts into one. *Fa* referred to the written laws promulgated by the rulers, *shu* referred to the means adopted by the rulers to control their subjects, and *shi* referred to the supreme power possessed by the rulers. Hanfeizi believed that a ruler should not be short of any one of the three. He thought that both punishment and reward should be no respecters of social status. Starting from the point of view that reality is in constant change, he advocated that the understanding of the world should progress along with the change of the world. He maintained that men were born selfish. For instance, some parents were happy when they got a baby boy, but they might kill their baby girl. Now that they even treated their own children in such a way, they surely would treat others with a selfish motive. The state could be stabilized only when *fa* was used to regulate the conduct of its people and adjust their interrelationship.

The articles in his book *Hanfeizi* are all well structured. Some fables are still well known among people today. For instance, the term *maodun* (contradiction) which we still use quite frequently today came out of the fable *The Spear and the Shield*.

18. 为什么称朱熹为理学家？他有哪些主要的主张？

朱熹（公元 1130 ~ 1200 年），字元晦，徽州婺源（今属江西）人，是南宋时期的哲学家、教育家。他在哲学上继承并发展了宋朝周敦颐、程颐、程颢关于理、气的主张，形成比较完整的客观唯心主义的理学体系，所以被后人称为理学家。

朱熹主张世界上理和气都是客观存在，“天地之间，有理有气。理者，形而上之道也，生物之本也；气者，形而下之气也，生物之具也”。他认为，理和气是不可分离的，理是“仁、义、礼、智”，气是“金、木、水、火”，二者统一，才有万物。比较起来，理在气先，理是存在于气当中的，并没有“别为一物”。他认为，宇宙起源在于阴、阳二气，而阴、阳二气也是一气所生。所以事物“只是一分为二，节节如此，以至于无穷”。对于人与人之间的关系，朱熹认为，万物皆有理，而所居地位不同，理的作用也不一样，“如为君须仁，为臣须敬，为子须孝，为父须慈，物物各具此理，而物物各异其用”。他认为，“天理”和“人欲”是对立的，要求人们放弃“人欲”，服从“天理”。

在认识与实践的关系上，朱熹认为知在行先。他说：“圣人教人，必以穷理为先，而力行以终之。”他长期从事教育，认为为学的宗旨在于“穷理以致其知，反躬以践其实”。也就是说，先要对世界上事物的“理”有所了解，然后付之实践。在治学处世上，他主张“居敬”（态度严肃认真）。

朱熹博览群书，对经学、史学、文学、乐律都有研究。他还吸收当时自然科学的成果，对自然现象及变化提出了一些见解，如说月亮光是太阳光的反射；在高山上发现残留的螺蚌壳，说明地质变迁，高山曾为大海等。朱熹著作有《四书章句集注》、《楚辞集注》以及门人辑录的《朱子语类》。

朱熹把理学推向一个完整的体系，到明、清两代，认为理学是儒学正宗。朱熹在日本等国也有很大影响。他的博览群书和精密分析的学风，为后世敬仰。

18. Why Is Zhu Xi Referred to as a *Lixuejia* (Rationalistic Philosopher of the Confucian School)? What Are His Main Thoughts?

Zhu Xi (1130—1200 A.D.), from Maoyuan, Huizhou (presently a part of Jiangxi Province), was a philosopher and educator in the Southern Song Dynasty

(1127—1279 A.D.). Philosophically, he carried on the thought of *li* and *qi* advocated by Zhou Dunyi, Cheng Yi and Cheng Hao of the Song Dynasty, and then developed his own philosophical doctrine of objective idealist rationalism. Owing to this achievement, he is generally held as a *lixuejia* (rationalistic philosopher) of Confucianism.

According to Zhu Xi, both *li* and *qi* exist on the earth. He said that *li* was the source for all the living things before taking shape while *qi* was the form for everything after taking shape. He thought that *li* and *qi* were inseparable. *Li* included benevolence, justice, rites and witness; *qi* included metals, wood, water and fire. Only when *li* and *qi* were combined together, could everything exist. Comparatively speaking, *li* came before *qi* and existed in *qi*. They were not two separate materials. He insisted that the universe came out of the blends of *yin* and *yang* while *yin* and *yang* came out of *qi*. Thus, everything came out of one and then produced more and more. As for interpersonal relationship, Zhu Xi thought that everything had its *li*. And the function of *li* varied in different materials depending on the position of the material. Say, kings should be benevolent, and the subjects respectful; children should be obedient and loyal, and fathers loving and kind. So everything had its *li* and the *li* of different materials varied. He noted that *li* and human desire were contradictory to each other and people should abandon their desires and obey *li*.

As for the relationship between knowledge and practice, Zhu Xi insisted that knowledge went before practice. He said that sagacious persons who taught others should first master *li* and then practise it. Having been involved in education for many years, he thought that the aim of education was to master *li* first and then to practise it personally. This means that first one should have some knowledge about the *li* of things in the world and then put it into practice. He held that people should be serious in both education and everyday life.

Zhu Xi was so widely learned that he studied Confucian classics, history, literature and music. He also utilized the new scientific achievement of the time and interpreted some natural phenomena. For instance, the following two records can be seen in his works: The moon reflects the light of the sun; the mussel shells discovered on the top of the mountain indicates geological evolution. His works include *Si shu Zhangju Jizhu* (*A Variorum of the Four Books*), *Chu Ci Jizhu* (*A Variorum of Elegies of Chu*) and *Zhuzi Yulei* (*The Quotations of Zhu Xi*) compiled by his disciples.

Zhu Xi developed the rationalistic Confucian philosophical school to a complete system. During the Ming and Qing dynasties (1368—1911 A.D.), the rationalistic philosophy was considered to be the authentic and orthodox school of Confucianism. Zhu Xi also had strong influences in Japan and other countries. He won respect from later generations as a scholar of profound knowledge and accurate analysis.

19. 道教是何时产生的？南北两大派是怎样发展起来的？

道教是中国土生土长的宗教。它源于先秦的道家，同时继承了中国古代的巫术。道教尊称老子为始祖，把老子的《道德经》奉为道教经典。

道教形成于东汉末年。东汉顺帝年间，方士张道陵（张陵）在四川鹤鸣山创立了天师道。因为入道的人或者被他的魔法治愈的病人都要交五斗米，因此，天师道又叫五斗米教。张道陵死后，他的孙子张鲁做了督义司马，并在汉中（今陕西汉中、南郑等地）建立了政权，实行政教合一的统治，这是利用宗教势力建立的第一个政府。另外，东汉末年，张角在河北创立了太平道，并利用太平道组织黄巾起义，这是中国早期道教的另一派别。由于起义于公元207年彻底失败，太平道从此销声匿迹。

南北朝时期，嵩山道士寇谦之对旧的天师道进行了改革，除去三张（张陵、张衡、张鲁）伪法，提出以封建"礼度"、儒家"佐国扶民"思想为主要内容，以礼拜炼丹为主要形式的新教义，在魏都平城建立天师道场，制定乐章诵诫新法，从而形成新天师道，这就是北天师道。南朝道士陆修静在修改道经的基础上，创立了南天师道。南北两派的天师道主要区别在于：北天师道在教义上基本是排佛的，而南天师道的教义则能吸收佛教的某些内容，和北天师道有很大区别。

唐代为李家天下，因为道教尊老子（李耳）为教主，所以唐朝始终尊崇道教并把道教当做李姓宗教。但当时的佛教由于吸收了道教和儒学等汉民族传统文化，已经变成了一种中国化了的宗教，并在唐代发展到了鼎盛时期。这时，儒、道、佛互相渗透，造成了三教合一的形势。正是在这种形势下，公元1167年，金代王重阳在山东创立了全真道教，其教义就是三教合一。到元朝初年，王重阳的弟子丘处机西游专门拜见成吉思汗，成吉思汗给他赐号"长春真人"，让他总领道教，这是全真道教在北方占统治地位的开始。在南方，也是在元朝初年，元成宗（公元1295～1297年）授张道陵第三十八代孙张与材为"正一教主"，总领天师道各派，统称"正一道"。这样，南北两大派自元朝开始形成并一直流传至今。

19. How Did Taoism Originate and Develop?

Taoism is a religion indigenous to China. Its origin lies in the Taoist school of thought of the Pre-Qin Period and ancient Shamanism. Laozi is held as the chief deity and first ancestor of Taoism. His work *Dao De Jing* is regarded as the basic canon of

Taoism.

Taoism was formed toward the end of the Eastern Han Dynasty (925—220 A.D.). During Emperor Shun's reign, Zhang Daoling, an alchemist, founded *Tianshidao* (celestial master) in Mount Heming of Sichuan. Since every member and those who were cured by his magic were to make a donation of *wu dou mi* (five pecks of rice), his group was also known as *Wudoumijiao*. After Zhang Daoling's death, his grandson Zhang Lu established a new Taoist sect in Hebei called *Taipingdao*, which was another sect in the early history of Taoism. He made use of *Taipingdao* to mobilize the peasants and organized the *Huangjin* peasant uprising. Due to the failure of the uprising in 207 A.D., *Taipingdao* vanished thereafter.

During the Southern and Northern Dynasties (420—589 A.D.), Kou Qianzhi, a Taoist priest of Mount Songshan (of Henan Province), reformed the old *Tianshidao*. He got rid of the old codes, took on Confucian thought of "assisting the government and helping the common people", and confined the main contents of his new religion to religious services and making immortality pills. He made the Wei's capital, Pingcheng, the place to perform rites and initiated some new codes and chants for his cult. So was shaped the new *Tianshidao*, also known as *Bei Tianshidao* (the northern celestial master sect). In the south, Lu Xiujing, a Taoist of Mount Lushan, assembled the collection of traditional Taoist scriptures, compiled them and created *Nan Tianshidao* (the southern celestial master sect). The main difference between these two sects was that the northern sect excluded Buddhism from its doctrine while the southern sect assimilated some ideas of Buddhism.

In the Tang Dynasty (618—907 A.D.), since Laozi (Li Er), the founder of Taoism, shared the same surname with the emperor, Taoism was revered as a religion for the Li family. However, at the same time, Buddhism absorbed Taoism, Confucianism and other Chinese traditional cultures and developed into a Chinese religion which entered its period of great splendor. At this time, Confucianism, Taoism and Buddhism were influenced by each other and had the tendency of combining with each other. In 1167, such a three-in-one combination, *Quanzhendao*, was founded by Wang Chongyang in Shandong. In the early years of the Yuan Dynasty (1271—1368 A.D.), Wang's disciple Qiu Chuji made a journey west and met Emperor Genghis Khan, who named him "*Changchun Zhenren*" and made him general master of Taoism. It was from then on that *Quanzhendao* occupied a dominant position in the north. At the same time, in the south, Zhang Yucai, who was Zhang Daoling's 38th-generation grandson, was made lord of the *Zhengyi* sect by Emperor Chengzong, and all schools of *Tianshidao* were formally called *Zhengyidao*. Thus, ever since the Yuan Dynasty, the two major sects of Taoism were founded and developed till today.

20. 佛教是什么时候传入中国的？汉化佛教有哪些主要宗派？

佛教传入中国汉族地区大约始于公元 1 世纪。根据史书《三国志注》记载：汉哀帝（刘欣）元寿元年（公元前 2 年）大月氏国（现新疆西部）的使者尹存到达长安（现西安西北部），并把佛经口授给博士弟子（汉代博士所教的学生）景卢。但是，多数人都认为，佛教是东汉明帝（刘庄，公元 58 ~ 75 年）时由中亚和印度传入中国的。关于这一点，在一些史书上还有汉明帝感梦求法的传说。相传，东汉永平七年（公元 64 年），明帝夜梦一金人在他的殿庭飞行。第二天他就问身边的大臣梦中所见金人的来历。太史官（掌管起草文书，测算天文历法、典籍等事）博毅说：西方有佛，他要人们敬仰崇拜，皇帝梦见的就是佛。皇帝听了之后，决定派蔡愔、秦景等 18 人去西域求法。公元 67 年，他们从西域把印度僧人迦叶摩腾和竺法兰请到都城洛阳。这三位僧人来时还用白马把佛经驮来。第二年，汉明帝命令在洛阳西门外建造白马寺，这便是中国第一座佛教寺庙。

东汉时期（公元 25 ~ 220 年），佛教在社会上的传播已经比较广泛，但当时的皇帝笃信道家学说，因此，佛教的地位并不稳定，释迦牟尼只是被当做一个普通的神来对待。

魏晋时期（公元 220 ~ 420 年），佛教在中国的影响迅速扩大。当时，由于统治阶级崇尚玄学，使玄学之风大盛。而佛教的教义，特别是“一切法皆空”的佛教思想与玄学有很多共同之处。因此，玄学和佛学很快结合成一体。南北朝时期（公元 420 ~ 581 年），佛教发展迅速，大批寺庙拔地而起，大量的佛经也翻译成了汉语。隋唐时期（公元 581 ~ 907 年），佛教在中国的发展达到了鼎盛阶段。由于皇帝对佛教的大力支持，寺院经济很发达，寺院的住持及和尚为了维持寺院的财产，师徒传承的制度就逐渐固定下来。正因为这样，具有组织意义的各种宗派渐渐形成。隋唐之时，由于小乘佛教在中国已经衰落，大乘佛教占了统治地位。人们所说的中国佛教的八大宗派都是属于大乘佛教。这八个宗派是：天台宗、三论宗、华严宗、禅宗、净土宗、密宗、律宗和法相宗。其中以禅宗势力最大，影响也最深远。唐代（公元 618 ~ 907 年）以来，全国寺庙百分之八十以上属于禅宗。

20. How Did Buddhism Spread in China? What Are the Buddhist Sects?

Buddhism was introduced into the regions inhabited by the Han people around the first century. According to *San Guo Zhi Zhu* (*Notes to Records of the Three Kingdoms*), during the reign of Emperor Ai of the Western Han Dynasty, in 2 B.C., an envoy named Yin Cun from Yuezhi (now the western part of Xinjiang) went to Chang'an (now the northwest of Xi'an) to impart Buddhist sutras verbally to a Chinese scholar named Jing Lu. But the commonly accepted date of the real entrance of Buddhism into China is during the reign of Emperor Ming (58—75 A.D.). There was a legend about him. This emperor was said to have had a dream in which he saw a shining golden image of a god flying over his palace. The emperor asked his minister what the golden image in his dream was. The minister told the emperor that in the Western Regions there was a Buddha, who demanded worship in China, too. The golden image he dreamed of was the Buddha. The emperor then sent a group of eighteen members to the Western Regions. They returned to the capital Luoyang in 67 A.D. with two Indian monks, Kasiapa Matanga and Gobharana, who used white horses to carry over the Buddhist sutras. The emperor ordered a temple called the White Horse Temple to be built in Luoyang. This is the earliest Buddhist temple in China.

However, at that time, the emperor worshipped Taoist doctrines, so the status of Buddhism was not stable yet and Buddha was only treated as an ordinary god. During the Wei and Jin dynasties (220—420 A.D.), the influence of Buddhism spread widely. Buddhist doctrines eventually became interwoven with traditional Chinese ethics and religious concepts. At that time, *xuanxue* (metaphysics) was very popular among the ruling class. The Buddhist doctrine of "believing that the whole universe is unreal" had a lot in common with *xuanxue*, and the two soon became one. During the Southern and Northern Dynasties (420—581 A.D.), the ruling class further helped the spread of Buddhism by building temples and monasteries and translating Buddhist sutras. By the Sui and Tang dynasties (581—907 A.D.), Buddhism had reached its peak in popularity and splendor.

At that time, the monastery economy grew rapidly and became very strong. The monks, in order to defend their property, set up different organizations. These organizations later became the different sects of Buddhism, among which were the Mahayana *Tiantai* sect, the *Sanlun* sect, the *Huayan* sect, the *Chan* sect, the *Jingtu* sect, the *Mi* sect, the *Lü* sect and the *Faxiang* sect. The *chan* sect was the most powerful and influential, covering eighty percent of the temples in China.

21. 中国佛教寺院中的殿堂分哪几个部分？供奉的神有哪些？三世佛是怎么回事？

中国的佛教寺院一般由山门、天王殿、大雄宝殿、观音殿、藏经殿等组成。

大雄宝殿为正殿，是供奉佛的大殿，里边供着佛教的缔造者释迦牟尼的佛像。但是在许多寺院的大雄宝殿里供奉着三尊佛，这叫三佛同殿。这三尊佛在殿内的安排也有两种不同的方式。一种是供奉“竖三世佛”。正中为现世佛即释迦牟尼，左侧为过去佛即燃灯佛，梵文为 Dipamkara，佛经说，他出生时，身边一切光明如灯，因此得名。如果按资格来分，他是释迦牟尼的老师，所以他叫过去佛。右侧为未来佛即弥勒佛，梵文叫 Maitreya，《弥勒下生经》说，他从“兜率天”下生在这个世界上，在龙华树下继承释迦牟尼的佛位而成佛，所以他是未来佛。另外的一组三世佛叫“横三世佛”。正中为娑婆世界的释迦牟尼佛，左侧为东方净琉璃世界的药师佛，右侧为西方极乐世界的阿弥陀佛。大雄宝殿的佛的两侧，近世多塑十六罗汉或十八罗汉。

观音殿是一般佛教寺院中都有的。大殿里供的是观音菩萨像。自从佛教传入中国，观音的造像经历了由男到女的变化。东晋、南北朝以前，观音的形象为男性，如敦煌石窟的观音雕像。隋唐以后，观音则变成了女性。观音菩萨在中国人的心目中是一位大慈大悲的救世主。

藏经阁主要有三部分组成。佛教的经典中第一部分是释迦牟尼本人的语录，第二部分是佛教的教规，第三部分则是阐述佛教教义的著作。

天王殿里供奉四大天王。这四大天王分别是：南方增长天王，身青色，持宝剑；西方广目天王，身白色，穿甲胄，手中缠绕一龙，掌碧玉琵琶一面；北方多闻天王，身绿色，穿甲胄，右手持宝伞；东方持国天王，身白色，穿甲戴胄，左手把刀，右手持鞘拄地。以上四位天王的形象，是中国早期，特别是唐代佛像画中的典型形象。宋、元以后，佛教进一步汉化，四大天王就成了四大金刚，四大天王手中所持的兵器也完全变了样。他们分别掌管风、调、雨、顺。

21. What Are the Arrangements of the Halls and the Deities in the Chinese Buddhist Temples?

A Chinese Buddhist temple normally consists of the Hall of the Heavenly Guardians, the Sanctuary of the Buddha, the Hall of Guanyin (the goddess of mercy), the repository for the scriptures and the main gate called *shanmen*.

The Sanctuary of the Buddha, the main hall in a Buddhist temple, often houses an image of Sakyamuni, the founder of Buddhism. In many temples, it houses three Buddha images: Dipamkara, the Buddha of the past; Sakyamuni, the Buddha of the present; and Maitreya, the Buddha of the future. According to Buddhist scripture, when the Buddha of the past was born, everything around him was bright. He was considered the teacher of Sakyamuni, so people called him the Buddha of the past. Another trinity often consists of Bhaisa Yaguru (the Buddha of medicine), representing the East; Sakyamuni, representing the native place; and Amitabha, representing Sukhayati, the pure land. Along both sides of the Buddha images, a group of sixteen or eighteen arhats are generally erected.

The Hall of Guanyin Bodhisattva exists in almost every Buddhist temple. After the introduction of Buddhism from India to China, the image of Guanyin changed from time to time. Before the Northern and Southern Dynasties(420—581A.D.), Guanyin was worshipped as a male Bodhisattva. After the Tang Dynasty(618—907A.D.), it became a female Bodhisattva, the goddess of mercy.

The repository mainly houses the Tripitaka, which consists of three parts. The first part is a collection of Sakyamuni's teachings, the second part is the Buddhist rules and regulations, and the third part is the exposition of the Buddhist doctrines.

There are four deities in the Hall of the Heavenly Guardians. They are virudhaka, the guardian of the south; Virupaksa, the guardian of the west; Vaisramana, the guardian of the north; and Dhrtaratra, the guardian of the east.

The guardian of the south is a blue one holding a double-edged sword. The guardian of the west is a white one with a dragon twisting in his hands. The guardian of the north is a green one in an armour with an umbrella in his right hand. And the guardian of the east is a white one in an armour, with a sword in his left hand and a sheath in his right hand. These were typical images of the four guardians portrayed in the paintings of the Tang Dynasty. After the Song and Yuan dynasties, along with the spreading of Buddhism among the Han nationality, the four guardians changed into four grand warriors and their weapons also changed. Their duties were to be in charge of *feng*, *tiao*, *yu*, *shun*— to make sure that there would be good weather and good harvests in the years to come.

22. 城隍是什么？城隍迷信是怎样兴起和发展的？

在旧中国，全国大大小小的城市里，都有城隍庙，有的城市还不止一座。看来城隍老爷的影响不亚于佛、道诸神。那么，城隍是什么意思呢？城，就是城市的意思，隍，即水庸，意思是无水的城堑。据《辞源》释义，城隍是一种神的名字。在八蜡（八种神）中，水庸之神居第七位。因此，祭水庸就是祭城隍之始。至于水庸何时演变成城隍，史无记载。实际上，城隍就是城市的保护神。

最早载于史书的城隍庙，是三国（公元 220～280 年）时吴国修建的芜湖城隍庙。它建于公元 240 年，迄今已有 1700 多年的历史。

据《礼记》记载，最早祭祀八蜡始于公元前 2300 年的尧。当时，每年秋收之后，于年底祭祀八种神，城隍也在祭祀之列。

城隍的职责是什么呢？是什么样的神呢？一般认为他是阴间世界管领亡魂之神，城隍老爷对他管辖之内的人，都有一本账，当一个人死了之后去阴曹地府的阎王殿报到时，这个人在阳间的行为表现都记录在案。从历史上看，到了明代（公元 1368～1644 年），祭祀城隍、大兴城隍庙以及对城隍加官晋升才真正兴盛起来。洪武二年（公元 1369 年），朱元璋即封京都城隍为“承天鉴国司民升福明灵王”，封开封城隍为“显圣王”。同时，又下令天下各府、州、县重建城隍庙，并按级别加封城隍为城隍王、城隍公、城隍侯及城隍伯。这种对城隍的崇拜一直延续到清朝末年。

城隍是人们心目中的阴间长官，所以，人们把过去的名人、英雄立为当地的城隍老爷，希望他们的英灵能保佑百姓，打击邪恶之鬼。不同的地区都有不同的城隍爷。如杭州的城隍庙里供的就是周新。周新是明朝浙江按察使，为人廉明刚直，后遭诬陷被杀。据传说，他死后不久，明成祖（朱棣，公元 1403～1424 年）忽见一人穿红袍立于日中，此人据说就是周新的鬼魂。这个鬼魂说：他的职责是惩治贪官污吏和盗贼。因此，周新后来就被封成“城隍爷”。类似的情况在上海和南宁也有。在上海的城隍就有三个：一是东汉大将霍光，二是元末明初的秦裕伯；三是清末爱国将领陈化成。在广西南宁的城隍庙里供的城隍却是苏缄。

22. What Is *Chenghuang*? How Did the Cult of *Chenghuang* Originate and Develop?

Chenghuang temples, big or small, could be seen everywhere in old China. In some cities, there were more than one *Chenghuang* temple. This might indicate that the influence of *Chenghuang* God was no less than that of those gods in both Buddhism and Taoism. Then, what is the meaning of *Chenghuang*? *Cheng* referred to city; while *huang* was the wat with no water—*shuiyong*. *Chenghuang* was said to be the name of a deity in *Ci Yuan* (*A Dictionary of Word Origins*). *Shuiyong* was the seventh deity of *Ba La* (the eight deities). The worship of *Shuiyong* was the beginning of worshipping *Chenghuang*. There were no records when *Shuiyong* was transformed to *Chenghuang*. Actually, *Chenghuang* was the protection god for cities.

The first *Chenghuang* temple recorded in historic books was built in Wuhu in 240 A.D. about 1700 years ago by the State of Wu, one of the three states during the period of the Three Kingdoms(220—280 A.D.).

Li Ji (*The Book of Rites*) recorded that the first man who worshipped *Ba La* was Yao, who lived about 2300 years ago. At that time, a ceremony was held every year after the autumn harvest to worship *Ba La*, among whom *Chenghuang* was included.

What was the responsibility of *Chenghuang*? What kind of god was it? It was usually said that it was the deity who took care of the souls of the dead. *Chenghuang* God kept a record for everyone in his charge. When someone died and went to the nether world to report, his deeds on the earth had been clearly recorded. To review Chinese history in retrospect, we can see that it was not until the Ming Dynasty(1368—1644 A.D.) that worshipping *Chenghuang*, building *Chenghuang* temples and conferring titles on *Chenghuang* had become popular. Beside granting titles to the two *Chenghuang*, one in the capital (present Nanjing) and the other in Kaifeng, Zhu Yuanzhang, the first emperor of the Ming Dynasty, also decreed to rebuild *Chenghuang* temples and conferred titles such as kings, princes, dukes and earls on different *Chenghuang* respectively in the second year (1369 A.D.) of the reign of Emperor Hongwu, This cult of *Chenghuang* lasted till the end of the Qing Dynasty (1644—1911 A.D.).

In ordinary Chinese people's eyes, *Chenghuang* was the magistrate of the nether world. For this reason, late heroes were taken as *Chenghuang* gods by the local people in the hope that the souls of these late heroes would protect the local people and dispel evils. There were different *Chenghuang* gods in different places. In Hangzhou, it was Zhou Xin, who used to be the judge in Zhejiang in the Ming Dynasty. Zhou was honest and straight, but was framed and killed. Legend goes that soon after the death of Zhou Xin, Emperor Chengzu (1403—1424 A.D.) of the Ming Dynasty saw a man in red robe standing in the sun, who was believed to be Zhou's soul. The soul said that his responsibility was to punish corrupt officials and robbers. Thus, later on, Zhou Xin was conferred the title *Chenghuang* God. Similar things happened also in Shanghai and Nanning. In Shanghai, there were three *Chenghuang* gods. One was Huo Guang, a general of the Eastern Han Dynasty (25—220 A.D.); the second was Qin Yubo, who lived at the turn of the Yuan and Ming dynasties; the third was Chen Huacheng, a general of the Qing Dynasty. In Nanning, the *Chenghuang* god was Su Jian, a hero in the Song Dynasty (960—1279 A.D.).

23. 为什么北京雍和宫有的佛像面目狰狞?

北京的雍和宫是喇嘛教的一座寺院。规模很大,共有七进院落,以高达 18 米的白檀木大佛和紫檀木的罗汉山以及乾隆皇帝的"洗三盆"而著称。在雍和宫的第四进院落的密宗殿和第六进院落的东配殿中,都有一些佛像,造型和其他佛像不同,全身和脸部都是青蓝色,头饰骷髅,颈挂人头,使人看了觉得可怕。这些佛像是属于密宗佛像。按教义讲,这些都是菩萨的化身,是为了铲除异端、镇压邪恶而现身的"愤怒相",俗称欢喜佛。其双身佛像是象征着智慧与禅定的结合。

密宗又称密派、密乘,是相对佛教中的显派而言的。相传是释迦牟尼传给弟子们的一种秘密修行方法。还有一种说法是:密宗是大乘佛教中部分派别与婆罗门教(印度古代的一种宗教,后经改革成为印度教)相互调和的产物。密宗认为佛与众生体性相同,如果人能手结密契(身密)、口诵真言(语密)、心观佛尊(意密),就能使"三业"(身、口、意)清净,与佛的身、口、意三密相应,可以即身成佛。密宗强调仪轨必须严格,奥秘必须密传。公元 8 世纪佛教的显、密两派都传入中国西藏,到 10 世纪后期,喇嘛教兴起,其教义包含了佛教中的显、密二宗,而以密宗为主。因此,雍和宫和不少喇嘛教的寺院殿中,都供有密宗佛像。

23. Why Do the Images of Buddha in Yonghe Lamasery in Beijing Have Ferocious Features?

Yonghe Lamasery in Beijing has a total of seven courtyards and it's noted for its 18-meter-high image of Buddha made of white sandalwood and the arhats hill made of indigo-blue sandalwood as well as the "washing bowl" of Emperor Qianlong of the Qing Dynasty (1644—1911 A.D.). In the *Mi* Sect Hall in the fourth yard and in the eastern side-hall in the sixth yard, some of the images of Buddha look quite different from others. With indigo-blue body and complexion, and with human skulls as decorations and human heads hanging around their necks, these Buddha images really look frightful. They are classified as the *Mi* Sect Buddha images. According to Buddhism doctrines, these are incarnations of Buddha with indignant looks to eliminate heterodoxies and suppress evils. They are also called "happy Buddha". The double-body images of the "happy Buddha" represent the blend of both wisdom and deep meditation.

Mi is the title for one of the schools of Buddhism, distinct from the *Xian* sect. As a legend goes, the *Mi* sect is a secret way in practising Buddhism which Sakyamuni handed down to his disciples. Another legend says that the *Mi* sect is the blend of some groups in the Mahayana doctrine and Brahmanism (an ancient Indian religion which has evolved into the present Hinduism). The *Mi* sect maintains that Buddha is the same by nature as all living creatures. If human beings can do secret gestures with their hands (body secret), recite Buddhism doctrine (language secret) and look at the Buddha with their hearts full of respect(mind secret), they can keep their bodies, mouths and minds calm and peaceful and turn into Buddha. The *Mi* sect stresses strict rules and secret delivery of profound mystery. In the eighth century, both the *Mi* and the *Xian* sects were introduced into the Tibetan area of China. In the late tenth century, Lamaism was on the upgrade. Though the doctrine of Lamaism contains both the *Mi* and the *Xian* sects, the *Mi* sect prevails. Therefore, there are Buddha images of the *Mi* sect style in Yonghe Lamasery and many other lamaseries.

24. 八仙包括哪些神仙?

道教八仙的故事在中国流传已经几百年了,影响很大,在戏曲、文学、绘画和工艺美术作品中常常可以看到八仙的形象。“八仙过海——各显神通”也是人们时常引用的一个与八仙有关的成语典故。

今天人们所熟知的八仙是下面八位神仙:钟离权、李铁拐、张果老、蓝采和、吕洞宾、何仙姑、韩湘子和曹国舅。其中何仙姑还是一位女仙。

钟离权,复姓钟离,名权,又称汉钟离,是一位坦胸露腹、头梳丫髻、手持棕扇的道人。有一种说法认为钟离权是八仙之首,八仙中的吕洞宾是他的弟子。另一种说法则认为钟离权是经李铁拐点化上山学道的。历史上唐朝(公元 618 ~ 907 年)确有一位名叫钟离权的道士,他嗜酒成性,行为放浪,大概就是这位神仙的原型。有关钟离权的传说早在北宋时代(公元 960 ~ 1127 年)就已经出现了。

李铁拐又称铁拐李,是个传说中的人物。他的名字实际上是他的绰号。因为他跛足,走路拄一铁拐杖,故而得名。传说他本来相貌堂堂,只因他的灵魂飞出身外去和师傅修行,回来时发现自己的躯壳已被徒弟焚化,不得已利用一具饿殍借尸还魂,结果变成了后来那副龌龊的样子。他的形象虽然不好,却乐善好施,他身背的葫芦里就放有治病救人的灵丹妙药,而且通常被认为是八仙之首。

张果老在历史上确有其人,姓张名果,是唐代的道士。只因他长相老,人们在他的名字后加上“老”以示尊敬。道情筒是他的法宝。他得道后,云游四方,传唱道情以劝化世人。和张果老形影不离的是一头毛驴。有趣的是这头毛驴不仅能日行千里,不骑时还可以折叠起来,十分方便。更有趣的是张果老倒骑在驴背之上,大概是教导世人凡事要回头看看。

蓝采和的故事最早出现在南唐(公元 937 ~ 975 年)。传说他穿破衣烂衫,一脚着靴,一脚跣露,手持大拍板行乞于闹市。据说蓝采和是五代(公元 907 ~ 960 年)时的伶人许坚,蓝采和只是艺名。他是经钟离权引度成仙的。

吕洞宾,姓吕,名岩,字洞宾,号纯阳子。他头戴纯阳巾,身背宝剑,是一副清秀道士的模样。在八仙中吕洞宾影响最大,传说故事最多。他被奉为全真道教的北五祖之一,故又称吕祖。在不少地方建有吕祖庙。吕岩是唐代人,传说他曾两次考进士不中,遂浪迹江湖,于 64 岁遇钟离权,被点化得道。在有关吕洞宾的传说故事中最有名的有“黄粱梦”、“钟离权十试吕洞宾”、“三戏白牡丹”和“飞剑斩黄龙”等。

何仙姑是一位手持莲花的女仙。传说她是唐代广州增城县人,原名是何秀姑。她 13

岁时入山采药，遇吕洞宾，吃了吕洞宾所赐的仙桃后得道成仙。何仙姑擅长占筮，能为人判断吉凶。

韩湘子原名韩湘，是唐代大文学家韩愈的侄孙。韩愈被贬潮阳行至蓝关时曾赠韩湘诗一首，诗中说："云横秦岭家何在，雪拥蓝关马不前。"韩湘子得道成仙大约从此附会而来。传说韩湘子有奇术，能使花卉顷刻开花。笛子是他的象征物，由此人们认为他是乐师尊崇的神。

曹国舅是八仙中出现最晚的一位，有关他的故事也最少。历史上确实有一位姓曹的国舅（皇后或妃子的兄弟），叫曹佾，是宋仁宗赵祯的国舅。曹佾性情温和，多才多艺，并能在政治动荡的时代明哲保身，活到72岁。传说他是被钟离权和吕洞宾引入仙班，成了一位头戴纱帽、身披红袍、手持尺板的神仙。

八仙的传说故事出现得有早有晚，张果、韩湘、吕岩早在唐代就有记载了。但是八仙凑在一起，成为一个神仙集团则是在元代（公元1271～1368年）。这一集团的形成经过了一个长时间的民间加工演化过程。八仙中有些有真人真事的影子，有些则纯属传说人物。关于他们的身世以及如何得道成仙亦是众说纷纭。但是把这些不同时代、相互无关的人物变成神仙，又把他们凑在一起并流传数百年至今，充分显示了民间文艺的丰富想像力和顽强的生命力。

24. Who Were *Baxian* (the Eight Taoist Immortals)?

The widespread legendary tales of *Baxian* have been told and retold for several centuries, whose images can be seen very often in theatrical, literary and artistic works as well as in arts and crafts. *Baxian guo hai, ge xian shentong* (the eight immortals cross the sea, each showing his or her special prowess) is a frequently quoted proverb derived from the story of these immortals.

The eight immortals known intimately to people today are Zhongli Quan, Li Tieguai, Zhang Guolao, Lan Caihe, Lü Dongbin, He Xiangu, Han Xiangzi and Cao Guojiu. He Xiangu is a female immortal among the eight.

Zhongli Quan, whose bisyllabic surname is Zhongli and given name is Quan, is also known as Han Zhongli. He is generally depicted as a Taoist priest who always holds a fan, his emblem, in his hand with his shirt unbuttoned and his hair tied into a bun on his head. Some people believe that he is the chief of *Baxian* and Lü Dongbin used to be his disciple. Other people say that he became converted to Taoism at the initiation of Li Tieguai. There was historically a Taoist monk in the Tang Dynasty (618—907 A.D.) named Zhongli Quan, who was unrestrained in manner and addicted in alcohol. He was most likely the model from whom the Taoist immortal Zhongli Quan was created.

Li Tieguai, also known as Tieguai Li, is a legendary figure. Tieguai was in fact a nickname given to him because he was crippled and had to use a *tieguai* (an iron walking stick). Legend has it that he was originally a man of handsome features. Once he went in his soul to practise Taoism with his converter, but when he returned, he found that his body had been cremated. He had no choice but to be reincarnated in the corpse of a starved lame man. Ugly as he was, he was kind and generous, and always ready to help the invalid with the miraculous cure in his bottle gourd he carried all the time. He is normally recognized as the chief of *Baxian*.

Zhang Guolao is a historical figure, a Taoist monk of the Tang Dynasty, whose real name is Zhang Guo. *Lao* (old) is added to his name out of respect for him and for his aged appearance. *Daoqingtong* (a musical instrument in the shape of a bamboo tube) is his emblem. After he attained immortality, he roamed about the world and sang to exhort people to do good. Zhang Guolao was always accompanied by a donkey and, very interestingly, the beast could not only cover a thousand *li* (half a kilometer) a day but also be folded up when he did not ride it. People may find it equally interesting that Zhang Guolao rode the animal backwards, by which he might suggest that people should always review what they have done.

The story about Lan Caihe was first told as early as in the 10th century. It is said that he was always in rags with one foot in a boot and the other bare. He was often found begging in busy streets with big clappers in his hand. It is believed that the story of Lan Caihe was based on the actor Xu Jian of the period of the Five Dynasties (907—960 A.D.) whose stage name was Lan Caihe. It was Zhongli Quan who converted him and made him enter on immortality.

Lü Dongbin is also known as Lü Yan and Chunyangzi. He was a handsome-looking Taoist priest with *chunyang* (the Taoist kerchief) on his head and a sword slung across his back. Among *Baxian*, he is the most popular one and a lot of stories have been told about him. He is revered as one of the five founders of *Quanzhendao* (wholly genuine) of Taoism in north China, and thus he is also called Lü Zu (ancestor). It is believed that Lü Dongbin lived in the Tang Dynasty. He failed twice in the national examination and then he started to live a wandering life. He met with Zhongli Quan, and learnt the secrets of Taoism and attained to immortality. The best-known stories about Lü Dongbin include *Huang Liang Meng* (*Golden Millet Dream*), *Zhongli Quan Shi Shi Lü Dongbin* (*Overcoming the Ten Temptations Emposed by Zhongli Quan*), *San Xi Baimudan* (*Teasing the White Peony Three times*) and *Fei Jian Zhan Huanglong* (*Slaying the Yellow Dragon*).

He Xiangu (*xiangu*—fairy) was a female immortal who always carried her emblem, the lotus. According to legends, her real name was He Xiugu who lived in Zengcheng, Guangzhou in the Tang Dynasty. At the age of thirteen, she encountered Lü Dongbin when she was collecting medicinal herbs in the mountains. Having eaten the divine peach Lü Dongbin gave her, she became an immortal. She was known to be skilled in divination and often told fortunes for people.

Han Xiangzi was originally known as Han Xiang, who was a grand nephew of Han Yu, a famous scholar of the Tang Dynasty. Once Han Yu was relegated and on his way to Chaoyang for his new post, he met Han Xiangzi and presented a poem to him. It is most likely that from this poem the story of Han Xiangzi evolved. It is said that Han Xiangzi's power was so magic that he could make flowers blossom instantaneously. His emblem was a flute and he was hence regarded as the patron of musicians.

Cao Guojiu (*guojiu*—brother of the wife or concubine of the emperor) had later records than the other immortals and there were less stories told about him. In history, there was indeed a person who had the surname Cao and was the brother of the emperor's wife. It was Cao You, the brother of Emperor Renzong's wife of the Song Dynasty (960—1279 A.D.). Cao You was good-tempered and talented. He could play safe at the time of political turbulence and lived to be seventy-two. It is said that he was converted and became an immortal co-initiated by Zhongli Quan and Lü Dongbin. He was often seen wearing a court headdress and a red official robe and his emblem was a pair of castanets held in his hand.

The legendary tales about the personages of *Baxian* took shape in different times, some as early as in the Tang Dynasty such as those of Zhang Guolao, Han Xiangzi and Lü Dongbin. However, it was not until the Yuan Dynasty (1271—1368 A.D.) that these tales were put together to form a story of the group and it took a fairly long time for this group to shape on the basis of facts as well as legends. There are various versions about the life experiences of *Baxian* and their ways to immortality. However, viewing from the fact that these unrelated personages from different times were made immortals and put together and that their stories have been told and retold for centuries till today, we can not but admire the highly imaginative power and great vitality of the folk art.

25. 门神的来历如何？为什么各地的关帝庙很多？

祭门神是中国古老的习俗。据记载，周朝（约公元前1100～256年）天子及诸侯每年都要祭祀门户、道路、井、灶、土地，即所谓"五祀"。官员和百姓也要祭祀门神。但是当时的门神只是泛指镇守大门的神灵。西汉（公元前206～公元24年）时，广川（今河北枣强县东北）惠王刘越的殿门前，画有武士成庆的像，穿短衣大裤，佩长剑。这可能是以武士为门神的开始。当时还传说古黄帝时候，有神荼（Shénshū）、郁垒（Yùlǜ）两位神仙，专门负责察看鬼的作为，在鬼门旁把守，如见有祸害人的恶鬼，就用苇索捆绑起来，去喂老虎。因此人们用桃木（古人相信桃木可以驱鬼）刻成凶恶的神荼、郁垒模样，春节时挂在门上，驱赶恶鬼。后来为了省事，又改为将神荼、郁垒神像画在桃木板上，挂在门前。也有用桃木板书写符咒挂在门前驱鬼的，称为"桃符"，后来演变成春联。

唐朝以后，用武将画像作为门神的逐渐多了起来。武将中画得最多的要算秦琼（秦叔宝）和尉迟恭（尉迟敬德）了。这两位武将是唐朝的开国功臣，相传唐太宗（李世民）在开国登基前杀人太多，因此做皇帝后夜晚常梦见恶鬼，不能安眠，秦琼、尉迟恭知道后，身着甲胄，手持兵器，夜晚守卫宫门两旁。从此唐太宗不再被恶鬼骚扰，得以安眠。后来，唐太宗觉得两员大将过于辛苦，命人将这两人的画像挂在宫门两侧，这就是秦琼、尉迟恭做门神的来历。民间为了使门神显得更威武，就把门神画成骑红马，手持锏锏或大刀。此外，还有以赵云、马超、薛仁贵等历代武将作为门神的。

过去人们除了在大门上张贴武将门神外，还有在内宅堂屋大门上张贴"文门神"的。用意大都是迎接吉祥幸福。这类门神头戴乌纱帽，身穿一品官服，手抱牙笏或吉祥器物。这就是俗话常说的"天官赐福"的天官。有时人们把天官与送子娘娘配对张贴，也有贴"和合二仙"（象征夫妻和谐、家庭幸福）的，还有贴刘海戏金蟾的。

中国各地关帝庙（又叫关圣庙、老爷庙）都很多。仅北京一地，据《京师乾隆地图》所记载，当时城内专祀关帝和以祀关帝为中心的庙宇就有116座，几乎占全城庙宇的十分之一。如果加上郊区、县的数字，可能超过200座，真可算供奉各种神灵庙宇之首位了。为什么关帝庙这么多呢？因为过去从皇帝到民间，都认为关帝爷是忠、孝、义、勇的化身。在历史上，这个人确实有过。他是三国（公元220～280年）时蜀汉大将，姓关名羽字云长，河东解县（今山西解虞县）人。年轻时投奔涿郡，跟随刘备起兵，刘备待他情同兄弟。建安五年（公元200年）刘备被曹操打败，关羽被曹操俘获。曹操爱其才，用献帝名义封他为汉寿亭侯，但是关羽仍然奔归刘备。刘备立为汉中王以后，拜关羽为前将军。在与曹军作战中，关羽水淹七军、擒于禁、斩庞德，威名远震。后来孙权派将袭击荆州，关羽兵败被杀。

这是建安二十四年(公元219年)的事。关羽死后41年,即公元260年,才被蜀后主刘禅追封为壮缪侯。

关羽死后,只有荆州一带有人奉祀他。到宋朝,关羽的地位才变得显赫起来,宋哲宗、徽宗都给他加了封号。明朝初年,《三国演义》的出版,也对提高关羽的威望起了推动作用。佛、道两教也都有关羽显圣、降伏妖魔的传闻,因此,"关老爷"的庙越来越多,连藏传佛教——喇嘛教地区也有关帝庙。

25. What Is the Origin and Development of the Door-gods? Why Are There So Many Lord Guan Yu's Temples Throughout China?

It is an old Chinese custom to offer sacrifices to the door-gods. According to historic records, in the Zhou Dynasty (c. 1100—256 B.C.), every year, the emperors and dukes would offer sacrifices to the door, road, well, kitchen, and land. These were the so-called "five worships". Officials and ordinary people would also offer sacrifices to the door-gods. However, the door-gods at that time were just deities to guard the gates. During the Western Han Dynasty (206 B.C.—24 A.D.), on the palace gate of Liu Yue, King Hui in Guangchuan (presently a part of Hebei Province), there was a picture of the warrior Cheng Qing in short jacket and long trousers with a sword in his hand. Perhaps, this was the beginning of taking a warrior as the door-god. It was also said that in the age of the Yellow Emperor, there were two immortals, Shenshu and Yulü, whose duty was to observe the behaviors of the ghosts and guard the ghosts' gate. If a ghost was found doing evil, they would tie it with a reed string and take it to feed the tigers. Since the ancient people believed that peach wood had the magic power of driving away ghosts, they carved pictures of Shenshu and Yulü on peach wood and hung them on the doors during the Spring Festival to ward off the ghosts. In order to make it simpler, people later on just drew their pictures on peach wood. Some people also wrote incantations on peach wood to drive away the ghosts. This is called "peach wood charms against evils", which developed into couplets pasted on gate posts or door panels.

After the Tang Dynasty(618—907 A.D.), more and more people began to use pictures of generals as the door-gods. Among all the generals painted as the door-gods, Qin Qiong and Yuchi Gong were the most popular. These two generals had rendered outstanding service to the founding of the Tang Dynasty. It was said that before Emperor Taizong (Li Shimin) ascended the throne, he had killed too many people. When he became the emperor, he often dreamed of ghosts in his nightmares and could not sleep well. Hearing this, Qin Qiong and Yuchi Gong offered to guard the palace gate every night with armour and helmets on and weapons in hands. From then on, Emperor Taizong was never again disturbed by ghosts. Some time later, the emperor thought that it would be too hard for the two generals to stand there every night. He then ordered the pictures of these two generals to be drawn and hung on the two sides of the palace gate. This was how Qin Qiong and Yuchi Gong became the door-gods. To make the door-gods look more imposing, ordinary people drew the door-gods riding on red horses with large knives in their hands. Other generals such as Zhao Yun, Ma Chao and Xue Rengui were also drawn as the door-gods.

Apart from pasting pictures of military generals on their gates as the door-gods, people also had "civil door-gods" on the doors of their central rooms. The purpose of doing this was to welcome good luck and happiness. The civil door-gods usually wore a black gauze cap and a uniform for the first-rank officials with a tablet or some other things symbolizing good luck in their hands. They were the commonly-called heaven officers in "Heaven Officers' Blessing". Sometimes, a heaven officer and a child-sending goddess were pasted together on the two sides of the door.

There are a lot of Lord Guan's temples throughout China. In the city proper of Beijing, there were 116 Lord Guan's temples in the reign of Emperor Qianlong of the Qing Dynasty(1644—1911 A.D.), accounting for one-tenth of all the temples in the whole city. If those in the counties and suburbs were added, the number would be above two hundred. It stands to reason that Lord Guan's ranked first among all the temples. Why were there so many Lord Guan's temples ? The answer lies in the fact that in the past, from the emperors to the ordinary people, everyone regarded Lord Guan as the incarnation of loyalty, filial piety, righteousness and bravery. Guan Yu was a real person in Chines history, who was a general serving Liu Bei in the Three

Kingdoms Period(220—280 A.D.). Once he was captured by Cao Cao, who intended to keep him by promising to confer him a title, he refused the request and managed to flee back to Liu Bei again. When Liu Bei was enthroned to be the king of Hanzhong, Guan was appointed to be front general. He was well-known for his countless outstanding military achievements. In 219, he was killed when he was arrested by the enemy. Forty-one years after his death, i.e. in 260, he was granted posthumously the title of Duke Zhuangmu.

At the beginning, only the people in Jingzhou area (presently part of Hubei Province) offered sacrifices to Guan Yu because it was believed that Guan Yu was seen in one of the temples in Jingzhou after his death. It was not until the Song Dynasty (960—1279 A.D.) that his status rose. Both Emperor Zhezong and Emperor Huizong granted him titles. In the early Ming Dynasty(1368—1644 A.D.), *San Guo Yanyi* (*The Romances of the Three Kingdoms*) was published, which greatly increased the escalation of Guan Yu's prestige. Both Buddhism and Taoism have stories of his power. More and more Lord Guan's temples were built in China, even in Lamaism regions.

26. 中国戏曲是如何产生和发展的?

中国戏曲产生的时间可追溯到远古时代。在古代,人们相信在人和神之间有一种特殊的人,他们是神的使者,可以传达神的意志,这些使者就是觋和巫。觋和巫为了取悦神灵,就用跳舞和口唱的形式表达他们的情感,这可以说是戏曲产生的雏形。后来,在春秋(公元前 770~前 476 年)时期,已经出现了专职的人员用说笑话、讲故事以及舞蹈和杂技形式在国王或国王客人面前献艺来取乐的事情。在当时来说,这种形式是音乐和表演相结合,也可以说是最古老的戏曲了。

到公元 500 年的时候,作为戏剧的核心部分——演唱、故事情节、舞蹈动作已经有机地结合在一起。唐代玄宗(李隆基,公元 713~755 年)时,已经开始设立教坊,教练年轻的艺人练习歌舞。因此,专业的演员在唐玄宗时才正式存在。直至今日,戏曲演员仍然称他们自己为梨园弟子,奉唐玄宗为戏曲祖师。从这一点上可以看出,戏曲演员把自己的演出当做一种职业,是在唐代才形成的。

提线木偶也是中国首先发明的艺术形式。在唐代,这种艺术形式向着两个方向平行发展,分别发展成喜剧木偶戏和悲剧木偶戏。木偶戏的发展对以后的戏曲有十分重要的影响。

但真正的中国戏曲文学的产生,是在宋代(公元 960~1279 年)。首先,宋代的平话、小说的产生为戏曲演员准备了充足的素材。这些小说内容经过改编都成了木偶戏或皮影戏的主要故事情节,也是宋代开始出现的杂剧的主要内容。这些艺术形式确定了剧曲艺术的基本原则。宋代曲谱和剧本的产生更是对戏剧发展的重大贡献。

隋唐以前,中国的诗一般都是为演唱而作。但到了唐代(公元 618~907 年),诗的韵律基本上变成了不变的格式,因此,千篇一律,有些呆板。这种情况在宋代逐渐发生了变化,为演唱所需要的韵律各异的词牌出现了,并在宋代大为流行。元代(公元 1271~1368 年)的戏曲在中国戏曲史上占有重要地位,取得了辉煌的成就,出现了 85 位剧作家,创作了 564 出戏剧。其中最有名的戏剧集就是《元曲选杂剧》,它包括 8 卷共 100 出戏。元代最有名的戏曲家有关汉卿、王实甫、马致远、白仁甫等。

明清时代(公元 1368~1911 年),中国戏曲发展到了繁荣的阶段。这两个时期,戏剧的主要形式就是传奇戏曲。这不仅因为戏的主要内容来源于传奇故事,而重要的是因为他们打破了以前戏曲的传统手法。明代以前,每个剧本都有四部分,即四场戏。对于传奇戏的剧作者来说,这种形式已经不适合了。因为短的剧本不能充分表现人物的性格,剧情也不能展开。这就需要内容更充实、篇幅更长的剧本问世。因此,这个阶段曾出现了长达

50至60场的大戏。有些戏类似于现代的连续剧，每一集既可以单独演出，又是整个戏的有机组成部分。这也相当于现代戏中的独幕剧。

明清时代，各种地方戏剧蓬勃发展，几乎每个省都有代表当地特色的剧种，如河北梆子、秦腔等。著名的京剧就是在清代乾隆年间形成的。

26. What Was the Origin of the Traditional Chinese Opera? How Did It Develop?

The origin of the traditional Chinese opera can be traced back to the very remote past. In the ancient times, people believed that between deities and human beings there were special persons who served as the envoys of the deities to pass on their wills. These envoys were known as *shi* and *wu*. To please the deities, *shi* and *wu* used dances and songs as a way to express their feelings. These dances and songs can be taken as the embryonic form of Chinese opera. Later, during the Spring and Autumn Period(770—476 B.C.), there were special actors who amused the kings and their guests with stories, jokes, dances and acrobatic feats—a combination of music and performance which could be regarded as the earliest form of opera.

By 500 A.D., the nucleus components of opera—dancing, singing and the plot—had been well integrated. During the reign of Emperor Xuanzong (713—755 A.D.) of the Tang Dynasty (618—907A.D.), school were established to teach young people to sing and dance. Therefore professional actors appeared at that time. Up till now, actors still regard Emperor Xuanzong of the Tang Dynasty as the opera founder. This fact also indicates that it was from the Tang Dynasty when opera actors began to take what they did as an occupation.

Marionette was also one of the art forms first created by Chinese. In the Tang Dynasty, this form of art developed along two parallel lines: one developed into tragedy puppet show; the other developed into comedy puppet show. The development of marionette had a great influence on the future development of opera.

However, it was during the Song Dynasty(960—1279 A.D.) that the real vital elements that built up the later Chinese literature of traditional opera came into being. The first contribution of paramount importance was *xiaoshuo* and *pinghua* (a kind of story-telling in local dialects), which supplied rich materials for opera actors. The plots were all adapted for the puppet shows or the shadow plays of the time, as well as for the main materials of *zaju* (poetic drama). These forms of arts set the basic principles for the traditional opera.

The appearance of music scores and scripts for opera in the Song Dynasty made a great contribution to the development of Chinese opera. Prior to the Sui and Tang dynasties, Chinese poems were basically written for singing. But during the Tang Dynasty, the meters in verse developed into unchangeable set forms, which in turn made Chinese poems more rigid and monotonous. During the Song Dynasty, this situation gradually changed. Poems of varied meters specially composed for singing grew out of the older patterns and flourished. In the Yuan Dynasty (1271—1368 A.D.), operas made brilliant achievements and played an important role in the history of traditional Chinese opera. During this period, there were 85 playwrights who altogether produced 564 plays.

The Ming and Qing dynasties (1368—1911A.D.) were the prosperous period for Chinese opera. During these two dynasties, the major form of opera was *chuanqi* (romantic tales). The significance of this development lay in the fact that these plays not only took legends and romances as sources for their contents, but also broke away from the orthodox ways of presentation. Prior to the Ming Dynasty, each play included four acts, which was too short for the playwrights to express the quality and temperament of their characters and to develop the stories in full. Thus, operas of immense length came into existence, some of which were composed of up to fifty or sixty acts or scenes. Like modern plays, each act may be considered as an independent play as well as an integrated part of the whole serial.

During the Ming and Qing dynasties, a lot of local operas, such as *Bangzi* of Hebei and *Qinqiang* of Shaanxi, also appeared. It was in the reign of Emperor Qianlong of the Qing Dynasty that the well-known *Jingju* (Beijing Opera) came into being.

27. 京剧是何时产生的？京剧有哪些行当？

1790年为庆祝乾隆皇帝(爱新觉罗·弘历)80寿辰，通过扬州盐商江鹤亭组织，旦角演员高朗亭率领徽剧三庆班进京，为皇帝及皇室成员演出。演出结束后，他们未返回安徽，而是留在北京，继续为北京的普通观众演出。在随后的十几年中，又有一批徽班进京献艺。这时最为著名的有三庆、四喜、和春和春台，称为四大徽班。随着徽班的进京，一个新的剧种——京剧开始了它的孕育时期。

徽剧原为安徽首府安庆(今安庆市)的地方戏。安庆是重要的交通枢纽，商业繁荣，与各地有广泛的联系，这使得徽剧在进京之前就已经吸收了不少地方戏的特长。徽班进京后，在新的环境中，面对新的观众，徽剧演员没有因循守旧，而是博采众长，积极向其他剧种，如京腔、秦腔、昆曲学习，不断丰富和改进了徽剧。1830年左右，汉调艺人进京，加入徽班演出，不仅壮大了徽班的演员阵容，而且把湖北汉戏的皮簧融于徽剧之中，这样，一个具有独特艺术风格的新剧种——京剧，就开始发展起来了。

作为一个独立的剧种，京剧的诞生大约是在1840年至1860年，即清咸丰、道光年间。这是广大徽汉演员几十年共同努力的结果。京剧是在徽剧汉剧吸收其他地方戏营养的基础上形成的，但京剧又不同于后者。京剧有了明确的角色分工；在念白上改用京字京韵，加以少量的方言俚语；在音乐上以西皮、二簧为主要曲调，并以胡琴为主要伴奏乐器；在表演上唱、念、做、打并重，并有固定的程式和规范。另外，京剧还有自己独有的剧目。

由于京剧是在融合各种地方戏的精华的基础上形成的，并运用京白，因此，它不仅为北京观众所钟爱，也受到全国人民的喜爱，成为中国戏曲最有代表性的一个剧种。

行当指中国传统戏曲角色的类别。京剧的行当分为四大类，即生、旦、净和丑。过去曾有末，近代已归入生行。

生是京剧中的男性人物。根据人物的年龄、性格和身份，生又划分为不同的专行，主要有老生、小生、文生和武生。老生又称须生，饰剧中中年或老年男性，大都为正面人物。小生则指英俊的青少年男子，或为书生，或为武将。在生的行当中，以唱、念为主的称为文生，而以武打见长的则为武生。

旦是京剧表演中的女性人物。在过去封建时代，男女不能同台，旦角也均由男演员担任，而现在则只有少数的男旦角演员了。根据角色的年龄、身份、性格及表演特点的不同，旦又分为正旦、花旦、彩旦、武旦和老旦几种。正旦又称青衣，因多穿青色褶子而得名，正旦一般是京剧中温顺贤慧的青年或中年妇女。在表演上以唱功为主。花旦一般为青年妇女。在性格上或天真活泼，或放浪泼辣。在表演上则侧重于做功和念白。彩旦也称丑旦，多为滑稽或奸刁的女性。化妆时彩旦在面部搽以白粉并涂以厚重的胭脂。在表演上与丑角基本相同。武旦是武艺高强、能骑善射的女性。表演上类似武生,着重武打。老旦指京剧中的老年妇女。唱腔与老生近似,用本嗓。表演及演唱均突出老年人的特点。

净亦称花脸,是性格、相貌、品质有特异之处的男性。净又分为文净和武净。文净以唱为主,武净则侧重武打。净角在化妆时均用夸张而又能突出人物特点的脸谱。

丑角又称小花脸或三花脸。丑角既可表现心地善良、语言幽默、动作滑稽的人物,也可表现灵魂丑恶、奸诈卑鄙的人物。根据人物的性格和身份,丑角又分为文丑和武丑。女性人物的丑角称为彩旦或丑旦。化妆时丑角的鼻部涂搽白粉,男丑角常有上翘的胡须,以表现出丑角滑稽的特点。

27. When Did *Jingju* (Beijing Opera) Emerge? What Are the Roles in This Opera?

In 1790, Emperor Qianlong was celebrating his eightieth birthday. Through arrangements by Jiang Heting, a Yangzhou businessman dealing in salt, the Sanqing Troupe of Anhui Opera headed by the female-role actor Gao Langting came to Beijing to offer congratulatory performances to the emperor and the royal family. For some reason, after the performances, they did not return home but stayed in Beijing to perform for the ordinary people. In the following dozen years, more Anhui Opera troupes came to Beijing, among which Sanqing, Sixi, Hechun and Chuntai were the most famous at the time. Following the entrance of the Anhui Opera troupes in Beijing, there started a gestation period of *Jingju*, a brand-new opera form.

Anhui Opera used to be the local opera popular in Anqing, then the capital of Anhui. Anqing was a hub of communication where trade was highly developed and there were wide contacts with the outside world. Anhui Opera had drawn much from other local operas even before it entered Beijing. Facing the new audience in the new environment in Beijing, Anhui Opera troupes did not stick to the old convention but learnt from other opera forms such as *Jingqiang*, *Qinqiang* and *Kunqu* so as to enrich and improve themselves. Around 1830, some *Handiao* performers from Hubei came to Beijing and joined the Anhui Opera troupes, which not only strengthened the cast of those troupes but also introduced *xipi* and *erhuang*, two types of music, into Anhui Opera. Thus

Jingju, a new opera form of unique artistic style, was to take shape.

Jingju as an independent opera form was born between 1840 and 1860 during the reigns of Emperors Daoguang and Xianfeng, which was the result of the joint efforts of the Anhui and Handiao Opera performers in several decades' time. *Jingju* originated in Anhui and Handiao Operas but is different from the two. In *Jingju* there is a clear division of roles; the language used is Beijing speech with a little use of dialects and slangs; *xipi* and *erhuang* are the chief types of music and *huqin* (two-stringed bower fiddle) is the major accompanying musical instrument; singing, recitation, performance and acrobatic fighting are all included and certain patterns have to be followed.

Because *Jingju* has combined the cream of various local operas and used Beijing speech, it is enjoyed not only by northerners but also by people from all over the country, and it has become the national opera, the most representative of Chinese drama.

There are mainly four different kinds of roles, namely *sheng*, *dan*, *jing*, and *chou*. There used to be another role called *mo*, which has merged into *sheng*.

Sheng is the male role in *Jingju*. *Sheng*, according to the age, personality and status of the characters, is subdivided into *laosheng*, *xiaosheng*, *wensheng* and *wusheng*. *Laosheng*, also known as *xusheng*, is a bearded middle-aged or old man who is in most cases a positive character. *Xiaosheng* is a handsome young man, who can either be a scholar or a military general. Those who specialize in singing and reciting are termed *wensheng*, while those who are skilled in stage-fighting, are called *wusheng*.

Dan is a general term in *Jingju* for all female roles. In the feudal society of old China, as men and women were forbidden to perform on the same stage, all the female roles were played by men. Today, however, there are very few female impersonators. According to the age, status, personality of the character and the style in acting, *dan* is further divided into *zhengdan*, *huadan*, *caidan*, *wudan* and *laodan*. *Zhengdan* is also called *qingyi* because she always wears a *qingyi* (black costume). *Zhengdan* is the type representing the gentle and virtuous young and middle-aged woman. In this type of roles much stress is given in singing. *Huadan* is the role for a maiden or a young woman, who is either vivacious or shrewdish in character. Emphasis is placed on acting and recitation in this type. *Caidan*, also called *choudan*, is the role for a woman of comical or crafty character. A *caidan* uses heavy make-up of rouge with a patch of white powder covering her nose while her acting is basically the same as that of a *chou* (clown). *Wudan* is the role for a woman of the military type who excels in riding and archery as well as in martial arts. Like *wusheng*, a *wudan* does a lot of stage-fighting. *Laodan* is the role for an old woman. In singing *laodan* uses the natural voice which is similar to *laosheng*. In both singing and acting the performer must try to indicate the special characteristics of an old woman.

Jing is also known as *hualian*, a role with a painted face, who is a man of special character, features and personality. *Jing* is further divided into *wenjing* (civilian type) and *wujing* (warrior type). *Wenjing* must lay particular emphasis on singing and *wujing* on acrobatic fighting. The face of a *jing* role is painted with a variety of coloured patterns which are not only an artistic exaggeration but also an indication of the personality of the character.

Chou (clown) is also called *xiaohualian*, or *sanhualian*. A chou may be a kind-hearted, humorous and funny fellow. However, he may also be very wicked or treacherous. *Chou* is also divided into *wenchou* (civilian type), and *wuchou* (a clown with martial arts). A female *chou* is normally called *caidan* or *choudan*. A *chou* always paints his nose powder-white and wears an upturned moustache so as to give a comic effect.

28. 京剧的脸谱代表什么？

脸谱是中国戏剧演员面部化妆的一种程式，有着悠久的历史。中国古代有一种傩舞，就是在驱鬼逐疫的祭祀仪式上跳的舞，跳这种舞时，舞者都戴上假面。这种傩舞在个别地区还发展为傩戏。另外，据说北齐(公元550～557年)兰陵王高长恭相貌英俊，武艺超群，在战斗中因为他貌美如妇人，不足威慑敌人，所以往往戴上凶恶的面具。在以后南北朝和隋唐乐舞中还有表现这一故事的节目。这种祭祀和乐舞中的假面无疑与后来产生的脸谱有密切的关系。在唐代的参军戏中仍然使用面具，但也开始用染面化妆来表现某些鬼神形象。到明代，在元杂剧的基础上，戏曲中各类角色的分工更细了，脸谱也逐渐规范化了。在清代，随着京剧的兴起，脸谱造型日趋完善，至清末脸谱已趋定型。

脸谱是中国戏曲特有的化妆艺术，是用写实和象征相结合的艺术夸张手法，从人物面貌上揭示人物的类型、品质和性格特征，并表示对人物的褒贬。

在某些剧种中，各种角色均勾画脸谱，而在中国最具代表性的京剧中，脸谱主要用于净角和丑角。丑角大都在鼻部涂抹小块白粉，谱式的种类较少。净角则有多种谱式，如“整脸”、“三块瓦脸”、“十字门脸”、“六分脸”、“碎花脸”和“厚脸”等等。

脸谱的颜色也各不相同，有红、黄、蓝、白、黑、紫、绿和金、银色等。一个脸谱的主色象征着人物的品质和气质。红色一般表示忠勇、正直；黄色象征枭勇、凶暴、沉着；蓝色象征刚强、骁勇、有心计；白色象征阴险、狡诈；黑色象征粗鲁、凶猛；紫色象征刚正、稳练、沉着；金色和银色则通常用来表示神怪。

脸谱艺术是戏曲中的化妆手段，也是一种富有装饰性的图案，成为中国画中的一个新的品种。

28. What Do the Facial Makeups Stand for in Beijing Opera?

The art of facial makeups in Chinese operas boasts a long history. In ancient China, there was a form of dance called *nuo* which was performed at ritual ceremonies to frighten off the ghosts and evil souls and to relieve people of epidemics. Masks were used by performers when they danced. In some areas the *nuo* ritual ceremonies were later transformed into theatrical performances. Another example of using masks was that of Prince Lanling of the Northern Qi Period (550—577 A.D.). It is said that Prince Lanling excelled in martial arts but was too handsome to terrorize the enemy. So he al-

ways wore a ferocious-looking mask in battles in order to overwhelm the enemy. This story was later brought onto the stage in the Southern and Northern Dynasties as well as in the Sui and Tang dynasties(420—907 A.D.). The masks used by the performers at the ritual ceremonies and in the performing art undoubtedly had a bearing on the origination of the facial makeups. In the Tang Dynasty(618—907 A.D.), masks continued to be applied in low comedy, and at the same time artists started to dye their faces in portrayal of super-human beings. In the Ming Dynasty(1318—1644 A.D.), division of roles among actors became more classified on the basis of the Yuan Dynasty(1271—1368 A.D.) operas and the facial makeups were gradually standardized. In the Qing Dynasty(1644—1911 A.D.), with the springing up of Beijing Opera, the art of facial makeups was increasingly perfected. And toward the end of the Qing Dynasty, the facial makeups for different categories of characters became finalized.

Facial makeups are a special art in Chinese operas which distinctly show the appearances of different roles as well as their dispositions and moral qualities by means of artistic exaggeration combined with truthful portrayal and symbolism. Facial makeups also serve to express praise or condemnation toward the characters.

In some local operas, facial makeups are applied to all the different roles while in Beijing Opera, the most representative of Chinese operas, facial makeups are limited only to the roles of *jing* and *chou*. A *chou* is characterized by his white-painted nose which gives a comic effect and there are relatively few facial makeup patterns for a *chou* role. There are a large variety of facial makeup patterns for *jing* in Beijing Opera, namely, "whole face", "three-tile face", "quartered face", "six-division face", "tiny-flowered face", "lopsided face", etc.

Different colours such as red, yellow, blue, white, black, purple, green, gold and silver are used for facial makeups. The main colour in a facial makeup symbolizes the disposition of the character. Red indicates devotion, courage and uprightness. Yellow signifies fierceness, ambition and cool-headedness. Blue represents staunchness, fierceness and astuteness. White suggests sinisterness, treacherousness, suspiciousness and craftiness. Black symbolizes roughness and fierceness. Purple stands for uprightness, sophistication and cool-headedness. Gold and silver colours are usually used for gods and spirits.

Facial makeups are not only a special art in Chinese operas, but also an art of ornamental design, and have become a new variety in Chinese painting.

29. 秦腔是中国地方戏的一种，它有什么特点？

秦腔是中国戏曲中历史较长、影响较大的一个剧种。现在主要流行于陕西、甘肃、宁夏、青海、新疆等地区。据记载，在明朝（公元1368～1644年）中叶已经有秦腔表演了。因为秦腔的起源在陕西、甘肃一带，古时这里为秦地，所以叫秦腔。一种说法认为，秦腔是在宋、金、元（公元960～1368年）铙鼓杂剧和陕、甘民歌的基础上发展起来的。清朝康熙末年至乾隆、嘉庆（公元1662～1820年）年间，秦腔流传到几乎全国各地，对不少剧种的曲调都有影响。秦腔的唱腔激越高亢，节奏鲜明。伴奏的乐器以板胡为主，配以笛子、京胡、月琴、唢呐等，以梆子击节，并有指板、干鼓、暴鼓、战鼓、大锣、小锣和大钹、小钹等打击乐器。现在陕西秦腔又分东、西、中、南四路。

秦腔的角色分四生、六旦、二净、一丑，共13门，各门都有出色的演员。各个行当的擅长的戏有：小生戏《长坂坡》、《抱妆盒》，须生戏《临潼山》、《斩韩信》，净（花脸）戏《斩单通》、《抱琵琶》，小旦戏《柜中缘》等。

秦腔演员不仅注重唱功，也重视表演工架和特技，如趟马、担柴、担水、喷火、扑跌等表演都十分考究。脸谱也有特色。

中华人民共和国成立后，秦腔在整理传统剧目、创作新剧和培养演员等方面都做了大量工作。经过整理、改编的传统剧目有《游龟山》、《赵氏孤儿》、《卖画劈门》、《三滴血》、《火焰驹》等。其中《三滴血》和《火焰驹》已经摄制成电影。

29. What Are the Characteristics of *Qinqiang*?

Qinqiang is one of the most influential varieties of operas that enjoys a long history. Presently, it is most popular in the northwestern provinces and autonomous regions like Shaanxi, Gansu, Ningxia, Qinghai, Xinjiang, etc. It is recorded that *Qinqiang* appeared as early as the middle of the Ming Dynasty (1368—1644 A.D.). Originated from parts of modern Shaanxi and Gansu, *Qinqiang* developed on the basis of Cymbals Drama of the Song, Jin and Yuan dynasties (960—1368 A.D.) and the folk songs of Shaanxi and Gansu. During a period (1622—1820 A.D.) of the Qing Dynasty, *Qinqiang* spread far and wide all over the country, imposing a great influence on a variety of operas. Its vocal music is sonorous and rhythmical. The music instrument used is mainly *banhu*, accompanied by *dizi*, *jinghu*, *yueqin*, and *suona* beating time with *bangzi and other percussion instruments like gongs, drums and cymbals. Nowadays in* the province of Shaanxi, *Qinqiang* is divided into four styles—east, west, center and south.

Qinqiang has a total of thirteen roles, including four *sheng*, six *dan*, two *jing* and one *chou*, all played remarkably by some splendid actors. The famous plays for the role of *sheng* are: *Changbanpo*, *Lintongshan* and *Zhan Hanxin*. The two pieces famous for the role of *jing* are: *Zhan Shan Tong* and *Bao Pipa*. The one famous for the role of *dan* is *Gui Zhong Yuan*, etc.

Qinqiang actors are not only good at singing, but also particular about performing skills, like trotting and galloping, carrying water and firewood, spewing fire and wrestling. The facial makeups are also unique.

Ever since the founding of the People's Republic of China in 1949, *Qinqiang* has been doing a lot in sorting out traditional plays, creating new works and training actors. Some of the revised traditional plays are *You Guishan*, *Zhaoshi Gu'er*, *Mai Hua Pi Men*, *San Di Xue* and *Huoyan Ju*, among which the last two have been made into movies.

30. 什么是傩舞？它与傩戏有关系吗？

傩(nuó)舞是中国很古老的一种舞蹈。原始社会时，人们在劳动之余，往往模拟捕猎生活中人兽角斗的情景取乐，在这个基础上就产生了傩舞，动作比较简单。后来变为祭祀仪式上禳魔驱疫的舞蹈，动作和演唱也变得复杂起来。据《礼记》等古籍记载，周朝(约公元前 1100 ~ 前 256 年)宫廷中，每年除夕都要举行大傩仪式，领头的人称为“方相”，手掌蒙上熊皮，穿着黑上衣，红下衣，执戈和盾，领着其他舞蹈者绕场跳舞，以驱鬼除祟。后来除了朝廷外，民间也用傩舞驱除邪祟。《论语·乡党篇》有“乡人傩，朝服而立于阼阶”的记载。汉朝(公元前 206 ~ 公元 220 年)宫廷每年在腊日(冬至后第三个戌日，这一天进行腊祭)前一天也要举行傩舞仪式，要选 120 个青少年，戴黑头巾，穿红衣裳，唱着驱鬼词，作方相与 12 兽舞，绕宫殿三圈，然后举火炬把“疫鬼”赶出宫门。以后历代朝廷与民间都有这种舞蹈，用意虽然在驱除鬼邪，但是也起到娱悦民众的作用。从宋朝(公元 960 ~ 1279 年)的《大傩舞图》中，可以看到 12 个戴着不同面具，佩带奇特饰物的人，手持帚、扇、斗、箕等物，边唱边曲折行进，以驱除宅妖、墓鬼。

由驱鬼除邪的傩舞，再加上一些民间流传的故事情节，逐步发展成戏曲，就是傩戏。傩戏演员一般戴面具演唱，表演仍然保持傩舞简单、粗犷的风格。傩戏流行于湖南、湖北、安徽、江西和广西等省、区，又叫“傩愿戏”、“师公戏”等。剧目有《孟姜女》、《柳毅传书》等。

30. What Is *Nuo* Dance? Is There Any Connection between *Nuo* Dance and *Nuo* Opera?

Nuo Dance is one of the oldest Chinese traditional dances. In the primitive society, during work breaks, people gathered together to entertain themselves by imitating the fight of human beings against beasts, which actually was part of their daily life. On the basis of this, *Nuo* Dance came into being. At that time, the dance was quite simple. Later on, it developed into a kind of dance to drive away evils and epidemics in praying and memorial ceremonies and its action and singing became more complicated. According to *Li Ji* (*The Book of Rites*) and some other classic books, on New Year's eve, grand *Nuo* Dance was, as a rule, performed in the royal court of the Zhou Dynasty(c.1100—256 B.C.). The leader of the dancers, called *fangxiang* would wear a black jacket, red pants, and gloves made of bear furs and with a spear and a shield in hand. They would dance around to drive away the evils. Later, people outside the royal court also started to use *Nuo* Dance to drive away the evils, which was recorded in *Lunyu* (*The Analects of Confucius*). In the Han Dynasty (206 B.C.—220 A.D.), *Nuo* dance was performed in the royal court at the end of the year. Usually, one hundred and twenty young men were chosen as dancers. They would chant evil-driving words, dance around the royal court three rounds, and then drive away the evils out of the palace gates with lighted torches. This kind of dances lasted for many dynasties in both the royal courts and among the people. Apart from its function of driving away the evils, it was also performed for popular amusements. In *Nuo Dance Painting* of the Song Dynasty(960—1279 A.D.), we can see twelve young men in different masks and colorful decorations and with brooms, fans, etc. in hands singing and dancing while zigzagging forward to drive away the evils.

With *Nuo* Dance as its origin, combined with legends, *Nuo* Opera was developed. *Nuo* Opera performers still wear masks and their performances remain simple and unconstrained. *Nuo* Opera is popular in Hunan, Hubei, Anhui, Jiangxi, Guangxi and other provinces and areas. It is also known as *Nuoyuan* Opera.

31. 唐朝的“十部乐”内容如何？什么是“坐部伎”和“立部伎”？

中国音乐和舞蹈历史都很长，古代人们在制造生产工具的同时，也制作出简单的打击乐器和吹奏乐器，如石磬、木鼓、骨哨等。人们在狩猎有所收获后，就敲击乐器，载歌载舞。也就是《尚书·舜典》所写的“击石拊石，百兽率舞”（人们装扮成各种兽形跳舞）。在祭祀和随后建立的王朝宫廷年节庆贺时，音乐和舞蹈成为仪式的一项重要内容。有些古代文献把音乐和舞蹈统称为乐。

音乐和舞蹈发展到唐朝，已经十分昌盛。随着国内各民族和国内外的文化往来的发展，有些少数民族和国外的乐、舞也传入唐朝宫廷。唐太宗（李世民，公元 627 ~ 649 年）时，在隋朝（公元 581 ~ 618 年）“九部乐”的基础上，有所增减，成为“十部乐”。包括《燕乐》（即宴乐，汉族乐舞，服饰华丽）、《清商乐》（汉、魏时汉族民间乐舞，后为宫廷采用）、《西凉乐》（中国西部少数民族的乐舞）、《高丽乐》（从朝鲜半岛传入的乐舞）、《龟兹乐》（即现在新疆库车一带的乐舞）、《天竺乐》（从印度等国传入的乐舞）、《康国乐》（中亚一带的乐舞）、《疏勒乐》（今新疆喀什一带的音乐舞蹈）、《高昌乐》（今新疆吐鲁番一带的乐舞）、《文康乐》（即礼毕，为汉族面具舞）。十部乐当中，以燕乐与清商乐为主。这些乐舞除了宫廷娱乐以外，每逢“千秋节”（唐太宗诞辰）、 招待异族使臣、朝贺之会和迎接唐三藏取经归来等重大庆典都要演奏。到唐朝末年，除燕乐外，大部已经失传。

“坐部伎”据说创立于唐太宗时，唐玄宗时又加以整理制作，是宫廷乐舞的一大类，因为演奏者坐于堂上，故名。为丝竹细乐合奏，舞蹈者约为 3 到 12 人，曲调典雅。内容为燕乐、长寿乐、天授乐、鸟歌万岁乐、龙池乐和小破阵乐等 6 部，每次由皇帝选点其中几部来演奏。“立部伎”是宫廷乐舞的另一大类，因演奏者立于堂下而得名。开始设于唐高宗仪凤年间，唐玄宗时除了整理前代节目外，还创制了新乐舞。包括安乐、太平乐、破阵乐等 8 部。舞蹈者有 64 人至 180 人，规模宏大，舞姿威武，加上用钲鼓伴奏，显得气势雄壮。

“坐部伎”和“立部伎”在安史之乱后，趋于衰亡。

31. What Were the Ten *Yue* in the Tang Dynasty? What Were *Zuobuji* and *Libuji*?

China has a long history of music and dance. In ancient times, along with the creation of production tools, people also made simple percussion instruments and wind instruments such as chimes, wood drums and bone whistles and so on. To celebrate good harvests, the ancient people would beat their musical instruments, dance and sing. Gradually, music and dance became one of the main programs in sacrifices and imperial celebrations. In some historical records, both music and dance were referred to as *yue*.

During the Tang Dynasty(618—907 A.D.), music and dance developed to a new height. With the development of cultural exchanges among various nationalities as well as between China and foreign countries, some music and dance from the minority nationalities and foreign countries were introduced into the royal court of the Tang Dynasty. In the reign of Emperor Taizong (627—649 A.D.), on the basis of the nine *yue* of the Sui Dynasty (581—618 A.D.), the ten *yue* took shape, which included: *Yan Yue* (music and dances of the Han nationality), *Qingshang Yue* (music and dances of the Han nationality popular during the Han Dynasty and the period of the Three Kingdoms(206 B.C.—280 A.D.), *Xiliang Yue* (music and dances of the minority nationalities in the western part of China), *Gaoli Yue*(music and dances from the Korean peninsula) , *Qiuci Yue* (music and dances from the present Kuche area in Xinjiang Autonomous Region), *Tianzhu Yue* (music and dances from India), *Kangguo Yue*(music and dances from central Asia), *Shule Yue* (music and dances from the area presently known as Kashi in Xinjiang Autonomous Region), *Gaochang Yue* (music and dances from the area presently known as Turpan in Xinjiang Autonomous Region) and *Wenkang Yue* (mask dances of the the Han nationality). Among the ten *yue*, *Yan Yue* and *Qingshang Yue* prevailed. Beside being used for entertainments in the royal court, these music and dances were also used on birthday celebrations for Emperor Taizong, in the receptions for missionaries from other nationalities and on the celebration for the return of Monk Sanzang who went to India for Buddhism scriptures, etc. But till the late Tang Dynasty, the ten *yue*, except *Yan Yue*, were lost.

It is said that *Zuobuji*, which was created in the reign of Emperor Taizong and improved in the reign of Emperor Xuanzong, was one of the court music and dances during the Tang Dynasty. It was called *Zuobuji* because all performers sat while performing in the court. Usually, 3 to 12 dancers danced to the ensemble of the traditional Chinese stringed and woodwind instruments. *Zuobuji* included *Yan Yue*, *Changshou* (longevity)

Yue, *Tianshou* (heaven-gifted) *Yue*, Niao Ge Wansui (long life) *Yue*, *Longchi* (dragon pool) *Yue* and *Xiao Puozhen* (minor operation) *Yue*. *Libuji* was another kind of court music and dances, which was so called because all performers stood while performing in the court. It started in the reign of Emperor Gaozong. And in the reign of Emperor Xuanzong, new music and dances were created on the basis of the old ones. All together, *Libuji* included *An* (comfort) *Yue*, *Taiping* (peace) *Yue*, *Puozhen* (operation) *Yue* and other five *yue*. Usually there were about 64 to 180 persons in the dance, looking grand and imposing.

Both *Zuobuji* and *Libuji* declined after the riot (755—757 A.D.) led by An Lushan and Shi Siming in the Tang Dynasty.

32. 中国人物画的产生与演变情况如何?

中国人物画早在战国时代(公元前475~前221年)就已经出现了。《说苑》中就记载了肖像画家敬君的故事。故事中说:齐王叫人修了一座华丽的亭子,于是让敬君作画,把新建的亭子画下来。由于敬君长年在国外生活,非常想家,他在作画时画的竟是他妻子的肖像!这可以被看作是中国最早的人物画了。

汉代和唐代人物画取得了很高的成就,有了很大的发展。据史书记载,汉武帝(刘彻,公元前140~前87年)曾下令让宫廷画家作周公摄政图,他把此画赐予大将霍光。当时,除了以汉民族的人为人物画主题外,表现其他民族的人物画也有不少。比如,汉成帝(刘骜,公元前32~前7年)就让画家把匈奴休屠王王后的肖像画好挂在他宫殿的墙上。在唐代,也有两位画家叫胡怀和胡虔,以画外国人物画而闻名。在人物画画坛上,特别需要指出的是:在东晋时,出了一位知名的人物画家顾恺之。他传世的惟一作品就是《女史箴图卷》,这幅画在义和团起义之前,一直藏于皇宫之内,义和团运动之后,流落海外,现藏大英博物馆。

对中国人物画产生重大影响的外来因素就是印度佛教的传入。佛教传入之后,佛像画在中国迅速兴起,并且发展很快。最早的佛像画家要算是三国时期吴国的曹不兴。南北朝时,是中国佛教大发展时期。在北方,这种宗教题材的作品主要以石窟雕刻艺术的形式出现。如云岗、龙门、敦煌等著名石窟就保存有大量的佛教艺术珍品。在南方则以大批表现佛教内容的壁画而闻名。不论在南方还是北方,都涌现出大批知名和不知名的高超艺术家。

佛教绘画艺术的发展,也促进了道教画的发展。道教徒看到佛教的艺术对传播佛教起了很大的促进作用,于是也仿效起来。南北朝时,著名的嵩山道士寇谦之与其他道教徒也开始画道教的神仙图。这一做法,也很快地在各地道观及民间传开。

唐代(公元618~907年),佛教和道教都得到空前的发展。很多有名的人物画家如吴道子、阎立德等,既是佛教的画家又是道教的画家。

人物画中的另一个领域是仕女画。在唐代,仕女画是作为一个专门的画科而出现的。但早期的仕女画是以《列女传》为主要题材。比如:蔡邕作的《小列女图》及王廙的《列女传仁智图》。唐代的仁女画传世作品仍有不少,张萱,周昉是仕女画的代表人物。唐代以后,特别是明代、清代也出现了一些著名的人物画家,其中仕女画家以唐寅、仇英、陈洪绶、吴俊卿为最有名气。

32. What Was the Origin of Chinese Portraiture? How Did It Develop?

The art of portraiture emerged as early as in the Warring States Period(475—221 B.C.). In the book *Shuo Yuan* (*Garden of Anecdotes*), there was a reference about a portrait painter, Jing Jun. The passage stated that when the ruler of the State of Qi had the construction of a new pavilion completed, he asked Jing Jun to make a drawing of it. Since he had been away from home for a long time and was very homesick, Jing Jun drew a picture of his wife instead of the new pavilion. This portrait could be taken as the earliest portraiture in China.

In the Han and Tang dynasties (206 B.C.—907 A.D.), the art of portraiture attained great achievements and development. According to historical records, Emperor Wu (140—87 B.C.) of the Han Dynasty ordered his court painter to draw a picture of Duke Zhou of the Zhou Dynasty (c.1100—221 B.C.) assisting the young child emperor in government, which he granted to his general Huo Guang. During this period, in addition to portraits of people of the Han nationality, there were also portraits of people of other nationalities. For instance, Emperor Cheng (32—7 B.C.) of the Han Dynasty had a portrait of the Queen of King Xiutu of Xiongnu (the old Mongols) drawn and hung on the wall of his palace. In the Tang Dynasty, there were two painters named Hu Huai and Hu Qian who were famous for their portraits of foreigners. In the matter of portraiture, a person who is worthy of special mentioning is Gu Kaizhi, a famous painter in the Eastern Jin Dynasty (317—420 A.D.). His painting that has been handed down from age to age is the illustrations *Nüshizhen Tujuan* (*Maxims for Ladies*). This scroll was kept in the imperial palace until the Boxer Uprising(1900), and then it was taken abroad. It is now kept in the British Museum.

The introduction of Buddhism from India was an exterior factor that has had a great influence on Chinese portraiture. In the wake of the introduction of Buddhism, paintings of Buddhist divinities rapidly spread and developed. Cao Buxing, a native of the State of Wu during the Three Kingdoms Period(220—280 A.D.), can be regarded as the first artist of Buddhist painting. During the Northern and Southern Dynasties (420—589 A.D.), Buddhism saw its fast development. In North China, the development of this religious-subject art was in the form of sculptures of Buddha and Bodhisattvas imaged in mountain caves. Grottoes such as Yungang, Longmen, Dunhuang and so on have kept a lot of Buddhist art treasures; in South China, a great number of frescoes of Buddhist subject appeared. In both North and South China, many great artists appeared.

At the same time, the development of Taoist painting was accelerated by the development of Buddhist painting. When they realized the role of Buddhist painting in the fast spreading of Buddhism, the Taoists started to follow suit. During the Northern and Southern Dynasties, Kou Qianzhi, a famous Taoist, and other Taoists began to paint celestials of Taoism. This practice was followed rapidly in many local Taoist temples.

In the Tang Dynasty (618—907 A.D.), Buddhism and Taoism both developed rapidly. Many well-known portrait painters such as Wu Daozi and Yan Lide were painters of both Buddhist portraiture and Taoist portraiture.

The painting of beautiful women was another field of portraiture. However, in the Tang Dynasty, the paintings of beautiful women appeared as an independent type of painting. The early paintings of this kind took their subjects mainly from the book *Lienü Zhuan* (*Biographies of Eminent Women*), for instance, *Xiao Lienü Tu* (Little Women) by Cai Yong. In the Tang Dynasty, there were also many painters whose works of this kind can be handed down age by age like Zhang Xuan and Zhou Fang. In the Ming and Qing dynasties (1368—1911 A.D.), there were also some noted portrait painters such as Tang Yin, Qiu Ying, Chen Hongshou and Wu Junqing.

33. 中国山水画产生和发展情况如何?

据史书记载,中国最早的山水画产生于东晋(公元317~420年)时期。戴逵的《吴中溪山邑居图》、顾恺之的《雪霁堂五老峰图》是最早出现的山水画。

顾、戴之后,山水画进一步发展,并且出现了专门评论山水画的论著。可见,山水画在当时已经比较流行。其中宗炳和梁元帝为有名的山水画评论家。

唐代(公元618~907年)是山水画发展的鼎盛时期,出现了许多有名的大画家,如吴道子、李思训父子、王维等人。吴道子被后世称为画圣,他的山水画一改前人细巧之积习,行笔纵放,如雷电交作,很有气势。李思训善画着色山水,他的儿子李昭道也是有名的山水画家,师其父而有自己的风格,后世称他们父子的山水画为大小李将军山水。王维襟怀高旷,迥超尘俗,首创渲淡画法。以水墨皴染之法而作破墨山水,以清淡闲逸为归。山水画发展到唐代,出现了山水画的南北两个画派。吴道子、李思训为北宗之祖,王维则为南宗之祖。

五代时期(公元前907~960年),山水画进一步发展创新。这个时期有名的山水画家有荆浩、关同、徐熙和黄筌。荆浩尤妙山水,善为云中山顶,四面峻厚,笔墨横溢。关同初师荆浩,刻苦钻研画道,中年之后,又学习王维的画法,自成一家。他喜作秋山寒林与村居野渡、幽人逸士、渔市山驿。他的画讲究用笔,笔愈简而气愈壮,景愈少而意愈长。徐熙善画花果、草虫。他的画"落墨以写其枝叶蕊萼,然后傅色,故骨气风神为古今绝笔。"黄筌善画禽鸟、山水,成一家之法。他画的花鸟,先以墨笔勾勒后傅以彩色,浓丽精工,称为双勾体。从徐、黄两个人的画来看,徐熙代表南宗,黄筌代表北宗。

宋代(公元960~1279年)山水画家最有代表性的要数李成、范宽、董源、巨然四人。李成初师关同,后来也自成一家。后人评论他的画时说:"其画精通造化,扫千里于咫尺之间。山林泽薮平远寒林写于笔下,其妙入神,古今一人。"范宽、董源、巨然的画都有"不装巧趣,皆得天真"的特点。

元代(公元1271~1368年)山水画家主要有黄公望、王蒙、吴镇和倪瓒四大家。黄公望则推为元季之冠,他师学董源、巨然,后来自成一家。他初居富春(今浙江富阳),领略江山自然之美。他总是随身带着纸笔,凡遇到美丽的景色就当场写生。后来移居虞山,使他有机会观赏虞山一年四季乃至每天早晚不同时间中虞山风光的变化。由于他师法自然,因此他的山水画风光秀丽,变化万千。

明代(公元1368~1644年)山水画分浙派、吴派和院派。浙派代表画家为戴进、蓝瑛,院派则以仇英、唐寅最有名气,吴派的画家主要有沈周、文征明等人。在浙派画家中,戴进当推第一，他的山水、道释、人物、花鸟、翎毛、走兽无所不工。沈周、文征明、董其昌、陈继儒被誉为吴门四大山水画家。

清代(公元1644～1911年)山水画家以四王为最著名。他们是王时敏、王原祁、王鉴和王翚。另外，佛门画家道济和八大山人也在山水画坛享有很高的声誉。

33. What Is the History of Chinese Landscape Painting?

According to historical records, the earliest landscape paintings emerged during the Eastern Jin Dynasty(317—420 A.D.). *Wuzhong Xishan Yiju Tu* (*The Landscape of Wu*) by Dai Kui and *Xuejitang Wulaofeng Tu* (*The Wulao Mountains in the Snow*) by Gu Kaizhi were regarded as two earliest paintings of this kind.

In the wake of Gu and Dai, landscape painting saw further development. And furthermore, some critical works on landscape paintings also appeared. It is evident that landscape painting was quite popular at that time. Among those critics, Zong Bing and Emperor Yuan of Liang of the Southern Dynasty were well-known.

During the Tang Dynasty (618—907 A.D.), the development of landscape painting reached its peak and many famous landscape painters, such as Wu Daozi, Li Sixun, Li Zhaodao, and Wang Wei, appeared. Wu Daozi was respected as a painting sage by later generations for his free and bold strokes and imagination, which revolutionized the previous style of painstaking delineation of details. Li Sixun was known for his painting of massive mountains and for his clever display of colors. His son, Li Zhaodao, developed his own style of great tenderness and finesse of spirit while learning from his father. Their paintings are named as "senior and junior Li's landscape painting". Wu Daozi and Li Sixun were taken as the founders of the Northern School of landscape painting. Wang Wei, a painter who carried the subjective element to the highest extent, surprised us by his free and fast strokes and by the novelty and strangeness of his conceptions. He began the method of *xuandan* painting, i.e. painting by woolly, light-colored ink-strokes in contrast to the method of painstaking fidelity to details. Wang Wei was regarded as the founder of the Southern School.

During the Five Dynasties(907—960 A.D.), landscape painting continued to attain a high development. Worthy of special mention among the painters of this period are Jing Hao, Guan Tong, Xu Xi and Huang Quan. Jing Hao specialized in drawing mountain peaks surrounded by clouds, with very impressive imagery. Guan Tong at first tried to imitate the style of Jing Hao, but later on gained a deeper insight into his art and learned the technique on strokes from Wang Wei. Guan was fond of making pictures of hills in autumn, forests in winter, rural habitations, country ferries, recluse scholars, fish markets, lonely messengers, etc. His special skill lay in achieving impressive effects with the use of a few strokes and conveying meaning by the use of simple scenes. Xu Xi specialized in painting flowers and fruits. He used to utilize mere drops of ink to form leaves and branches and flower buds, and then spread on them a light layer of color, which gave the picture an antique and distinguished effect. Huang Quan, in his pictures of flowers and birds, first made sketches and then filled them with colors—a method which became known as *shuanggouti* (double-sketch method). In the matter of their landscape paintings, it is evident that Xu represented the Southern School, while Huang represented the Northern School at that time.

During the Song Dynasty(960—1279 A.D.), the most representative landscape painters included Li Cheng, Fan Kuan, Dong Yuan and Ju Ran. Li Cheng once was a follower of Guan Tong, but later on developed an independent style of his own. His painting was like long distance panoramas swept into view under the magic of his brush. He delineated the successive ranges and peaks of mountains from a distance to depict woods, forests, ponds and rivulets. The other three also succeeded in creating a sense of reality in pictures of distant hills and in changing colors without and artificial sign.

During the Yuan Dynasty(1271—1368 A.D.), the famous landscape painters were Huang Gongwang, Wang Meng, Wu Zhen and Ni Zan. Huang Gongwang learned the style of Dong Yuan and Ju Ran, but later on modified it and developed his own style. Huang lived in Fuchun (present Fuyang in Zhejiang Province), where he could see around him every day all the natural beauty of the hills and rivers. And it was his habit to have a brush and paper with him all the time so that he could make a sketch whenever an inspiration came upon him. Later on, he settled down in Yushan (Zhejiang Province), where he had the opportunity to observe the changing hues of Yushan hills at different times of the day and different seasons of the year. Because of his instant inspiration and his close proximity to nature, his painting of hills and dales possessed the manifold beauty and ever-changing aspects.

During the Ming Dynasty (1368—1644 A.D.), landscape painting developed into three schools, i.e. *Zhe*, *Wu* and *Yuan*. Dai Jin was known to be the leader of the *Zhe* school. His paintings of gods, human beings, animals, flowers and feathered fowls were exquisite. Qiu Ying and Tang Yin represented the *Yuan* school. Shen Zhou, Wen Zhengming, Dong Qichang and Chen Jiru were known as the four great landscape painters of the *Wu* school.

During the Qing Dynasty (1644—1911 A.D.), the famous painters included the four Wangs: Wang Shimin, Wang Yuanqi, Wang Jian and Wang Hui. Monk Daoji and *Badashanren* (the eight famous recluse monks) were also among the well-known painters.

34. 中国书法的发展分几个阶段？各个阶段中书法艺术是如何发展的？有哪些著名的书法家？

中国书法和中国绘画一样，是中国传统艺术中最重要的部分。我们可以把书法的发展分为三个阶段。第一阶段是先秦时期（公元前221年前），这是书法艺术的早期。第二阶段从公元前206年算起，至公元907年，也就是西汉至唐朝末年，这是书法艺术的成熟期。第三阶段是从五代开始至清朝末年（公元907～1911年），这是书法艺术具有独特个性的发展阶段。

商代（约公元前1600～约前1100年）甲骨文的发现，是文字史上的重大事件。甲骨文被认为是中国最古老的文字，也可以说甲骨文是书法艺术最早的作品。

钟鼎文是与甲骨文相似的文字，是甲骨文的进一步发展，商代末期已经出现在青铜器上。钟鼎文又叫金文，西周（约公元前1100～前771年）时期的金文据统计有4000多个。同时，周代早期，还有一种文字是用漆写在竹片上的，叫蝌蚪文。钟鼎文之后发展起来的一种新文字叫籀文，也就是大篆。石鼓文就是大篆字体的代表作品。

到了秦朝（公元前221～前206年），李斯规范了全国的文字，这种文字就是小篆。其传世的作品有泰山刻石和琅琊台刻石。除了小篆，在当时，有一个叫程邈的，发明了另一种新的字体——隶书。

从西汉到唐朝末年，历经1000多年。在这个阶段，书法和绘画一样，被承认为一门艺术，两者并驾齐驱，具有同等的价值。汉代，书法中流行的字体有两种，即篆书和隶书。整个汉代，隶书占了统治地位，是官方通用字体。隶书虽然发明于秦朝，但真正得到发展，则是汉朝（公元前206～220年）的事。特别是到了东汉（公元25～220年），出现了八分书，八分书的特点是字的形体“似八字势”，所以叫八分书，结构上有俯仰的变化。当时，最著名的八分书书法家首推蔡邕，他的代表作品是《熹平石经》。晋代（公元265～420年）以后，书坛发生了很大变化，形成了楷书为主、行草为辅的局面。至于其他字体的使用，则偏重于艺术欣赏。楷书的出现在汉末、魏晋时期。它是在八分书和魏晋隶书的基础上发展起来的一种新字体。一般认为楷书的首创者是钟繇。晋代以后，楷书就成了官方和私人文书的正规字体。在楷书方面，王羲之写的《黄庭经》、《乐毅论》、《孝女曹娥碑》最为著名，人们把王羲之称为“书圣”，他的儿子王献之，在师法其父的同时，发展了自己的风格，也是有名的书法家，在书法史上并称“二王”。

行书是隶书的另一种变化形式，是桓灵二帝（公元147～188年）时，由刘德升首先创立的。最早形式的行书叫行押，后来才发展成为独立的书写字体——行书。

草书分章草和今草。章草是史游发明的。汉元帝(刘奭，公元前48～前33年)时他写的《急就章》就是最早的章草书法作品。汉代的张芝，师法杜度、崔瑗并加以发展，开拓出草书的新的字体——今草，被誉为“草圣”。大书法家王羲之评论他自己的草书时说过，他的草书和张芝草书的水平一样高。由此，可以看出：从汉至晋，张芝在草书领域内享有最高的声望，他的名字成了草书艺术完美的代名词。唐代的孙过庭、张旭、怀素都是非常有名的草书名家。

唐代(公元618～907年)的书法艺术可以说达到了顶峰，出了很多大书法家，如欧阳询、柳公权、虞世南、颜真卿等，一直到现在，他们的传世作品仍被人们当作学习书法的范本。自唐以后，在书法界，人们认为要想出名，必须发展自己独特的风格。因此书法风格在唐代以后进入了个人风格大发展的阶段。宋代(公元960—1279年)出现了苏东坡、黄庭坚、米元章、蔡襄等风格各异的大名家。元代，赵子昂又开一代楷书新风，他的书法作品对后来的影响也很明显。到了明(公元1368～1644年)、清(公元1644～1911年)，书法界创新的人仍然不少，著名的人物有宋濂、董其昌、文征明、八大山人、金农、何绍基、吴昌硕、郑板桥、康有为等人。

34. How Did Chinese Calligraphy Develop? Who Were the Famous Calligraphers?

Chinese calligraphy, like Chinese painting, ranks among the most important of traditional Chinese fine arts. We may divide the developmental history of Chinese calligraphy into three periods. The Pre-Qin Period (before 221B.C.) may be called the ancient period, or the period of early beginnings. From the Western Han Dynasty (206 B.C.—24 A.D.) to the end of the Tang Dynasty (618—907 A.D.) is the second period, or the period of maturity. From the Five Dynasties (907—960 A.D.) to the end of the Qing Dynasty (1644—1911 A.D.) is the modern period, or the period of individualistic development.

The discovery of *jiaguwen* (oracle bone inscriptions) is a very important event in the Chinese language research. *Jiaguwen* was seen as the most ancient characters in China. Therefore, they were the earliest pieces of Chinese calligraphy.

Zhongdingwen, which have many similarities with *jiaguwen* and can be seen as the development of *jiaguwen*, are inscriptions on bronze vessels in the late Shang Dynasty (c.1600— c.1100 B.C.). *Zhongdingwen* is also called *jinwen* (inscriptions on ancient broze objects). According to statistics, characters of *zhongdingwen* in the Shang Dynasty numbered up to more than four thousand. At this time, there was another form of writing called *kedouwen* (tadpole script), which was painted on bamboo slips. Following *zhongdingwen* appeared *dazhuan* (greater seal script), which is called *zhouwen* (scripts in the Zhou Dynasty (c.1100—221 B.C.)). *Shiguwen* is the representative of *dazhuan*.

During the Qin Dynasty (221—206 B.C.), Li Si succeeded in standardizing Chinese writings, which is called *xiaozhuan* (lesser seal script). Examples of *xiaozhuan* of this period are *Taishan Keshi* (stone inscription on Mount Tai) and *Langyatai Keshi* (stone inscription on langya Terrace). At the same time, a man called Cheng Miao invented *lishu* (official script).

The second period spanned more than one thousand years from the Western Han Dynasty to the end of the Tang Dynasty. During this period, just like painting, calligraphy was also regarded as an art of great value and importance. In the Han Dynasty, the most popular calligraphy forms were *zhuanshu* and *lishu*. Throughout the Han Dynasty, *lishu* possessed a prevailing position as the official script. Although it was invented in the Qin Dynasty, *lishu* saw its real development in the Han Dynasty. In the Eastern Han Dynasty, *bafenshu* was invented. The characteristic of this script is that the right and the left sides of a character turn against each other. The most famous calligrapher in this line was Cai Yong, whose greatest work was *Xiping Shijing* (the stone classics in the 4th year of Emperor Xiping's reign during the Han Dynasty). From the Jin Dynasty (265—420) on, *kaishu* (regular script) became the chief object of cultivation, with *xingshu* (running hand) and *caoshu* (cursive script) as subordinate forms. Other styles were not important. *Kaishu* appeared during the periods of the late Han Dynasty and Wei and Jin dynasties. Zhong You was considered as its inventor. Later on, Wang Xizhi, whose known calligraphies are *Huangting Jing*, *Yueyi Lun*, and *Xiaonü Cao'e Bei*, was considered as the greatest calligrapher of all times. His son Wang Xianzhi was also a great calligrapher, who learned the style of his father and created a style of his own. In the Chinese calligraphic history, they were called "the two Wangs".

Xingshu is a modification of *lishu*. This style was created by Liu Desheng in the reigns of Emperors Huan and Ling of the Han Dynasty. At the very beginning, it was called *xingya*, and later on became an independent form.

Caoshu including *zhangcao* and *jincao* was invented by Shi You in the reign of Emperor Yuan (48—33 B.C.) of the Han Dynasty. *Jijiuzhang* written by him in the reign of Emperor Yuan is a work in *zhangcao* (a coarse style formed by breaking up the forms of *lishu*). During the Han Dynasty, Zhang Zhi developed a new style of *caoshu*—*jincao* by learning the style of Du Du and Cui Yuan with his own creation. For this sake, he was called "the sage of *cao*". When the great calligrapher Wang Xizhi made comments on his own works, he said that his works in the cursive script was as good as that of Zhang Zhi. It is thus evident that from the Han Dynasty to the Jin Dynasty, Zhang Zhi's name remained a symbol of perfection in this branch of calligraphy. During the Tang Dynasty, Sun Guoting, Zhang Xu and Huai Su were famous calligraphers of *caoshu*.

The development of calligraphy reached its peak during the Tang Dynasty. Many great calligraphers like Ouyang Xun, Liu Gongquan, Yu Shinan and Yan Zhenqing appeared, and their works are still used as calligraphy textbooks up to now. After the Tang Dynasty, it was realized that only calligraphic works with unique personal style could be recognized. The development of calligraphy in the post-Tang Dynasty was characterized by individualistic development. During the Song Dynasty (960—1279 A.D.), Su Dongpo, Huang Tingjian, Mi Yuanzhang and Cai Xiang were all noted calligraphers of different styles. In the Yuan Dynasty (1271—1368 A.D.), Zhao Zi'ang initiated a new development of *kaishu*. Zhao's works also had an influence on the development of calligraphy. Dong Qichang, He Shaoji, Zheng Banqiao, Kang Youwei were among the famous calligraphers of the Qing Dynasty.

35. 印章是怎么来的？它是怎么发展的？

在人们的日常生活中，经常要使用印章。印章最初是一种政治权力的象征，古时候任免官吏都要用印章作为凭证；官府发布文告、往来公文，也要加盖公章。后来，文人、士大夫又把它作为一种身份凭证。

在中国各个历史年代，印章有着不同的叫法。秦始皇（嬴政）统一中国（公元前221年）后，规定了皇帝专用的印章叫“玺”，一般私人用的印章只能叫“印”。到了汉代（公元前206～公元220年），人们又把将军用的印分离出来，单独叫“章”。从这时候起，人们把官家和私人的印、武官们的章总称为印章。宋代（公元960～1279年），有人专门刻了一种印章，用来盖在自己收藏的图画、书籍上，人们把这种印章称为图章。至今仍有许多人这么称呼。

印章的最初使用和人们现在使用的火漆印很相像。在发明纸以前，人们只能把字写在竹简上。平时官府公文和私人书信往来，为了不致泄露内容，就用绳子把竹简捆扎起来，在打结的地方凿一个方形的槽，在槽内填入带有粘性的泥丸，最后在泥丸上捺上图章。泥丸干燥后，成为坚硬的土块，叫作“封泥”。《史记》上记载的“青泥封书”就是这个意思。后来纸张和绢帛逐渐取代了竹简、木片，印章开始打在纸张和绢帛上了。

印章有雕琢、浇铸和陶土烧制三种制作方法。材料有金、银、铜、铁、玉、石、骨、木、瓷、玻璃、水晶等。3000多年来，随着汉字的发展演变，印章上的字体也在不断演变，表现出来各个时代的不同特征。还有人把书法、绘画、图章三种艺术结合于一体。据说元代大画家王冕曾经用花乳石来刻印章。他每画完一件作品，都把印章盖在上面，很受当时人们的欣赏。

印章的大小也不一样。战国（公元前475～前221年）的印章中有一厘米见方的，甚至有比黄豆粒还要小的。东晋（公元317～420年）的印章比较大，有一枚道教徒雕刻符咒的印章，在四寸见方的枣木上，刻了120个字，这已是一篇短文章了。南北朝（公元420～581年）时期出现了更大的木印，木印长1尺2寸，宽2寸5分，简直是一块相当大的木版雕刻。由于印章的大小和质地不同，它们的轻重也不一样。例如战国的一种特殊的印章只有几克重，而故宫博物院珍宝馆陈列的三方清代金印，每方重40多公斤。

35. What Was the Origin of the Seal? How Did It Develop?

Seals are very frequently used in everyday life. It was initially a symbol of political power, and was used to authenticate a signature or document on the appointment or removal of governmental officials in the past. All the official announcements and documents should be affixed with an official seal. Later, the literati and officialdom also took it as a sort of identification to show their social status.

Seals had different names in different dynasties in the Chinese history. After the unification of China by Qinshihuang in 221 B.C., it was stipulated that only the emperor's seal could be called *xi*, and those of the common people could only be called *yin*. By the Han Dynasty (206 B.C.—220 A.D.), the seals of generals got the special name *zhang* so as to differentiate them from those of the common people. Later on, the seals got a general term *yinzhang*. In the Song Dynasty (960—1279 A.D.), people started to use a new kind of seal which was specially carved for the purpose of affixing on their collections of paintings and books. It was called *tuzhang*, a term which is still used by many people today.

The use of seals in the beginning was quite similar to the wax-sealing of today. Before paper was made, people could only write on bamboo slips. In order to keep the government documents and personal letters from being peeped at by others, people used to tie the bamboo slips with strings. They cut a square hole at the knot, filled it with a sticky clay ball, and pressed their seal on it. When drying up, the clay ball became a hard lump and was called the "sealing clay". You can find the sentence "sealing the letter with black clay" in *Shi Ji* (*Records of the Historian*). Along with the gradual replacement of bamboo slips, seals came to be affixed on paper and silk.

There are three ways to make a seal: carving, casting and clay-baking. The materials used range from gold, silver, copper, iron, jade, stone, bone, wood, porcelain to crystal and glass. The script on the seals developed along with the development and evolution of characters over the past three thousand years, displaying different features of different times. Some people combined the three forms of art—calligraphy, painting and seal-carving—into one. It was said that Wang Mian, a great painter in the Yuan Dynasty (1271—1368 A.D.), liked to carve his seals with a special type of stone and affix his seals on each of the works he finished, and this received much admiration from the people at that time.

The size of the seal also varies. In the Warring States Period (475—221B.C.), there were seals as small as one square centimeter or even smaller than a grain of soybean. Seals in the Eastern Jin Dynasty (317—420 A.D.) were fairly big. There was one carved on a piece of 4-square-Chinese-inch jujube wood, on which 120 characters of Taoist magic figures were carved. In the Northern and Southern Dynasties (420—581A.D.), there was an even larger wood seal. It was 1.2 Chinese-foot long and 2.5 Chinese-inch wide—simply a large piece of wood engraving. Owing to the different sizes and materials of the seals, their weights also differ. For example, a special seal in the Warring States Period was as light as several grams, while each of the three gold seals of the Qing Dynasty (1636—1911 A.D.), which are now on display in the Palace Museum, weighs more than 40 kilograms.

36. 驰名世界的"唐三彩"有什么特点?

"唐三彩"是中国唐朝开始生产的一种陶器。以釉色绚丽、造型细腻雄健著称于世界。

中国陶器的生产历史悠久,早在8000年前新石器时代的文化遗址中,就发现了陶制的碗、钵、壶、罐、鼎等。还有材料说,在江西万年县仙人洞发现的一批陶器残片,据测定距今已有近万年的历史。到唐朝(公元618~907年),陶器生产工艺有了飞跃的发展。当时,人们日用品已由陶器转向瓷器,"唐三彩"器皿主要是用作墓葬中的明器。"三彩"中是以褐色、黄色和蓝色为基本色,在此基础上,还用了白色、赭黄、浅黄、褐红、翠绿、深绿、天蓝、藏蓝、茄紫等色彩。不同品种的含铅釉料,在窑内900度高温焙烧过程中,釉层流动,使各种颜色呈现出深浅不同的层次,各种颜色互相浸润融合,表现出人工与天然结合的艺术效果。使人叹为观止。

"唐三彩"陶器的种类,有人物、动物、器物、建筑、生产工具模型以及琉璃瓦等。其中人物类有天王、力士、文武官员、贵妇人、侍女以及胡人、杂技人等。动物中常见的有健壮的骏马、昂首嘶鸣或伫立欲行的骆驼,有的有商人骑在骆驼上,其他动物有麒麟、老虎、驴、牛、猪等。器物有壶、樽、盘、钵、杯、碗、盒等。各种模型有住房、仓库、厕所和车、钱柜等。可以说,"唐三彩"反映了当时社会生活的各个方面。

从雕塑造型来看,"唐三彩"比过去也有了很大进步。秦汉陶俑的形象较为单一,表情也较呆板。而"唐三彩"人物和动物的造型是千姿百态,表情也各有差异:妇女们大都文静端庄,面含微笑;武士则怒目圆睁,剑拔弩张;文官有的严肃庄敬,气派非凡,有的则蛮横狡诈,令人厌恶。其手法融合了北方雕塑的浑厚和南方雕塑细腻的特点。对西域人物深目高鼻的逼真造型显示出唐朝与西域诸国文化和贸易交流往来频繁。

继"唐三彩"之后,辽代(公元916~1125年)也生产过"辽三彩",但是质地不如"唐三彩"。辽代以后,多彩陶器生产逐渐衰落。而"唐三彩"在工艺美术史上占有无法替代的辉煌的一页,至今仍为人们看作不可多得的高级艺术品。

36. What Are the Characteristics of the World-famous *Tangsancai*?

Initially made in the Tang Dynasty (618—907 A.D.), *tangsancai* (tri-colored glazed pottery of the Tang Dynasty) is well-known for its gorgeous glaze and exquisite shape.

The production of pottery has a long history in China. Pottery bowls, pots, jars and cooking vessels were found in the cultural relics of the New Stone Age about 8000 years ago. Another record says that some broken pieces of pottery found in a cave in Jiangxi Province were determined to enjoy a history of nearly 10000 years. It was in the Tang Dynasty that the technology of pottery making achieved a great leap forward. At that time, more and more daily utensils were made of porcelain instead of pottery. *Tangsancai* were mainly used as articles buried with the dead in the graves. They are based on brown, yellow, and blue, with white, reddish brown, light yellow, jade green, dark green, sky blue, purplish blue and purple added and mixed. Fired in kilns of 900℃, different kinds of colors soak and blend in harmony and manifest an artistic combination of artificial and natural work.

The variety of *tangsancai* ranges from human figures, animals, utensils, architecture, model tools to tiles. Human figures are mainly kings, warriors, officials, madams, maids, people of minorities and acrobats. Animals include horses, standing camels, kylins, tigers, donkeys, oxen, and pigs. Utensils include pots, plates, cups, bowls, boxes and drinking vessels. Models are usually houses, warehouses, toilets, vehicles and money safes, etc. So we can say that *tangsancai* covers all aspects of social life at that time.

The modeling of *tangsancai* was also a great improvement over the past. In the Qin and Han dynasties (221 B.C.—220 A.D.), most of the pottery figurines are monotonous with dull facial expressions, while *tangsancai* shows an infinite variety of postures and faces: gentle and dignified women, scary-looking warriors, serious and crafty officials, etc. Its technique is a combination of the vigor of North China and the delicacy of South China. From the figures with deep eyes and high noses characteristic of people in the Western Regions, we can see the frequent cultural and economic exchanges with the states in the Western Regions in the Tang Dynasty.

Following *tangsancai*, there was *liaosancai* of the Liao Dynasty (916—1125 A.D.) Unfortunately, with inferior quality of the material, the production gradually declined thereafter. But *tangsancai* occupies such an irreplaceable position in the history of Chinese art and craft that even today it is still regarded as high-grade and precious works of art.

37. 中医诊病的独特理论——四诊与八纲的内容是什么？

中国是世界四大文明古国之一，中医的历史可追溯到远古时代。几千年来，中国人民在与疾病进行斗争的过程中，积累了丰富的经验，从而使中医形成了一整套独特而完整的理论体系。这些理论主要包括阴阳五行理论、脏腑理论、辨证施治理论以及药物学、针灸学等方面的理论。这些理论带有朴素而鲜明的辨证唯物主义思想，体现对立统一的规律。同时，几千年的临床实践也证实了中医的科学性。

中医是如何看病的呢？中医看病包括两个部分，即诊断方法和辨证施治。传统中医诊断病的方法为：望诊、闻诊、问诊和切诊，通常叫四诊。四诊在中医临床运用时具有各自独特的作用。望诊是中医大夫用自己的视觉对病人的神、色、形、态以及舌、舌苔进行有目的的观察，还通过对分泌物、排泄物的色质异常变化进行仔细观察，以测知内脏的病变。一般以神色和舌诊为重点。闻诊包括听声音和嗅气味两个方面。听声音主要是通过病人语言、呼吸、咳嗽等来听其声音的高低强弱。嗅气味是大夫凭嗅觉诊察病人呼吸及排泄物的气味，以辨别疾病的寒、热、虚、实等方面的情况。问诊是中医大夫在病人主诉病情的同时，对病人或其陪诊者有目的地询问发病时间、起病过程、治病经过、生活起居、病痛所在、病因、病史以及其他有关情况，是全面了解病情和病史的重要方法。切诊分为触诊和切诊两个部分而以脉诊为主，脉诊是中医临床不可缺少的基本诊断方法。

辨证施治主要是指八纲辨证。八纲就是通过四诊把诊察到的错综复杂的临床表现联系起来加以具体分析，然后归结为八个方面的症候。它们指的是阴、阳、表、里、寒、热、虚、实这八个方面。八纲用来辨别和概括疾病的性质、病因、病变部位以及机体抗病能力的强弱。

尽管疾病的症状非常复杂，但基本上都可以归纳为以上所说的八个方面。如果从总体上来分，疾病也可以分为两大类，即阴症和阳症。表、热、实症属于阳的范围；里、寒、虚属于阴的范围。所以称阴阳为八纲中的总纲，有统领其他六纲的作用。

强调阴阳的重要性正是中医最基本的特点。本来，阴阳理论是中国古代的一种宇宙观，它认为宇宙间的一切事物都是阴和阳的统一体，这两个方面相互依存又相互排斥，并且在其盛衰的变化中相互转化。这种阴阳理论是最基本的宇宙理论。几千年来，阴阳学说和中医实践结合在了一起，并且成为中国传统医学的一种指导理论。中医认为：人身和宇宙的情形是一致的，宇宙是大天地，而人身则是一小天地；正如阴阳是宇宙的支配力量一样，阴阳也是人体的支配力量，人体的健康取决于阴阳的和谐存在。

和阴阳学说结合在一起的是五行理论。五行学说是中国古代哲学的一个流派。这五行是指金、木、水、火、土。它们之间的相生、相克、相乘、相侮是宇宙间一切事物运动和变化的基本规律。这个学说也在中医学上得到了具体的应用。它把人体的五脏分属于五行,即肝属木,心属火,脾属土,肺属金,肾属水。中医就是利用五行相生、相克、相乘、相侮的关系来解释五脏的病变和病变原因。

虽然我们说疾病症候可以分为八类,但它们之间并不是毫无联系而孤立存在的。它们可能同时交叉存在,并且在疾病发展过程中还可能相互转化。以寒、热症为例,有些病本是寒症,却出现了热病的症候,而热症有时却呈现寒症的症候,这些都是假象。因此,根据八纲进行辨证施治时,为了正确地诊断疾病,得出正确的结论,不仅要求大夫对八纲掌握得好,而且还要善于注意这八个方面之间的复杂关系以及出现的假象,要透过假象看清实质。只有这样才不至于误诊。

总之,四诊和八纲是传统中医诊治疾病的指导理论和基础。

37. What Are *Sizhen* (the Four Diagnostic Methods) and *Bagang* (the Eight Principles)?

China is one of the four countries in the world with an ancient civilization. The history of traditional Chinese medicine can be traced back to antiquity. Through several thousand years of medical practice, the Chinese people have accumulated a wealth of experience in fighting against illnesses and thus creating a unique and integrated system of theories, such as the theories of *yin* and *yang* (the positive and negative forces) and *wuxing* (the five elements—water, fire, metal, wood and earth), of viscera, of treatment based on the differentiation of symptoms and signs, of pharmacology, of acupuncture and moxibustion, etc. These theories are imbued with the law of the unity of opposites and with the theory of dialectical materialism. The traditional Chinese medicine has been proved to be a science by thousands of years of clinical practice.

The traditional Chinese medical diagnostics includes two parts: the method of diagnosis and the determination of treatment based on the defferentiation of symptoms and signs. The method of diagnosis is composed of *sizhen*—inspection, auscultation and olfaction, inquiry, and palpation, of which each has its own clinical function. Inspection is the method to see the patient's expressions, complexion, physique, posture, tongue and the fur on it and the color of secretion and excrement in order to know the situation of the internal organs. Expressions and the tongue are the most important of them all. Auscultation and olfaction are the method to listen to the patient's sounds and to smell the odour of his/her breath and discharge. The changes of his/her sounds through his/her talking, breathing and coughing and his/her odour can tell chills, fever, hypofunction and hyperfunction. Inquiry is the method to inquire the patient or his /her companions about the onset, the cause and course of the illness, the chief complaints (especially pain), the past history, the living habits and other relevant conditions. As to palpation, pulse feeling is the chief item.

Bagang are *yin* and *yang*, exterior and interior, cold and heat, deficiency and excess. They are analyzed and summed up from the data obtained by *sizhen* to reveal the affected site, the nature and the cause of the disease. In spite of the complexity of diseases, they could be basically summed up into *bagang*. They may be classified as *yin* syndromes or *yang* syndromes in view of the general classification of the disease. Of *bagang*, *yang* includes exterior, heat and excess while *yin* covers interior, cold and deficiency. Thus *yin* and *yang* syndromes are the general principles of *bagang*.

A cardinal feature of the Chinese medicine is fixed on *yin* and *yang*. *Yin* and *yang* is a view on the universe, which holds that everything in the universe is in an entity of *yin* and *yang*. The two forces not only depend upon each other and oppose each other, but also tend to transform and alternate in waxing and waning. They are considered to be the basic law of the universe. For thousands of years, combined with traditional Chinese medical practices, this theory has become one of the guiding ideologies for traditional Chinese medicine. As these two forces dominate the universe, they control the physical organism, too. Health is dependent upon their existence in proper proportions.

The theory which goes together with *yin* and *yang* is *wuxing*, one of the schools of the ancient philosophy in China. The relations between *wuxing* are interpromotion, interaction, overaction and counter-action, which are believed to be the common law of the motions and changes of the creatures in the universe. Its application to traditional Chinese medicine is to subsume the various viscera of the human body into the category of *wuxing*. For example, liver is subsumed to wood, heart to fire, spleen to earth, lungs to metal, kidney to water, so as to explain the relations among the physiological and pathological changes of the viscera.

Bagang do not mean that the eight symptoms of diseases have nothing to do with each other. Actually they are closely connected and inseparable. For example, there may be coexistence of cold with heat syndromes, or heat with cold syndromes. They are also transformable from each other in the course of the disease. The patient may appear to have cold syndromes but has heat syndromes in nature. In order to get a correct diagnosis, a doctor must have a good command of *bagang* and also know very well about the coexistence of different syndromes.

In summary, *sizhen* and *bagang* are the guidance and the basis of traditional Chinese medicine diagnostics.

38. 中医十大古典名著是哪些人写的？基本内容是什么？

据估计，从最古老的《黄帝内经》算起，到清代末年，一共出版了大约 10000 种中医药书籍。这是祖国传统医学的巨大财富。在这浩翰的书库中，有 10 种医书是学习、研究中医必读之书。下面就分别做一简单介绍。

一、《黄帝内经素问》

《黄帝内经》是中国最古老的医书。它是以黄帝和他的大臣歧伯一问一答的对话形式写成的。这本书写于战国（公元前 475 ~ 前 221 年）时期，其内容包括两部分，即《素问》和《灵枢》。《素问》是《内经》的第一部分，它本来有 9 卷，后经唐代王冰修编而变成了 24 卷。主要讲述关于脏腑、经络、病因的基本理论以及治疗和针灸的原理。这些原理的阐述又是以阴阳理论和五行理论为基础的。

二、《灵枢》

《灵枢》分为 12 卷。主要讲经络系统，详细论述了针灸方面的问题。因此，《灵枢》篇又被称为《针经》。

三、《黄帝内经太素》

这本书是隋朝（公元 581 ~ 618 年）由医官杨上善编写的，是最早研究和论述《黄帝内经》的医著之一。此书是学习、研究《内经》的主要参考书。

四、《难经》

这是由中国最早的名医秦越人（亦称扁鹊）所著的。书中通过 81 个问题，论述了中医的基本理论，提出了用“望、闻、问、切”来诊断疾病的“四诊”，讲述了通过切脉来了解发生疾病的生理和病理因素。此外，该书还涉及到经络学说及针灸穴位的理论，是研究中医脉学的一部很有价值的参考书。

五、《伤寒论》

《伤寒论》是东汉（公元 25 ~ 220 年）名医张仲景的著作。晋代（公元 265 ~ 420 年）王叔和将其改编为 10 卷。《伤寒论》是对东汉以前医学理论和实践的科学总结。该书的中心议题是根据六经理论对热病进行辨证施治。张仲景提出的六经辨证论是东汉以后临床治病的指导原则。后来的温病理论就是在六经辨证论的指导下发展起来的一种新理论。《伤寒论》被医学界誉为“中药方剂之祖”。

六、《金匮要略方论》

《金匮要略方论》是张仲景原作《伤寒杂病论》的第二部分。晋代王叔和修撰第一部分时，此书的第二部分《杂病篇》已散佚。到了宋代，林亿和孙奇对第二部分进行了整理，命名为《金匮要略》,此书奠定了中医临床治病的基础。

七、《神农本草经》

这是中国最古老的药物学著作,相传为神农所作。实际上该书写成于战国时期或秦汉时期(公元前 221 ~ 公元 220 年)。《本草经》中所载药物大多数为植物性药物。该书对这些药的名称、别名以及药性、药味、生长环境都作了详细的描述。因此,这本书是传统医学中药物学的基础。

八、《脉经》

《脉经》是两晋(公元 265 ~ 316 年)王叔和编著的,是中国最早的脉学专著,也是最系统的脉学专论。本书分 10 卷,论述了三部九候的诊脉方法和 24 种脉象,还就每一经脉中各种病症所表现出的脉象以及杂病、妇女儿童热病等方面进行了详细的阐述,从而奠定了中国脉学的基础。

九、《针灸甲乙经》

《针灸甲乙经》是魏晋时期(公元 220 ~ 420 年)皇甫谧所著,全书分 10 卷,是中国最早的针灸学专著。包括《素问》、《针经》的释义和《明堂孔穴针灸治要》三部分。该书系统论述了经络理论、脉学理论以及针灸穴位的分布和针灸治病的穴位选择。

十、《中脏经》

《中脏经》系六朝(公元 317 ~ 618 年)时期写成的医书,作者的名字无从考查。有人认为是三国(公元 220 ~ 280 年)时期华佗所作。据推测,该书可能出自华佗徒弟之手。全书分 3 卷。论述如何通过脉诊来诊断人体五脏六腑的虚、实、寒、热以及采用的治疗方法。这是第一部以脏腑辨证的理论为指导诊治疾病的医学著作。

38. Who Were the Authors of the Ten Classics of Chinese Medicine? What Were Their Contents?

It was estimated that there were about 10000 Chinese medicine books altogether, with the most ancient *Huangdi Neijing* (The Yellow Emperor's Canon of Internal Medicine) and all others written before the end of the Qing Dynasty included. What an enormous treasure of traditional Chinese medicine! Among all these books, the following ten are necessities for students and researchers of traditional Chinese medicine.

1. *Huangdi Neijing Suwen* (*Plain Questions of the Yellow Emperor's Canon of In-*

ternal Medicine)

Huangdi Neijing is the earliest medical book in China. It took the form of a catechism, a dialogue between the Yellow Emperor and his minister Qi Bo. The book was compiled during the Warring States Period (475—221 B.C.). It consisted of two parts: *Suwen* (*Plain Questions*) and *Lingshu* (*Miraculous Pivot*). *Suwen* originally covered 9 volumes, which was later revised into 24 volumes by Wang Bing of the Tang Dynasty (618—907 A.D.). The contents of this book mainly included the fundamentals of physiology current at that time, such as internal organs, meridians and collaterals, etiology, diagnosis, principles of treatment, acupuncture and moxibustion. Discussions were based on the theories of *yin* and *yang* and of *wuxing* (the five elements—wood, fire, earth, metal and water).

2. *Lingshu* (*Miraculous Pivot*)

Lingshu covers 12 volumes. It stressed on the channels and collaterals and discussed acupuncture and moxibustion in details. So it is also called *Zhen Jing* (*The Canon of Acupuncture*).

3. *Huangdi Neijing Taisu* (*Fundamentals of the Yellow Emperor's Canon of Internal Medicine*)

The book was compiled by the physician Yang Shangshan of the Sui Dynasty (581—618 A.D.). The book is an important reference to the study of *Huangdi Neijing*.

4. *Nan Jing* (*The Classic on Medical Problems*)

This book was written by one of the earliest noted physician Qin Yueren, also known as Bian Que (in the 1st—2nd century B.C.). It dealt with fundamental medical theories through 81 problems and put forward *sizhen* (the four methods of diagnosis). The discussion of pulse-taking in this book was so thorough and comprehensive that it made the book a good introduction to the theory of arteries and veins.

5. *Shanghan Lun* (*Treatise on Febrile Diseases*)

The book was written by a famous doctor Zhang Zhongjing of the Eastern Han Dynasty (25—220 A.D.) and was revised into 10 volumes by Wang Shuhe of the Jin Dynasty (265—420 A.D.). It served as a summarization of the medical theories and experiences before the Eastern Han Dynasty. The essence of the book was the analysis and treatment based on the differentiation of symptoms and signs of febrile diseases according to the theory of the six pairs of channels. The diagnosis and pulse-taking in each phase, the principles of treatment and the prescriptions were also discussed in detail. The development of the doctrine of seasonal febrile diseases was based on this book. As a result, this book was honored as "the originator of proved prescriptions".

6. *Jingui Yaolüe Fanglun* (*Synopsis of the Prescriptions of the Golden Cabinet*)

The book was written by Zhang Zhongjing and was originally the second part of his book *Shanghan Lun*. When Wang Shuhe rearranged the first part, this second part was lost. It was not until the Song Dynasty(960—1279 A.D.) when Lin Yi and Sun Qi revised this part into 3 volumes and named it *Jingui Yaolüe Fanglun*. This book has laid the foundation for clinical treatment in traditional Chinese medicine.

7. *Shennong Bencao Jing* (*Shennong's Herbal Classic*)

This was the earliest extent monograph on Chinese medicinal herbs. It was believed to be a product of the 1st century B.C. with its authorship accredited to the ancient emperor Shennong (the divine farmer). Actually, it came into existence in the Qin and Han dynasties, or the Warring States Period (221B.C.—220 A.D.). A great part of this book was about herbs, giving minute descriptions of their formal names, nick names, properties and natures, flavors, growing environments, and functions in ailment or poisoning. This book served as the basis of traditional pharmaceutics and phytopharmacy.

8. *Mai Jing* (*The Pulse Classic*)

This book was written by Wang Shuhe in the 4th century. It was the earliest monograph about pulse-taking and a comprehensive treatise on pulse-taking before the Jin Dynasty(265—316 A.D.). In the 10 volumes, it discussed the methods of pulse-taking and 24 kinds of pulse conditions. It also gave a further exposition about the pulse conditions for diagnosis of different diseases in each channel, and discussed miscellaneous diseases as well as febrile diseases in women and children. It laid the foundation for diagnostics in traditional Chinese medicine.

9. *Zhenjiu Jiayi Jing* (*A-B Classic of Acupuncture and Moxibustion*)

This 10-volume book was written by Huang Fumi living in both the Wei and the Jin dynasties (220—420 A.D.). It was the earliest book on acupuncture, including the essence of *Suwen*, *Zhěn Jing* and *Mingtang Kongxue Zhenjiu Zhiyao* (*The Principles of Acupuncture and Moxibustion Treatment*) in accordance with the illustrations of the channels and acupoints. The selection of acupoints for the treatment of various diseases was discussed.

10. *Zhongzang Jing* (*Treasured Classic*)

This book was written between 317 and 618 A.D. by an unknown author. Some people believed that it might be written by Hua Tuo of the Three Kingdoms Period (220—280 A.D.) or by some of Hua Tuo's disciples. The book in 3 volumes explained how to diagnose the hypofunction or hyperfunction, cold or heat of the vital organs by means of pulse-taking in order to determine a disease and predict its prognosis. It was an original version of analysis and differentiation of diseases through pathological changes of the viscera and their interrelationships.

39. 中国最早的法医学著作是谁写的？其内容如何？

中国的法医学历史悠久。远在《礼记·月令》中就有临刑法官“瞻伤、察创、视折、审断”等项记载，这就是中国古代法医学最早的萌芽。汉、唐之际（公元前 206 ~ 公元 907 年），又积累了一定的法医学知识，但缺少专著。五代（公元 907 ~ 960 年）时的《疑狱集》是中国现存最早的法医著作。到宋朝（公元 960 ~ 1279 年）时法医知识进步较快，有关法医检验的书籍如《内恕录》等接连问世，但其内容较为粗陋，体系还不完备。真正称得上是中国也是世界历史上第一部系统的法医学专著的，是南宋（公元 1127 ~ 1279 年）时宋慈所著的《洗冤录》。这部书完成于宋理宗淳祐七年（公元 1247 年），而西方最早的法医学专著，是 300 多年以后才由意大利人菲德里在 1602 年写成的。

宋慈（公元 1186 ~ 1249 年），字惠文，一生曾四任高级刑法官。他长期从事审判工作和现场执法检验的实践，深入钻研历代法医文献，因而积累了丰富的法医检验知识和经验。在综合前人成就的基础上，他历尽两年之工，校勘订正，终于编辑成《洗冤录》一书。全书共 5 卷。卷一载条令和总说；卷二验尸；卷三至卷五详载各种伤、死情况。该书内容丰富，范围极广，对人体解剖、尸体检验、现场检查、死伤原因鉴定、自杀或谋杀的各种现象、各种毒物和急救及解毒方法等，有很多精辟的记述，牵涉到了内科、外科、妇科、儿科、骨科等诸方面的专门知识。与近代法医学相比，不但论述的项目和范围基本相吻合，而且内容也具备了现代检验方面所需要的初步知识。书中记载的洗尸、人工呼吸法、迎日隔伞验收、夹板固定伤断部位，以及银钗验毒、明矾催吐洗胃、蛋白解砒毒等等，都是合乎科学道理的。此书十分重视自杀、他杀或病亡的细致差别，案例详明。如对自缢与假自缢、溺死与非溺死、烧死与假烧死、自刑与杀伤等都详尽判别，并列举了各类猝死的情况，书末还附有各种急救药方。

《洗冤录》中的许多内容载述翔实、见解独特，在法医学上具有较高的科学价值。当然，由于时代的局限，当时的科学还不够发达，书中有些观点难免缺少科学依据甚至带有迷信色彩。

自 13 至 19 世纪，《洗冤录》这部杰作在中国沿用达 600 多年之久，成为历朝审判官员案头必备的参考书。元、明、清三朝的法医学著作，大都以它为蓝本来引证、考释。在近代，此书还被传至国外。荷兰人 1862 年将其译成荷兰文，后又被译成法文、德文以及朝、日、英、俄等文字。

39. Who Wrote the First Book on Medical Jurisprudence in China? What Is Its Content?

Medicolegal investigation has a long history in China. The earliest record of this could be found in the book *Li Ji* (*The Book of Rites*). In the Han and Tang dynasties (206 B.C.—907 A.D.), more knowledge was accumulated, but still there was not a monograph. The book *Yi Yu Ji* (*Difficult Cases*) written in the Five Dynasties(907—960 A.D.) was the earliest one extant. Medical jurisprudence achieved a quick progress and development in the Song Dynasty (960—1279 A.D.) and books on medicolegal investigations came out one after another, e.g. *Nei Shu Lu* (*Clear Conscience*). But the content was still crude and the system was far from perfect. The one that was qualified to be called the first systematic monograph on medical jurisprudence in China, and in the world as well, should be *Xi Yuan Lu* (*Manual of Forensic Medicine*) written by Song Ci in the Southern Song Dynasty(1127—1279 A.D.). The book was finished in 1247, while the earliest one in the West was written more than 300 years later in 1602 by an Italian named Phideli.

Song Ci (1186—1249 A.D.), also known as Huiwen, had assumed the post of a penal code justice four times in his lifetime. Owing to his long-time practice in administration of justice and inspection of the scenes of crimes and his intensive study of the documents through the ages, he accumulated abundant knowledge and experience in the field of medical jurisprudence. On the basis of the achievements made by his predecessors, he spent two years collecting and emending and finally compiled the book *Xi Yuan Lu*. There are five chapters in the book. Chapter One is about regulations and a general introduction; Chapter Two is about postmortem; Chapters Three to Five keep a record of all kinds of wounds and deaths. This book has rich contents and brilliant expositions dealing with a wide range of scope from dissection, autopsy, inspection of the scenes, appraisal of causes of wounds and deaths, to different kinds of suicides and murders as well as all kinds of poisons and various means of first aid and detoxification, covering the specialized knowledge of internal medicine, surgery, gynaecology, paediatrics, orthopaedics, etc. Compared with books of modern times, this book not only deals with identical subjects and covers equally broad scopes, but also presents the basic knowledge required by modern inspections. The practices recorded in the book, such as bathing a corpse, giving artificial respiration, putting the broken parts in splints, testing the poison with a silver hairpin, inducing vomiting with alum to bathe the stomach, detoxicating the poison of arsenic with egg white, etc. all tally with scientific knowledge. And it pays special attention to the tiny differences between suicide, murder and death resulting from illness. These are explained with detailed cases, such as how to distinguish deaths caused by suicidal hanging or by drowning and burning from murder that were made to look like these. The book also included various kinds of abrupt and sudden deaths, and an appendix of prescriptions for emergency treatments.

With its full and accurate record and distinctive ideas, *Xi Yuan Lu* is of high scientific value in the history of medical jurisprudence. Owing to the limitations of the time and the inadequacy of scientific development, it is only natural that some of the viewpoints in the book lack scientific basis or are even superstitious beliefs.

From the 13th century all the way to the 19th century, *Xi Yuan Lu* had been used continuously for more than 600 years, and had become a required reference book for examing officers. Most of the books on medical jurisprudence written in the Yuan, Ming and Qing dynasties (1271—1911 A.D.) were based on it. The book was transmitted abroad in modern times and was translated into Dutch in 1862, and then into French, German, Korean, Japanese, English, Russian, etc.

40."劈山救母"讲的是什么故事?

"劈山救母"是一个广为流传的民间神话故事。传说,有一个书生叫刘彦昌,他进京赶考,路过华山时,到了山上的圣母祠。圣母祠里住着一个仙女,她是玉皇大帝的外甥女,人们称她为"三圣母"。这一天,正当三圣母在祠中载歌载舞时,忽见外面有人进来,于是她急忙登上神座,变作一尊塑像。在这匆忙之中,她的飘带被香案挂住了。刘彦昌一进祠殿,就被三圣母的美丽容貌和温柔的气质迷住了,他情不自禁地提笔在飘带上写下了表达爱慕之情的一首诗。这一切三圣母都看在眼里。由于她早就向往着人间爱情的幸福生活,所以,当她看到这位纯真、朴实的年轻人时,终于不顾天上的禁令,勇敢地和刘彦昌结成了夫妻。

一年以后,他们有了一个儿子,取名沉香。一家人过着和睦幸福的生活。但是,这件事叫三圣母的哥哥二郎神知道了,他就把三圣母抓走了,压在华山之下。这个幸福的家庭就这样被二郎神给拆散了。年幼的沉香看到母亲被压在华山之下,大哭大叫。他的哭声被善良的霹雳大仙听到了。大仙见沉香可怜,于是就把他带入另一座大山之中。后来,沉香长大了,每天在大仙的指导下练习武艺,学了一身好本领。大仙还用法术点化沉香脱了凡身。

15年过去了。当沉香知道自己的身世和母亲的遭遇时,就急忙想救出母亲。霹雳大仙放他出山。临行前,霹雳大仙送给他一把开山神斧。沉香在去华山的路上,结识了四位神仙。他们对沉香的不幸表示同情,答应一定帮沉香救出母亲。

沉香来到二郎庙,哀求舅舅二郎神放出他的母亲。二郎神不但不听沉香的请求,还想把他杀死,于是,两人打了起来。四位神仙赶来助战,他们和沉香一起打败了二郎神。沉香急忙来到华山脚下,大声呼喊母亲。当沉香听到母亲那悲凉的回答时,他恨不得马上见到自己的亲生母亲。于是他举起神斧,向华山猛劈过去。顿时,华山被劈成两半,三圣母重见天日。后来,母子俩又找到了流浪在外的刘彦昌,一家人终于团聚了。

40. What Is the Story of *Pi Shan Jiu Mu* (*Cleaving the Mountain to Rescue the Mother*)?

Pi Shan Jiu Mu is a popular legendary tale. It was said that on his way to the capital, a young man called Liu Yanchang passed by Mt. Hua and walked into the

Temple of the Third Goddess, where lived a female deity who was a niece of Jade Emperor, the supreme sovereign in Heaven. People called this deity the Third Goddess. On that day, when she was singing and dancing, the Third Goddess heard someone coming into the temple hall. So, she hurriedly ascended the pedestal and resumed the form of a statue. But her long draping scarf was caught by the alter table. Entering the hall, Liu was so attracted by the beautiful image of the goddess that he wrote a poem on the scarf expressing his love and admiration for the goddess. The goddess saw all of these. Since she had longed for a happy life on the earth and was moved by the pure and honest love of the young man, she took the bold step of marrying him in defiance of the ban from Heaven.

In a year's time, they got a son, who was named Chenxiang. The family lived in perfect bliss. But finally, the goddess's borther, God Erlang, got to know it. He took his sister away from her family and put her under Mt. Hua. Thus, a happy family was broken up. When the cries of the motherless boy were heard by the kind-hearted god of thunder, he took Chenxiang under his custody in his mountain abode thousands of miles away. The boy was brought up and trained in fighting skills and magic arts by the god of thunder, who also gave him an invulnerable body to replace his mundane form.

Fifteen years passed, as Chenxiang grew up to be a strong young man, he got to know all the story about his family. He was anxious to rescue his mother. For this purpose, the god of thunder gave him a magic axe. On his way to Mt. Hua, he made friends with four gods, who, in sympathy with him for his sufferings, promised to render him their assistance.

Chenxiang then came to God Erlang and entreated his uncle for mercy to release his mother from under the mountain, but was refused. So the uncle and the nephew clashed in a fierce fight. With the assistance of the four gods, Chenxiang defeated his uncle. He called to his mother, and she answered from under the dead weight mountain. The boy raised high his magic axe and cleft the mountain apart, so the goddess was rescued.

Later on, the mother and the son also located the father, who had been roaming around, and the family finally reunited.

41."麒麟献书"是什么故事?

这是讲麒麟献书给孔子的神话故事。麒麟是古代传说中的吉祥动物,它的样子像鹿,头上只有一只角,身上长满了鳞甲,它的尾巴像牛的尾巴。

相传,有一天夜里,在孔子半睡半醒的时候,他看到远处有一道红光,这道光好久没消失。孔子感到很奇怪,就想,是不是有什么圣贤来给我指点来了呢?当时,孔子还不是一个大学问家,他虽然到处求教,但是没有什么大的收获。由于孔子求知的欲望很强,所以,当他看到这种奇异的现象时,就迫不及待地马上把跟他同行的两个弟子喊醒,坐上车,朝着有红光的地方奔去。走着走着,天渐渐地亮了。忽然间,孔子看到河岸上有一个小男孩正用石头打一只麒麟,孔子急忙跑到河边。小男孩看见有人来了,就把麒麟藏到一堆干草中,还骗孔子,说麒麟朝别处跑了。孔子见小孩撒谎,很生气,就径直走向草堆,扒开干草一看,里边有一只受伤的麒麟。它望着孔子,好像在求孔子救它一命。孔子就把衣服脱下盖在麒麟的身上,还小心地给它包扎伤口。麒麟好像要对孔子表示感激似的,舔孔子的手。舔着舔着,忽然从嘴里吐出三部书来。孔子想这一定是天书,麒麟也是神兽。

孔子得了天书之后,苦心钻研,进步很快,最后终于成了一个大学问家,被人们尊称为"至圣先师"。

41. What Is the Story of *Qilin Xian Shu* (*A Unicorn Presents Books*)?

The legendary tale told that once a *qilin*, a fabulous animal, delivered some books to Confucius. *Qilin* was a Chinese legendary animal known as the Chinese unicorn by Western writers. It looked like a deer, but with a single horn on its head, large fish scales on its body, and a tail like that of an ox.

Legend goes that once when he laid half asleep, Confucius saw a red glow rise and stay indispersed at a certain spot in the distance. He was surprised and puzzled, asking himself: could this mean that some sage has appeared to give me enlightenment? Confucius had not become a famous scholar yet prior to this event. Although he had travelled to many places to pursue knowledge, he had not made any significant accomplishment. Confucius was very eager and keen to pursue knowledge. Now that he saw this strange scene, he immediately woke up the two disciples who were travelling with him, got into a carriage and hurried in the direction of the light. The day was approaching dawn as they went toward the light. Suddenly, Confucius saw on the riverbank a boy beating a unicorn hard with stones. He hurried to the riverside. When the boy saw someone approaching, he hid the unicorn in a stack of hay, and even lied to Confucius and told him that the animal had run in another direction. Confucius was very angry for the boy's lying. He walked directly to the stack and pushed aside the hay, where he saw the animal wounded and pitiably looking up to him for help. Confucius took off some of his own clothes and carefully dressed the wound of the unicorn with it. The unicorn licked Confucius' hand as if it wanted to express its gratitude. While it was doing so, three books came out of its mouth. Confucius believed that these must be books from Heaven and the animal must be a divine.

From then on, Confucius worked hard studying these books and made rapid progress. Eventually, he became the greatest sage and educationist in China.

42."麻姑献寿"是什么故事?

"麻姑献寿"是有名的民间神话故事。

相传,勤劳美丽的麻姑原是江西建昌(今江西南丰、广川等县)人,后来在山东牟州(今山东莱芜东)东南的姑余山修炼成仙,东汉桓帝(刘志,公元147~167年)时,又投胎转世在一户姓蔡的人家。转世后,她曾施展魔法,掷果成珠,把宝珠分给穷苦老百姓。最后成仙升天。据传说,麻姑曾三次目睹东海变为桑田。人们根据麻姑的故事,就创造出一句中国成语"沧海桑田"。

麻姑献寿的故事内容大致是这样的:相传,农历三月初三是西天昆仑山的神仙西王母的寿辰,每逢这一天,王母娘都设蟠桃会宴请各路神仙。四海龙王和天上的仙女都来祝寿。有一次,四位花仙带着盛开的鲜花邀请麻姑一块去给西王母拜寿。但这时,麻姑还没有把寿礼准备好,她就来到绛珠河边,用灵芝酿成仙酒,把酒带到蟠桃会献给了西王母。

正是由于这样的故事在民间广为流传,所以在民间就有了在给年长妇女祝寿时赠送《麻姑献寿图》的习惯,图面上一般都画着麻姑双手持仙酒或仙桃献礼的样子。

虽然麻姑献寿只是一个神话,但历史上确有为麻姑树碑立传的事。唐代大历六年(公元771年),在江西临川(今临川市)就为麻姑立了碑,大书法家颜真卿亲自撰写碑文。碑文全称《大唐抚州南城县麻姑山仙坛记》,后遭雷击而毁。据记载,唐碑被毁后,元代建昌府知府梁伯达重刻碑文。

42. What Is the Story *Magu Xian Shou* (*Magu Presents Her Birthday Gift*)?

Magu Xian Shou is a well-known ancient myth.

Legend goes that Magu was a pretty and industrious girl from Jianchang (present Nanfeng and Guangchuan of Jiangxi Province), who later attained immortality through self-cultivation at Guyu Mountain, southeast of Mouzhou (east of Laiwu of Shandong Province) and got reincarnated in the Cai family during the reign of Emperor Huan of the Eastern Han Dynasty(25—220 A.D.). After her reincarnation, she once exerted her magic power by throwing fruits into the air and turning them into pearls, which she distributed among the poor. Finally she disappeared by ascending to Heaven again.

According to legend, she had personally witnessed three times that the Eastern Sea turned into mulberry fields. It is from this legend that the Chinese idiom "the blue sea turns into mulberry fields" came.

The third day of the third lunar month was supposed to be the birthday of Xiwangmu (Heavenly Queen Mother) who lived in Mt. Kunlun in the far west. Every year on that day she would have a banquet of immortality peaches prepared, and invite the divinities and deities of all quarters and descriptions, including the Dragon Kings of the four seas, the fairy maidens of Heaven, and so on. One year, when the four flower fairies with different flowers in blossom were on their way to the peach banquet, they asked Magu to go with them. But at that moment, Magu had not yet had her birthday gift prepared. So, she walked up to the Crimson-pearl River and brewed some divine wine there with *lingzhi* (an elixir plant). Magu brought the wine to the assembly of celebration and presented it to the Queen Mother.

It is this story that gives rise to the custom of presenting a *Magu Xian Shou* picture to an aged woman on her birthday. In the picture, Magu often holds a bottle of divine wine or a tray of divine peaches.

Although it is just a legendary tale, it is so widely spread that Magu has been glorified with monuments in the history. In the year 771 in the Tang Dynasty, Yan Zhenqing, a great calligrapher, wrote a story of Magu and had it engraved on a stele and erected in Linchuan, Jiangxi Province, which was destroyed by lightning later. It is also recorded that during the Yuan Dynasty (1271—1368 A.D.), Liang Boda, the prefect of Jianchang Prefecture, re-engraved the story on another stele.

43."商山四皓"是什么故事?

"商山四皓"讲的是西汉(公元前206~公元24年)初年的故事。刘邦在起兵前已和吕雉(就是后来的吕后)结了婚,并且有了他们的第一个儿子刘盈。后来在夺取政权的征战中,有一次刘邦大败而逃,跑到一个老百姓家里躲避。就在这一家,他看中了一个姑娘,于是和她成了亲,这个姑娘就是后来汉高祖刘邦的另一个夫人戚夫人,刘邦和戚夫人也有一个儿子叫如意。

刘邦登基称帝之后,把刘盈封为太子,把如意封为赵王。后来,刘邦特别喜欢如意,就想把如意立为太子,让他将来继承皇位。这个消息传到吕后耳里,她大为恼火,就找开国功臣张良商量对策。张良深知变换继承人将会引起诸王、贵族之间的混乱。因此,张良向吕后献策,要她请四位老者出山辅佐太子,并告诉了她四位老人的名字。这四位老人是秦末汉初有名的学者,他们是:东园公、角里、绮里季、夏黄公。这四个人每个都是通古晓今、运筹帷幄的人物,只是由于秦末战乱而隐居商山。由于这四位学者当时都已是满头银发,所以后人称他们为商山四皓(皓:白的意思,引申为老翁)。四位老人看太子刘盈是个诚实善良的年轻人,因此答应做他的老师。有一次,刘邦与太子刘盈一起吃饭时,发现刘盈背后站着四位长者。当刘邦知道这几位老人正是商山四皓,并且成了太子的老师时,不禁大吃一惊。刘邦认识到太子刘盈羽翼已丰,要想废刘盈而另立如意为太子已是不可能的了,只得改变了原来的主意。刘邦死后,刘盈继承了皇位,他就是西汉的第二个皇帝——汉惠帝。

43. What Is the Story of *Shangshan Sihao* (*The Four Hoary Venerable*)?

The story of *Shangshan Sihao* took place in the early Western Han Dynasty (206 B.C.—24 A.D.). Before launching armed struggles, Liu Bang, the founding emperor of the Western Han Dynasty, had got married with Lü Zhi, who later became his queen. With Lü Zhi, Liu Bang got his first son named Liu Ying. During his subsequent battles, Liu Bang once was defeated and had to flee for his life. In a household, where he took refuge, he met a girl and found her shapely and attractive. Enamored, he married the girl. who was later known as Lady Qi. With Lady Qi, Liu Bang got another son, named Ruyi.

When Liu Bang ascended the throne, he designated Liu Ying, his first-born son, as the crown prince and granted his second son Ruyi the title of the Prince of the State of Zhao. Later on, Liu Bang was increasingly fond of his second son Ruyi and had the idea of making him the crown prince to inherit the throne. When the queen became aware of the intention, she was on tenterhooks. She took counsel with Zhang Liang, one of the founding ministers of the Han Dynasty. Zhang knew clearly that changes in the lineage of succession would bring about chaos in the country and unrest among the princes and the lords. He gave the queen his advice , asking her to invite the four accomplished scholars, Dongyuangong, Luli, Qiliji and Xiahuangong, to assist the crown prince. They were all distinguished scholar-statesmen in the late Qin Dynasty and the early Han Dynasty, and were known for their outstanding achievements and rich knowledge in both history and current affairs, as well as for their wisdom to work out strategies. It was only because of the turmoil of the times that they became disillusioned with their official careers and escaped the world into delusion in Shangshan. Since they all had hoary hair, they were called "*Shangshan Sihao*" (the four hoary venerable). They were pleased to become mentors of the crown prince because they had heard of Liu Ying as a sincere and kind young man. One day, when the emperor had dinner with Liu Ying, he was surprised to see four elders standing behind his son. He learned that they were none other than *Shangshan Sihao*. It was at that moment that he realized that popular sympathy had gone to the crown prince, and that as the prince had become full-fledged, it was impossible to replace him. In this way Liu Ying eventually become the second emperor of the Western Han Dynasty.

44. 为什么中国人尊敬崇拜龙，并且自称“龙的传人”？

龙在中国人的心目中，是充满神奇力量的吉祥神物，自古以来受到人们的尊崇。1987年，考古工作者在河南濮阳发现的一座古墓中，墓主尸体两侧有用蚌壳摆成的龙、虎图形。据考证，这是距现在6000多年的仰韶文化时期的墓葬，也是迄今为止中国发现的最早的龙图形。说明早在新石器时代，中国就有崇拜龙的事实了。东汉许慎在《说文解字》中，将龙的神异描写为：“鳞虫之长，能幽能明，能细能巨，能短能长，春分而登天，秋分而潜渊。”历来史书典籍和传奇小说中，对于龙的无边威力和神奇变化有过数不清的描绘。以龙为名的江河湖泊、市、县、乡镇也遍布全国各地。

古代传说中，有黄帝乘龙升天的神话。而把龙与皇帝本身合而为一的，则始于汉高祖刘邦。据《史记》说，刘邦的母亲“梦与神遇”，当时电闪雷鸣，刘邦的父亲见到一条蛟龙在上面，于是刘邦母亲怀孕，生下了刘邦。自此以后，历代皇帝都自称为“真龙天子”。他们的居室、衣服、日用器具以至陵墓都饰以龙的图案。而民间则以“龙王爷”为统治江河湖海的主宰，说它管行云布雨。所以每逢旱年，人们常叩拜龙王，祈求下雨。在过去每年印制的历书上，书首都标明本年为几龙治水，以预卜旱涝。在民间节日活动中，龙又是喜庆与幸福的象征。如逢年过节人们要龙灯，端午节赛龙船等。

龙的来源说法不一，大体上有三种说法：一种认为，远古时期人们看到天上的霹雳闪电，认为在那神秘的力量中一定存在着一种实体，那就是龙；另一种认为龙的原型是鳄鱼，因为鳄鱼冬天冬眠，到初春苏醒，而且在大风雨前发出如雷的吼声，与古书上所说龙的习性一样；第三种说法认为龙起源于氏族时期的蛇图腾，并在氏族发展与合并过程中，吸收了其他几种动物图腾的特点，形成了一种带有多种动物特点的新图腾。所以古文献中有“伏羲龙身，女娲蛇躯”的说法，说这两个人“兄妹为婚”。现存的汉代石刻还有上述的画像。看来，第三种说法较为可信。因为龙是综合了几种动物特征的“神物”，所以对它的特点的描绘也不相同。大体上说，其头像驼（或马），其角像鹿，其眼像虾（或兔），其身像蛇，其鳞像鱼，其爪像鹰（或狗），其耳像牛（或狐），其尾像鬣狗。

千百年来，人们尊崇龙，喜爱龙，把它看作中华民族品格与精神的象征。因此，有人说中国人是“龙的传人”。

关于龙生九子，俱不成龙的传说，在古书记载中也不尽相同。其中一种说法是：龙的九个儿子第一叫赑屃（bìxì），好负重，多刻于碑座；第二叫螭（chī）吻，长得像兽，为屋顶兽头；第三叫蒲牢，好吼，为过去铸的钟上的钮；第四叫狴犴（bì'àn），像虎，有威力，多刻于牢狱门上；第五叫饕餮（tāotiè），贪食，立于鼎盖；第六叫蚣蝮（bāxià），性好水，多刻于桥柱；

第七叫睚眦(yázì),性好杀,刻在刀环上;第八叫金猊(ní)或狻猊(suānní),性好烟火,刻在香炉上;第九叫椒图,形似螺蚌,性好闭,刻在门铺首(就是衔门环的兽头)。

44. Why Do the Chinese People Respect and Love Dragons and Call Themselves "Dragon's Descendants"?

In Chinese people's eyes, the dragon is an auspicious deity full of magic power. It has always been respected by the Chinese people. In 1987, an old tomb was unearthed in Puyang, Henan Province. On either side of the buried corpse, a dragon figure and a tiger figure formed with mussel shells were found. According to textual research, this was the ruins of a tomb of the Yangshao Culture Age some six thousand years ago, and this was the first dragon figure discovered in China up to now. All this indicates that even as early as in the Neolithic Age, the Chinese people already paid respect to the dragon. There are countless descriptions through the ages on the unlimited power and magical changes of the dragon. Rivers, lakes, cities, counties, and villages named after the dragon are found everywhere in China.

In the ancient mythology, there was a myth to the effect that the Yellow Emperor went to Heaven on the back of a dragon. It was Liu Bang, the first emperor of the Han Dynasty(206 B.C.—220 A.D.), who associated the dragon with the emperor. According to *Shi Ji* (*Records of the Historian*), Liu Bang's mother once "met a god in her dream". Just at that moment, lightning flashed and thunder rolled. Startled, Liu Bang's father looked up and saw a dragon in the sky. Hereafter, the mother was pregnant and gave birth to a boy, who was named Liu Bang. From then on, every emperor called himself "heavenly son of the real dragon", and decorated their rooms, clothes, daily utensils, and even tombs with patterns of dragons. Common people regarded to the "dragon king" as the ruler of rivers and lakes who could marshal clouds and rain. So, whenever there was a drought, people would pray the dragon king for rain. On the front covers of the old Chinese lunar calendars, there used to be words telling how many dragons would harness the flood that year. In the folk festive days, dragons also served as a symbol of joy and happiness. For example, there were dragon lantern festival in the New Year and dragon boat race on the fifth day of the fifth moon.

There are various sayings about the origin of the dragon. Roughly, there are three widely accepted ones among them. One saying states that in the remote antiquity, seeing lightning and thundering in the sky, the ancient people thought there was an entity existing in the magical power, which they believed was the dragon. The second believes that the primary form of the dragon is that of a crocodile because the crocodile hibernates in winter and wakes up in early spring, and roars when rain and storm are coming. All these accord with the characteristics and habits of the dragon described in ancient books. The third goes as follows: Primarily, dragons originated from the totems of the Clan Age. In the course of clan development and annexation, by absorbing characteristics of other animal totems, dragons gradually became a new totem with the characteristics of other animals incorporated. It was recorded in some ancient books that Fuxi had a dragon body, and Nüwa, the girl, had a snake body. The third saying is proved by the stone sculpture of the Han Dynasty with a picture similar to that described in the third saying. It stands to reason that the third saying is more credible. As a "deity" with the characteristics of several kinds of animals, descriptions on the appearance of the dragon vary. Generally speaking, it is a mixture: with camel's (or horse's) head, deer's horns, prawn's (or rabbit's) eyes, snake's body, fish's scales, eagle's (or dog's) paws, ox's (or fox's) ears, and hyena's tail.

For thousands of years, the Chinese people have respected and liked dragons, regarding them as a symbol of the character and spirit of the Chinese nationalities. Therefore, the term "descendants of the dragon" is used to refer to the entire Chinese nation.

There are different records on the nine sons of the dragon in ancient books. One record says that Bixi, the eldest son of the dragon, is good at carrying weight and is carved on tablet seats; the second son, Chiwen, looks like a beast and is the head of roof beasts; the third son, Pulao, is good at roaring and is cast on chimes; the fourth son, Bi'an, looks like a tiger and is engraved on jail doors; the fifth son, Taotie, is gluttonous and is put on the cover of cooking vessels; the sixth son, Baxia, is fond of water and is carved on bridge posts; the seventh son, Yazi, is fond of killing and is carved on knife rings; the eighth son, Jinni (also known as Suanni), likes smoke and fire and is carved on incense burners; the ninth son, Jiaotu, looks like a snail and a mussel. Being fond of closing, he is engraved on the knockers of gates.

45．“龙凤呈祥”中将凤与龙并提，凤是一种神鸟吗？

凤凰是中国传说中的神鸟。自古以来，人们就把凤凰看作百鸟之王和祥瑞的象征。据《礼记·礼运》说：“麟、凤、龟、龙，谓之四灵。”传说如果凤凰出现，则天下安宁。所以《论语》中记载孔子的话说：“凤鸟不至，河不出图，吾已矣夫！”意思也是指凤鸟不出现，说明当时政治不清明。凤凰的形状，据郭璞为《尔雅》作的注说：“鸡头，蛇颈，燕颌，龟背，鱼尾，五彩色，高六尺许。”还有些古籍介绍了凤凰的习性，如：只栖息于梧桐树、只吃竹实、饮灵泉、不啄活虫、不折生草、百鸟跟随等。实际生活中，凤凰这种鸟是不存在的。

那么，凤凰的来源如何？总的说来，它是来源于图腾崇拜中的鸟图腾。《诗经·玄鸟》中说：“天命玄鸟，降而生商。”《史记·殷本纪》中，也有关于殷商先祖契的母亲吃了玄鸟卵后有孕而生契的事。可见，商族是以鸟为图腾的。在鸟图腾的基础上，演变出神鸟凤凰。古人原来把凤凰分开来说，凤是雄性，凰是雌性。后来发展到龙凤相配，龙为雄性，凤凰变成一体，为雌性。皇帝既然是“真龙天子”，皇后也自然是凤鸟所化了。

45. Dragon and Phoenix Are Mentioned Together in the Chinese Saying “Dragon and Phoenix Show Good Luck”. Is Phoenix a Magic Bird?

Phoenix (*fenghuang*) is a legendary bird in Chinese myth. It has been regarded as the head of all birds and a symbol of auspice for thousands of years. In *Li Ji* (*The Book of Rites*), unicorn, phoenix, tortoise, and dragon are considered as four fairies. It is said that social stability usually follows the appearance of a phoenix. According to the notes that Guo Pu made for the book *Erya* (*Literary Expositor*), the phoenix has a chicken's head, snake's neck, swallow's jaw, tortoise's back and fish's tail. It is colorful and is about two meters tall. Some ancient books also describe the habit of the phoenix: living on phoenix trees, eating bamboo, drinking spring water, never eating any live insects, never breaking any live grass, and always being followed by other birds. Actually, there has never been such a bird.

Where did the phoenix originate? Generally speaking, it originated from a bird totem. In *Shi Jing* (*The Book of Songs*), we can find such words: The Shang Dynasty (c.1600—c.1100 B.C.) was founded when a black bird from Heaven came down to the earth. In *Shi Ji* (*Records of the Historian*), there is a story saying that Xie, the ancestor of the Shang people, was born when his mother ate an egg of a black bird. Thus, we can say that in the Shang Dynasty, birds were taken as totems. On this basis, the magic bird, phoenix, was created. The ancient people named the male phoenix *feng* and the female *huang*. Later on, people believed that phoenixes were supposed to be matched with dragons. As dragons were male, phoenixes (both *feng* and *huang*) were supposedly female. Now that emperors are the sons of the dragon, empresses are naturally the embodiment of the phoenix.

46. 民间传说中有“鲤鱼跳龙门”的说法，它的来历与含义是怎样的？

“鲤鱼跳龙门”是中国民间古老的传说。龙门是山西省河津县和陕西省韩城县之间黄河流经的一段峡谷。河水到这里水流湍急，奔腾而下。据传说每年春天，有无数从江河游来的鲤鱼，逆流游到这里，奋力往上跳，由于水流急，上游河床又高，每年只有少数（有的说72条）能跳过去，一旦跳过去，有雷火烧其尾，就变成龙。因此，跳龙门被借喻为人们荣升高位或声名显赫的变化。也有指士人被声望高的人接谈而增高其身价，叫“登龙门”。范晔《后汉书》中的《李膺传》说：“膺以身名自高，士有被其容接者，名为登龙门。”唐朝大诗人李白在《与韩荆州书》中说：“一登龙门，则声价十倍。”正是因为这些，“鲤鱼跳龙门”在民俗中被看成地位升高的象征。

实际上，跳龙门的鱼并不是鲤鱼。据尹荣方先生考证，那是古时称为鳣、鲔，现在称为鲟的一种鱼。它体长约两米，嘴和背与传说中的龙相类似。鲟鱼的习性是在春天溯流而上产卵繁殖。在这个季节，雌雄鱼互相追逐，常跳出水面。而腾出水面的鱼鳍充血发红。这种情景被古人观察到，又加以渲染神化，就成为鱼跳龙门、雷火烧尾而成龙的传说了。

据尹荣方先生研究，鲟鱼跳龙门之所以传成鲤鱼跳龙门，是因为古人把鳣与鲤混为一谈的结果。清朝段玉裁为《说文解字》所做的注中说：“古人多云鳣鲔，出巩穴，渡龙门为龙，今俗语云鲤鱼跳龙门，盖牵合为一，非一日矣。”这个推断，尹先生认为是有道理的。

46. What Are the Origin and Meaning of the Saying "*Liyu Tiao Longmen*" (Carps Jump over Longmen) in Chinese Folk Legend?

The saying *liyu tiao Longmen* is a folk legend of great antiquity. Longmen refers to the canyon between Hejin County of Shanxi Province and Hancheng County of Shaanxi Province, through which the Yellow River runs. Coming to this section, the water runs fierce and fast and falls rapidly down to the lower part. It is said that every spring, countless corps will swim against the current and try their best to jump up to the upper section. However, the water runs so rapidly and the gap between the upper river bed and the lower river bed is so big that only a few of them can succeed. The successful ones will be blazed by lightning on their tails and then turn into dragons. Therefore, people who are promoted or enjoy higher fame are likened to *tiao Longmen*. Those whose fame are enhanced by meeting well-known figures are called *deng* (climbing) *Longmen*. In the biography for Li Ying in *Hou Han Shu* (*History of the Later Han Dynasty*) by Fan Ye, there is such a passage: "Li Ying is a well-known figure. Those who are interviewed by him are called *deng Longmen*." In his Letter to Han Yu, an official, Li Bai, the greatest poet in the Tang Dynasty (618—907 A.D.) said: "Once jumping over Longmen, one's fame will be greatly enhanced". For these reasons, the term *liyu tiao Longmen* is regarded as a symbol of promotion.

Actually, it is not carps that jump over Longmen. According to the research done by an expert, it is the fish which is called sturgeons today and were called *chan* or *you* before. This sort of fish is about two meters long and its mouth and back look like that of a dragon in the legend. Every spring sturgeons swim to the upper section of the river to lay eggs and breed. During this period, female and male sturgeons chase one another, jumping out of the water now and then with their fins red. This scene, detected by ancient Chinese, has been played up and deified into the legend that carps having jumped over Longmen would be blazed by lightning on the tail and then turn into dragons.

According to the expert, in the past, people could not tell carps from sturgeons. Owing to this confusion, the fact that sturgeons jumping over Longmen is mistaken as carps jumping over Longmen. In his notes for *Shuo Wen Jie Zi* (*Explanation and Study of Principles of Composition of Characters*), Duan Yucai of the Qing Dynasty (1644—1911 A.D.) said that people in ancient times used to believe that *chan* and *you* having jumped over Longmen would turn into dragons. The present proverb *liyu tiao Longmen* is totally due to this confusion.

47. 中国民间传统的吉祥话中常用桃来象征长寿，这是为什么？

原产地是中国的桃，作为一种水果，汁多味甜，自古以来受到人们的喜爱。桃和长寿联系到一起源于神话传说。据说西王母瑶池所种桃树三千年一开花，三千年一结果，吃一颗这种仙桃可以增寿六百年。有的古籍中对仙桃有不同的描写，如宋朝《太平御览》中说："东北有树焉，高五十丈，其叶长八尺，广四五尺，名曰桃。其子径三尺二寸，小狭核，食之令人知寿。"从上述的神话与古籍描写来看，古人已把桃和长寿联系起来，并且由此产生了不少吉祥图像和民俗。如：寿星在画像中常常是一手持杖，一手托桃。旧时人们在为老人祝寿时，常蒸一些米粉或面粉制作的桃，名为"寿桃"。历代画家绘桃以象征长寿的也很多。清末吴昌硕在一幅桃画上题诗："琼玉山桃大如斗，仙人摘之以酿酒。一食可得千万寿，玉颜常如十八九。"表达了人们对健康长寿的美好愿望。

实际上，古人对桃树很是推崇。在《夸父追日》神话中，描述夸父在渴死前，把手杖抛出，化为一片桃林。在《诗经》中，有一篇是"桃之夭夭，灼灼其华。之子于归，宜其室家。"用鲜红娇艳的桃花，象征美满的婚姻生活。古人还相信桃木可以避邪驱祟，所以在桃木上书写或画一些符号挂在门上，以后发展成门神和春联。

47. Why Has Peach Been Taken as the Symbol of Longevity in China?

Peach is one of the fruits of Chinese origin and tastes juicy and sweet. It has enjoyed favour from the Chinese people since ancient times. The connection between peach and longevity can be traced back in a myth. It is said that the peach trees planted in Yaochi, the orchard of Xiwangmu (Heavenly Queen Mother), only blossom once within three thousand years, bear fruit once within another three thousand years. If you eat one peach, your life will be lengthened by six hundred years. A variety of descriptions of the peach can be found in some ancient Chinese books. For instance, the description in a book written in the Song Dynasty (960—1279 A.D.) goes: "In the northeastern part of Yaochi, there is a kind of tree named peach, standing 50 *zhang* (a traditional Chinese measure unit approximately equivalent to 3.33 meters) in height and having leaves as long as 8 *chi* (a traditional Chinese measure unit approximately equivalent to 33.33 centimetres) and as wide as 4 to 5 *chi*. The fruit is 3.2 *chi* in diameter and its core is small and narrow. Those who eat the fruit can live long lives." The above myth and description from ancient books show that ancient Chinese had linked peach with longevity and also had produced a lot of auspicious images and folklore. For instance, the god of longevity in Chinese paintings always has a walking stick in one hand and a peach in the other. In the past, it was the custom to make steamed buns in the shape of a peach, named "longevity peach", as birthday presents to the aged. Many painters in the past also symbolized longevity with peach in their paintings. In a peach picture painted in the late Qing Dynasty (1644—1911 A.D.), the following words can be seen: "The peaches in Mount Qiongyu, big as a *dou* (a measuring tool to mete out grain), are plucked by fairies to brew wine. Drinking the wine, one can not only enjoy longevity but also look as young as 18-year-old." These words express the strong desire of the Chinese people for good health and longevity.

Actually, the ancient Chinese praised highly of peach trees. In the myth *Kuafu Zhui Ri* (*Kuafu Chasing the Sun*), before his death, Kuafu threw the stick out of his hand, which then turned into a peach orchard. In *Shi Jing* (*The Book of Songs*), there is a poem " The prosperous peach trees are in full bloom. Since our son has returned home, it is a good time for him to get married." In this poem, fresh and beautiful peach blossoms are used to symbolize happy marriage. The ancient Chinese also believed that peach wood could ward off evils and drive away ghosts. For this reason, peach wood panels with painted or written signs to be hanged on doors gradually developed into the door-gods in China and Spring Festival couplets.

48. 过去春节前后民间有“送灶王”、“迎财神”的活动，关于这两位神有什么传说？

人们对灶王爷的祭祀，大约与人类用火烹烧食物有关。自从学会用火，人类文明就向前迈进了一大步。所以自古以来，人们对火、灶都很崇敬。先秦时期，祭灶属于“五祀”之一。这种对火的尊崇，逐步发展到附会于具体的神灵身上。灶神究竟是谁？历来说法不一。《礼记·月令》中把炎帝、祝融说成主灶之神；道教则用张奎《经说》中的说法，说灶神是居于昆仑山中的一位“老母”，不仅掌管人间灶火厨房，而且把人们行善为恶记录下来，禀报给天帝。大约后来受了整个社会男尊女卑的影响，灶神变成男神，原来女灶神变为“灶王奶奶”。另一种说法，见于唐朝段成式的《酉阳杂俎》，说：“灶神名隗，状如美女。又姓张名单，字子郭，夫人字卿忌，有六女皆名察洽。”《酉阳杂俎》上说，灶神常在农历月末上天告人间罪恶，并根据罪恶大小，减去罪人寿命。因为这样，人们祭灶早先是在农历四月及传说中灶王爷生日八月初三。

随着时间的推移，灶神上天禀报的时期也变为每年一次，而且是善恶都报告。人们祭灶的日期也逐步改为农历腊月二十三或二十四。北方祭灶时，供桌上主要摆设饴糖（北京俗称关东糖，因做成南瓜形，又叫糖瓜）；南方则用糯米团，其作用是要粘住灶王爷的嘴，让他少说本户的坏话。也有在供桌上预备一碗清水、一碟草料，供灶君的马享用的。祭拜以后，把灶王神像烧掉，送他上天，待农历除夕再换贴新像。旧时有腊月二十三“过小年”的说法，可见对祭灶的重视。

过去农历除夕，北方人吃过饺子、南方人吃过年饭以后，就该迎接“财神”了。也就是买一张木版印刷的财神像供奉起来。

也许是由于古今人们求财心切，对于财神究竟是谁，也就有多种说法。其中流传最广的当推赵公明了。据传说赵公明的姓名是赵朗，公明是他的字，终南山人氏。秦时避世山中，汉代张道陵入山修行，收他做徒弟，让他骑黑虎，守护丹室。待丹炼成后，张道陵分给他吃，遂能变化无穷，为张道陵守玄坛（即斋坛），被天帝封为“正一玄坛赵元帅”。他手下有招宝、纳珍、招财、利市四神。所以人们祈求招福进财，多供奉这位赵公元帅。神像中的赵公明顶盔披甲，手执钢鞭，身跨黑虎，形象威猛。

民间也有供奉“文财神”的。这种财神像是长髯官服，一副文官模样。据说这是殷纣王的叔父比干。比干被纣王杀害剖出心肝 。据传说比干是自己取出心抛给纣王，因为吃了姜子牙给的灵丹妙药，所以健康如常。因为没了心，所以办事公道，不偏不倚，深受人们爱戴，成为财神。另一种说法是越王句践手下的大臣范蠡，在帮助越王打败吴国后，隐身江湖，经商致富，自号“陶朱公”。他发财以后，并不贪财，而是周济乡亲，所以成为财神。

48. There Were Some Folk Festive Activities like *Song Zaowang* (Seeing Off the God of the Hearth) and *Ying Caishen* (Welcoming the God of Wealth) during the Spring Festival in the Past. Were There Any Stories about These Two Gods?

The custom of offering sacrifices to *zaowang* (the god of the hearth) might have something to do with the use of fire in cooking. When man began to know how to use fire, human civilization made a great progress. Therefore, people always show great respect to fire and the hearth. During the Pre-Qin period (before 221 B.C.), offering sacrifices to the hearth was one of the "five offerings". Afterwards, the esteem towards fire gradually evolved and some specific deity was created. As to the question who the god of the hearth was, there has never been an agreed saying. In *Li Ji* (*The Book of Rites*), Emperor Yan and Zhu Rong were described as the gods of the hearth; while Zhang Kui, a Taoist, believed that the god of the hearth was an "old lady" living in Mt. Kunlun, who not only took charge of fire and the hearth, but also kept records of the good and bad deeds of the people and then made reports to the ruler in Heaven. Probably due to the influence of the thought that men were superior to women, the god of the hearth replaced the goddess of the hearth, who was then called *zaowang nainai* (the hearth grandma). There is another saying in a book written in the Tang Dynasty (618—907 A.D.): "The god of the hearth, by the name of Gui, looks like a beautiful woman. His another name is Zhang Dan. He had six children." According to another book, at the end of every month in the Chinese lunar calendar, the god of the hearth would go to Heaven to report the bad deeds of the people, in the light of which one's life span would be determined. For this reason, people used to offer sacrifices to the god of the hearth in the fourth moon, and on the third day of the eighth moon, which was believed to be his birthday.

As time went on, the god of the hearth visited Heaven only once a year. Furthermore, his report began to include both the good and the bad deeds. The twenty-third or the twenty-fourth day of the twelfth moon became the date when people would offer sacrifices to the god of the hearth. Northerners would offer malt candies on the altar while southerners would offer glutinous rice balls. Since they are sticky, people believed that they could stick his lips together to prevent him from speaking evil. A bowl of water and a plate of hay were sometimes offered to his horse. The last procedure was to set his portrait on fire, which meant to send him off to Heaven. A new picture would be put on the wall on the eve of the Spring Festival. In the past, lunar December 23 was called "the Minor New Year", which was an indication of the great importance people attached to the god of the hearth.

On the eve of the Spring Festival, northerners would eat *jiaozi* (crescent-shaped Chinese dumplings) while southerners would eat *nianfan* (New Year dinner). After that, it was time to welcome *caishen* (the god of wealth), namely, to put a new picture of the god of wealth on the wall.

Who is the god of wealth? It also has many different stories. The most widely accepted one is Zhao Gongming. It was said that Zhao Gongming was from Mount Zhongnan. During the Qin Dynasty (221—206 B.C.), he went to live in a mountain as a hermit. Then, during the Han Dynasty (206 B.C.—220 A.D.), he became a disciple of Zhang Daoling (founder of Taoism) who came into the mountain to practise Taoism. He was asked to ride on a black tiger to guard the pellet room for Zhang. When the pills of immortality were ready, Zhang gave him some. Zhao took the pills, which enabled him to change into various shapes, and he was then asked to guard the altar for Zhang. The god of Heaven then granted him the title of Marshal Zhao. Under him, there were four other deities: the treasure attracter, the jewelry taker, the fortune usher, and the market guard. So, people would worship Marshal Zhao for fortune and treasure. In pictures, Zhao Gongming wears a helmet, has a steel whip in his hand, and rides on the back of a black tiger, looking powerful and fierce.

Wen caishen (the civil god of wealth) was worshipped as well. In pictures, this god usually has a long beard and wears the uniform for civil officials. It was said that this god was Bi Gan, uncle of King Zhou of the Shang Dynasty (c.1600—C.1100

B.C.). Bi Gan was killed by the king for his heart as medicine. It was said that Bi Gan took his heart out by himself and threw it to the king. It was a miraculous medicine given by Jiang Ziya (a great person then) that kept Bi Gan as healthy as before. With no heart, Bi Gan was fair towards everyone, and was beloved and esteemed as the god of wealth. Another story says that the civil god of wealth was Fan Li, an official of King Gou Jian of the State of Yue. When the king had defeated the State of Wu with Fan's help, Fan withdrew from the officialdom to do business. Yet he was not interested in money. When he became rich, he handed out his money to the poor in his neighbourhood, and thus, he was also regarded as the god of wealth.

49. 什么是阴阳？它对中国文化有何影响？太极图体现了什么理论？

在中国古代，阴阳观念被认为是宇宙基本规律。阴阳这个概念最早出现在《书经》中的《洪范》篇。

阴和阳的原意是指山的背阴面和向阳面。但是自古以来这两个字不仅表示亮与暗两个方面，而且表示男性与女性、刚与柔、上与下。阳象征着力量和创造力，是与天联系在一起的；阴则表示弱、女性，与地联系在一起。天是在上方，总是运动着的；地在下方，是静止不动的。因此，阳象征着动；阴象征着静。在思维领域里，阴是复杂的、女性的、直觉的思维；而阳则是清晰的、男性的、理性的思维。阴是贤圣平静的沉思；阳是君王强有力的创造活动。阴阳思想渗透在中国文化的各个方面并决定了中国人传统生活方式的特点。中国是一个农业国，中国人非常熟悉太阳和月亮的运动规律以及季节的变化。他们从季节的更替和生物的生死现象看到了阴阳的相互影响，看到了寒冷的冬天与炎热的夏天之间的相互作用的关系。同时，这种季节性的变化也影响了人们日常吃的食物。在中国人看来，食物也可分为阴阳两大类。要使身体强健，人们选择食品就应本着能使身体内部保持阴阳平衡的原则。

传统中医的理论基础也是在于使人体保持阴阳两方面的平衡。人体的疾病被认为是体内的阴、阳平衡遭到破坏所造成的。中医大夫治病的原则也就是调和阴阳。如果人体内阳气虚弱就要补阳，病人要服用能够补充阳气的药物；如果阴虚，就要补阴。按照中医的观点，人体本身就分为阴阳两部分。前面为阴，背面为阳；体表为阴，体内为阳；在体内的器官也分为阴阳两部分。所有这些部分要保持平衡都是通过“气”在经络中不断运行来实现的。当阴阳之间的通道被阻塞时，人就会生病。治疗疾病的大夫就是要使“气”通畅。我们常见的针灸治病，其原理就是通过针刺或艾灸相应的穴位来刺激和恢复“气”的运行。我们可以说，中医学是阴阳理论最系统最实际的体现。

阴和阳都是处在不断变化之中，最能表达阴阳运动性质的就是中国古代的太极图。这个图中，黑色表示阴，白色表示阳，阴和阳是对称的，但这种对称并不是静止的。这种对称暗示着有力的无休止的运动。当阳循环运动到开始之点时，阴正好达到它的顶峰，又让位于阳。阴阳循环的过程也是阴阳消长的过程。图中的两个小圆点象征着这样的思想：当其中一方达到自己的极端时，它已经孕育着对方的种子。“物极必反”就有这个意思，世界上任何事物的发展都表现为来和去、张和缩的循环形式。中国人相信，一种局面发展到极端就会走向它的反面。与此有关的太极理论是北宋周敦颐在研究《周易》的基础上提出来的新学说。这种学说认为:太极是最原始的、绝对的实体。由于它的一动一静,产生出宇宙万物。周敦颐说:“立天之道曰阴曰阳,立地之道曰柔曰刚,立人之道曰仁曰义。”从而奠定了宋明理学的理论基础。太极图就是根据“太极图说”的理论在北宋年间出现的。

49. What Are *Yin* and *Yang*? What Are Their Influences on Chinese Culture? What Is *Taijitu*?

In ancient China, *yin* and *yang* were considered to be the basic law of the universe. This was started for the first time in *Shu Jing* (*The Book of History*).

The original *yin* and *yang* referred to the shady and sunny sides of a mountain. From very early times, *yin* and *yang* represented not only darkness and brightness, but also female and male, and gentleness and stableness. *Yang*, the strong, male, and creative power, was associated with the heaven, whereas *yin*, the dark, feeble, female and maternal element, was related with the earth. The heaven is high above and full of movements while the earth, in the old geocentric view, is down below and motionless. *Yang* is the clear and rational male intellect; *yin* is the complicated feminine intuitive intellect. *Yin* is the quiet, contemplative stillness of the sages; *yang* refers to the strong, creative action of kings. *Yin* and *yang* permeate into Chinese culture and feature the way of life. As being in an agriculture country, the Chinese have been very familiar with the law of the movements of the sun and the moon and the changes of the seasons. Seasonal changes and the resulting phenomena of life and death of the living things were thus seen by them as the clearest expressions of the interplay between *yin* and *yang*. They also have seen the relations of the interplay between the cold and dark winter and the bright and hot summer. The seasonal interplay of the two forces is also reflected in the food we eat, which contains elements of *yin* and *yang*. A health diet should also observe the principle of balancing *yin* and *yang*.

Traditional Chinese medicine, too, is based on the balance of *yin* and *yang* in the human body, and an illness is considered as a disruption of this balance. Therefore, the doctor is to help the patient to balance his/her *yin* and *yang*. The human body is divided into *yin* and *yang*. So it is with the internal organs. The balance between all the organs is maintained by a continuous flow of *qi* (vital energy), along a system of channels. Whenever the flow between *yin* and *yang* is blocked, the body falls ill. There are many ways to cure people of their illness. Acupuncture is one of the common ways. The principle is that by sticking needles into the acupuncture points, the flow of *qi* can be stimulated and restored. We can say that Chinese medicine is the most practical embodiment of *yin* and *yang*.

Yin and *yang* have always been in a state of incessant changes. *Taijitu* (the Grand Terminus) is the best presentation of the movements of *yin* and *yang* with the black for *yin* and the white for *yang*. The two dots in *Taijitu* symbolize the idea that when one of the two forces reaches its extreme, the seed of its opposite has already been born.

This philosophy was further developed by Zhou Dunyi, a philosopher of the Northern Song Dynasty (960—1127 A.D.). He advanced the theory of *taiji* (the absolute, or the terminus), holding that *taiji* was the most primeval and most absolute entity, and its movement and stillness created everything in the universe. Zhou was quoted as saying that the way of the heaven lay in *yin* and *yang*; the way of the earth consisted of flexibility and strength; and the way of men depended on humanity and justice. His teachings prepared the theoretical foundation for neo-Confucianism that prospered during the Song and Ming dynasties.

50. 二十四节气是怎么回事？

中国人的祖先从生产的实际需要出发，在战国（公元前475～前221年）末期独创了二十四节气。成书于这个时代的《黄帝内经》中，已有二十四节气的说法。书中说："五日谓之候，三候谓之气。"一年有七十二候，也就是有二十四节气。但现在用的二十四个节气的名称，在西汉（公元前206～24年）《淮南子》一书中才全部出现。

二十四节气，是古人根据一年中太阳在黄道上位置的变化情况来确定的。他们把变化的时间分成二十四个阶段，每阶段约半个月，分列在十二个月里。因为二十四节气的日期在阴历的每一年里大体上都是固定的，所以，每一个月里一定有两个节气，节气的日期，每年稍有变化，前后不过一两天的出入。二十四节气基本上反映了黄河中、下游流域气候变化的规律，长期以来为农民所乐用。

下面按其顺序对每个节气作简要的说明。

1. 立春：立是见的意思，春是蠢动，是植物开始有生气之意。这一天表示春天开始。
2. 雨水：开始下雨的意思。
3. 惊蛰：蛰伏地下的昆虫和小动物开始活动。
4. 春分：这一天太阳直射赤道，南北半球昼夜平分。
5. 清明：气候开始转暖，万物欣欣向荣。汉族大部分地区有清明节扫墓的习惯。
6. 谷雨：开始种植蔬菜和谷。
7. 立夏：表示春天结束，夏天开始。
8. 小满：表示小麦等夏收作物籽粒逐渐饱满。
9. 芒种：表示大麦、小麦成熟。黄河中、下游大部地区开始播种秋季作物。
10. 夏至：在北半球，这一天是一年中白天时间最长、黑夜时间最短的一天。
11. 小暑：表示气候开始炎热。
12. 大暑：表示一年中最热的时候。
13. 立秋：表示秋天开始。
14. 处暑：表示炎热的夏天已经过去。
15. 白露：表示天气开始变得干燥。
16. 秋分：在北半球，白天和黑夜等长。
17. 寒露：天气明显转凉，北方有的树开始落叶。
18. 霜降：天气继续变冷，早晚有时有霜出现。
19. 立冬：秋天结束，冬天开始。

20. 小雪:华北地区开始降雪。

21. 大雪:有些地区开始下大雪。

22. 冬至:一年中白天最短、黑夜最长的一天。过去,这一天皇帝在天坛祭天。

23. 小寒:天气寒冷,但没有冷到极点。

24. 大寒:一年中最冷的时候。大寒过后,天气不那么寒冷,春天又要开始了。

50. What Are the 24 Solar Terms?

Based on the practical needs of agriculture, Chinese people initiated the 24 solar terms towards the end of the Warring States Period(475 B.C. ~ 221 B.C.). The term "solar terms" can be found in *Huangdi Neijing* (*Yellow Emperor's Canon of Internal Medicine*). In this book, every five days was called a *hou*, and every three *hou* made a *qi*. Therefore, a year was divided into 72 *hou*, or 24 *qi*. But the names for these solar terms did not appear until the Western Han Dynasty (206 B.C.—24 A.D.) in *Huainanzi*.

The 24 solar terms were determined by the changes of the sun's position in the zodiac all through the year. A complete circle of the changes was divided into 24 segments, and each segment is about half a month. In the lunar calendar, the date of each solar term is basically fixed, with minor changes within one or two days. As a reflection of the regularity of the changes of the climate in the areas of the middle and lower reaches of the Yellow River, the 24 solar terms are still being used by the farmers.

The following is a brief chronological introduction of all the solar terms.

1. *Lichun*: the Beginning of Spring, about on February 4th.
2. *Yushui*: the Beginning of Raining, about on February 19th.
3. *Jingzhe*: Waking of Hibernating Insects and Small Animals, about on March 6th.
4. *Chunfen*: the Spring Equinox, when the day and night are of equal length, about on March 20th.
5. *Qingming*: Pure Brightness, about on April 5th. The weather gets warmer. For the Han people this is the time to sweep the family graveyards.
6. *Guyu*: about on April 20th. This is the time when millet and other vegetables

are sown or grown.

7. *Lixia*: the Beginning of Summer, about on May 6th.
8. *Xiaoman*: Wheat becomes plump-eared, about on May 21st.
9. *Mangzhong*: about on June 6th, indicating the ripeness of barley and wheat. It is time to start growing autumn crops.
10. *Xiazhi*: the Summer Solstice. This day has the longest day time of the year. It falls on about June 21st.
11. *Xiaoshu*: about on July 7th. This indicates the beginning of hot weather.
12. *Dashu*: about on July 23rd. This is the hottest day of the year.
13. *Liqiu*: the Beginning of Autumn, about on August 8th.
14. *Chushu*: about on August 23rd. This marks the end of summer, indicating the heat is over.
15. *Bailu*: about on September 8th. This is the time when the weather starts to get drier.
16. *Qiufen*: the Autumn Equinox, about on September 23rd. The day and night are of equal length.
17. *Hanlu*: about on October 8th. The weather gets distinctively colder, and leaves begin to fall.
18. *Shuangjiang*: continuation of coldness and appearance of frost in the early mornings and late evenings, about on October 23rd.
19. *Lidong*: the Beginning of Winter, about on November 7th.
20. *Xiaoxue*: about on November 22nd. It starts snowing.
21. *Daxue*: about on December 7th. In some areas, heavy snow starts.
22. *Dongzhi*: the Winter Solstice, about on December 22nd. This day has the shortest daytime of the year. It is on this day that the Chinese emperors went to the Temple of Heaven to worship and offer sacrifices to Heaven in the old time.
23. *Xiaohan*: about on January 6th, indicating cold days, yet not the coldest days.
24. *Dahan*: about on January 21st. This is the coldest time of the year. After this, it will get warmer gradually and spring is to come.

51. 十二生肖是何时形成的？

十二生肖即十二属相，是中国古代特有的一种民俗现象。它是一种以动物名称纪年的特殊方式。所谓十二属相就是用十二地支和十二种动物相对应搭配而成，每一种动物代表一年。在许多场合，当一个人被问及他的年龄时，他往往只告诉他的属相。比如：属牛或属龙等。可见十二属相在民间的影响是很深的。

首先，我们看一下十二地支和十二种动物的结合问题。一般认为这种结合始于东汉（公元25～220年），在公元1世纪已经比较流行。因为在汉代才正式使用天干地支纪年法，把十二地支和十二种动物结合在一起也表示年，似乎是合乎逻辑的。这一点在许慎的《说文解字》中可以得到证实。《说文解字》在解释“巳”字时说：“巳为蛇象形”，另外，在公元1世纪成书的《吴越春秋》中有这样的记载：“吴在辰，其位龙也，故小城南门上反羽为两鲵鳑以象龙角；越在巳地，其位蛇也，故南大门上有木蛇，北向，首内，示越属于吴也。”这段话中，辰和龙相对应，巳和蛇相对应。由此我们更有理由认为：这种十二地支配十二种动物的结合方式，在公元1世纪时已经普遍使用。

十二地支和十二种动物的配合是按顺序排列的，他们的顺序就是子鼠、丑牛、寅虎、卯兔、辰龙、巳蛇、午马、未羊、申猴、酉鸡、戌狗、亥猪。上面说到这种对应关系在东汉时期已经形成，但动物十二支用来与人的生年联系在一起，是否始于东汉，史无明证。认为始于东汉的学者，也不过是推测而已。据史书记载，明确表明生年和属相关系，至晚在南北朝（公元420～581年）时期已经有例证。《南齐书五行志》中有“东昏侯属猪”，“崔慧景属马”等记载。到了唐代（公元618～907年），十二生肖更为流行。在铜镜的纹饰上以及其他工艺品中都有十二生肖的图案。

51. When Did *Shi'er Shengxiao* (the Twelve Animals of Chinese Zodiac) Come into Being?

Shi'er shengxiao or *shi'er shuxiang* is a kind of Chinese folk custom. It is a way to designate the years in the names of the animals. The twelve animals actually represent the twelve earthly branches, one animal symbolizing one year. On many occasions, when someone is asked about his age, he will reply by naming the animal of the year in which he was born, e.g. the year of the ox, or the year of the dragon, etc.

Thus it is evident that the twelve animals are deeply rooted among the people.

It is generally agreed that the association of the twelve earthly branches and the twelve animals started in the Eastern Han Dynasty(25—220 A.D.) and gained popularity in the first century A.D. Since the lunar calendar was formally adopted in the Han Dynasty, according to which the years were designated by the heavenly stems and the earthly branches, it is therefore logical to combine the twelve earthly branches with the twelve animals to designate the years. This can be verified in the book *Shuo Wen Jie Zi*. Its explanation of the character *si*, one of the twelve branches, goes like this: "It is a pictographic character indicating the shape of a snake." We can also find records in another book, *The Annals of Wu and Yue*, written in the first century. There was a passage about the relevance between *chen* (another earthly branch) and the dragon and between *si* and the snake, which further proved that the combination of the branches and the animals was already widely adopted in the first century.

This combination follows a certain order, which goes like this: *zi-shu* (rat), *chou niu* (ox), *yin-hu* (tiger), *mao-tu* (rabbit), *chen-long* (dragon), *si-she* (snake), *wu-ma* (horse), *wei-yang* (ram), *shen-hou* (monkey), *you-ji* (rooster), *xu-gou* (dog), and *hai-zhu* (boar). It is still uncertain whether the association of it with people's years of birth started in the Eastern Han Dynasty. According to historical records, the clear reference to animals as indications of the years of birth appeared as late as in the Southern and Northern Dynasties(420—581 A.D.). It became more prevalent in the Tang Dynasty (618—907 A.D.) and the patterns of the twelve animals were very popular on handicraft articles then.

52. 为什么喜庆的日子要舞狮、舞龙?

舞狮、舞龙为中国民间喜庆节日的传统习俗。每逢节日,欢乐的人们舞狮、舞龙,含有祝福吉祥如意、兴旺发达的意思。

远古时代,狮子曾广泛分布于亚、欧、非洲大陆。由于冰河浩劫等原因,欧亚大陆的狮子逐渐减少。中国的狮子在数十万年以前已经灭绝。汉朝(公元前206~公元220年)通西域后,汉武帝(刘彻,公元前140~前87年)派张骞出使西域月氏(今阿富汗一带)、安息(今伊朗)等国,这些国家曾向汉朝皇帝赠送过狮子等异兽。这些狮子引起了人们极大的兴趣。

据考证,中国舞狮活动始于魏晋南北朝(公元220~581年)时期。据《宋书》卷七十六《宗悫传》记,南北朝时的宋文帝元嘉二十二年(公元445年),宋军伐林邑,"林邑王范阳迈倾国来拒,以具装被象,前后无际,士卒不能当。"宗悫想到狮子能威服百兽,便令士兵连夜用麻布"制其形,与象相御,象果惊奔,众因溃散,遂克林邑"。从此,舞狮在军中开始流行,很快又传到民间。从那时起,人们便把雄健、威武的狮子视为吉祥、勇敢的象征,又模拟狮子的形象和动作逐渐形成狮舞,在庆典喜日以此为乐,并驱魔避邪。故有"避邪狮子"之称。

到唐代(公元618~907年),舞狮已发展成为一种优秀的民间艺术,不但在民间、军中流传,而且正式列入宫廷燕乐乐部。在"立部伎"中舞狮被正式取名为《五方狮子图》。其舞蹈为:由舞者披上缀毛的"狮皮",扮成五个不同颜色的"狮子"。立在东、西、南、北、中五个方位上,装演狮子的各种情态。此外,还有逗引狮子的狮子郎,同时还有由140人组成的庞大的伴唱队,高唱《太平乐》歌以助舞。著名诗人白居易有诗《西凉伎》描写舞狮子:"西凉伎,假面故人假狮子,刻木为头丝作尾,金镀眼睛银贴齿,奋迅毛衣摆双耳,如今流沙来万里。"

明清时期,舞狮更为广泛流行,形成了许多流派。有北方舞狮和南方舞狮之分。北方舞狮又有河北双狮、安徽青狮和湖南狮子之分。北方舞狮的外形与真狮相似,全身狮披覆盖,两人配合而成,其中一人武士打扮,手拿绣球作为引导。舞动时,配以锣鼓伴奏,因而显得更加生动活泼。南方舞狮流行于广东。广东舞狮由两人配合,一人舞狮尾,一人舞狮头。另有一人或两人戴大头佛面具在前边引狮、戏狮。

在喜庆的日子里,很多地方还有舞龙的习惯。龙在中国古代传说中是一种代表力量和吉祥的神奇动物。人们把龙看成是美好愿望的象征。人们之所以舞龙,是因为古人相信龙是管雨的,用舞龙这种形式,正是为了取悦龙王,保证农业风调雨顺、五谷丰登。《后汉书·礼仪志》注中就记载了当时人们在祈雨时,舞动代表金、木、水、火、土的黄、青、白、红、黑各色长龙的活动。到唐宋(公元618~1279年)时期,舞龙已成了很流行的习俗。在长期的发展中,舞龙也形成了许多不同的形式。主要有龙灯、布龙等。现在,由于科技的发达,舞龙的活动变得越来越丰富多彩,并且成为一种纯粹的娱乐活动了。

52. Why Do People Perform Lion and Dragon Dances on Days of Jubilation?

Lion and dragon dances during festivals are part of the traditional custom in China. People celebrate on these happy occasions and express their best wishes for good luck and prosperity.

In ancient times, lions used to be found all over Asia, Europe, and Africa. Due to the glacial and other natural disasters, lions in Eurasia gradually decreased in numbers. Over several hundred thousand years ago, lions were actually extinct in China. In the Han Dynasty (206 B.C.—220 A.D.), Emperor Wu dispatched Zhang Qian as his special envoy to Yuezhi, Parttia and other states of the Western Regions. These states presented lions and other rare animals to the emperor. These lions aroused people's great interest.

According to textual research, lion dances in China started from the Wei, Jin and Northern and Southern dynasties(220 A.D.—581 A.D.). It was recorded in the "Biography of Zong Que", Chapter 76 of *Song Shu* (*The History of the Song Dynasty*), that in 455 A.D., the troops of Song attacked Linyi. "The ruler of Linyi led all his people to fight back. They drove large numbers of elephants clad in armor, and the Song troops could not withstand the attack." Thinking of the fact that lions overpower all other animals, Zong Que ordered his soldiers to make life-size models of lions to ward off the elephants. And the elephants were frightened and fled pellmell, so the soldiers fled and Linyi was occupied. Ever since then, lion dances became popular among the troops, and then among the people. From that time, people came to regard the mighty and powerful lions as the symbol of good luck and bravery. They imitated the lion's image and movements, and lion dances took shape gradually. Lion dances were performed on festivals and on days of celebrations. They were also performed for the purpose of warding off evil spirits. So lions got the name of "evil-shunning lions".

As late as in the Tang Dynasty(618—907 A.D.), lion dances had been developed into a kind of excellent folk art not only popular among the people and troops, but also officially listed in the imperial court entertainment programs. In the famous *Libuji* (standing perfomance), it was formally named as *Wufang Shizi Tu* (five-direction lion dance). The performers will wrap themselves in furry skins of lions and acted as five lions of different colors, standing at the five directions of east, west, south, north and the center, and imitating the various actions and movements of lions. There were also boys to tease the lions. In the meantime, there was a big vocal accompaniment composed of 140 people, singing a tune of peace to liven the dance up. There were lines of vivid descriptions in Bai Juyi's famous poem *Xiliang Ji*.

In the Ming and Qing dynasties (1368—1911 A.D.), lion dances became even more popular and developed into many styles, mainly the northern style and the southern style. The northern style was subdivided into Hebei double-lion dances, Anhui blue-lion dances and Hunan lion dances. The lion of the northern style looked very much like the real animal, with a lion wrapping covering all over, and his partner clad as a warrior, holding a silk ball to lead out the lion. The dance was particularly vivid and lively with the accompaniment of gongs and drums. The southern style was popular in Guangdong. The lion was performed by two people, one moving the tail, and the other the head. And there was another performer or two wearing big Buddhist masks to lead out the lions, teasing and playing with them.

On festivals and other happy occasions, many places also have the custom of performing dragon dances. The dragon is a mythical animal, and a symbol of power and auspiciousness in ancient Chinese legends. People regard the dragon as the symbol of best wishes, and the dragon dance came from the belief that dragons were in charge of the rain. So people tried to please the dragon by performing dragon dances, so that he would give them favorable weather and good harvests. In "The Annals of Etiquette" in *Hou Han Shu* (*History of the Later Han Dynasty*), there was a note which described how people prayed for rain with their dragon dances. And in the Tang and Song dynasties (618—1279 A.D.), dragon dances became very popular and took on various forms in the process of its development, such as dragon lanterns and cloth dragons, etc. Nowadays, due to the development of science and technology, dragon dances have become an interesting and colorful recreational activity for the people.

53. 对联是怎样演变来的？

对联又叫对子、楹联、楹帖，是意思上相关、形式上对偶的两句话。第一句叫上联，贴或悬挂在右边；第二句叫下联，贴或悬挂在左边。两联的字数相等，两句中相同位置上的词要字数相等、词性一致、平仄协调。在成熟于唐代的律诗中，第三句和第四句、第五句和第六句要求对偶，如“野火烧不尽，春风吹又生”。这种对偶句促进了对联的产生。

相传，中国人民早在春秋（公元前 770 ~ 前 476 年）时期就有挂桃符的习俗。挂桃符就是用桃木制成板条，上面画符号或神荼和郁垒二神像，钉在门上用来驱邪避鬼。到了唐代末年就开始有人用对偶的吉祥语代替桃符上的神像。现在人们知道的最早的一副对联是五代十国（公元 907 ~ 960 年）时后蜀皇帝孟昶亲自写在桃符上的“新年纳余庆，佳节号长春”。这副对联距今已有 1000 多年。后来人们又用大红纸代替桃木板书写对联。

过春节时人们贴在大门上的对联又称春联。春联一词始于明代（公元 1368 ~ 1644 年）。明太祖朱元璋曾于一年除夕传旨要求家家贴春联。从此，过年贴春联之风俗更盛了。

除春联表示喜庆之外，对联还用于许多其他地方。中国有许多名胜古迹。一些庙宇、殿堂的柱子上一般都有楹联。这些楹联为湖光山色、亭台楼阁增加了不少情趣。有的楹联字数较少，有的则很多。清代诗人孙髯翁写的昆明大观楼长联有 180 个字，被称为“古今第一长联”。其实比这副长的对联还有。清末洋务派首领张之洞的一副题屈原湘妃祠长联竟有 400 字之多。

过去，行业联的使用也非常普遍，各行各业都有自己的行业联。常常从一副对联即可判断出一个店铺经营什么。如书店有“欲知千古事，须读五车书”的对联；旅店的行业联有“欢迎春夏秋冬客，款待东西南北人”。

人们有时也常用对联这种形式来激励自己或勉励别人。如“书山有路勤为径，学海无涯苦作舟”就是一副激励人们勤奋学习的并为许多人所喜爱的对联。

除此之外，对联也常用于贺喜、祝寿、哀悼死者及一些其他场合。

53. How Did *Duilian* (Couplets) Develop in the History?

Duilian, also known as *duizi*, *yinglian*, *yingtie*, etc., is made up of two sentences which are interrelated in meaning and antithetic in form. The first line is called *shanglian* and is put up or hung on the right side, and the second line is called *xialian* and is placed on the left side. Not only are the two lines required to have an equal number of characters, the words that stand in the same position in each of the two sentences must be identical in number of characters and parts of speech and harmonious in tone. In *lüshi*, a standard form of poetry of eight lines matured in the Tang Dynasty (618—907 A.D.), the four lines in the middle have to be rendered in two pairs of antithetical sentences. "*Ye huo shao bu jin, chun feng chui you sheng.*" (Not even a prairie fire can destroy the grass. It grows again when the spring breeze blows.) are two such lines from a Tang poem. Such antithetical sentences certainly had a bearing on the origination of *duilian*.

Legend has it that as early as in the Spring and Autumn Period (770—476 B.C.) there was the custom among the Chinese people of hanging *taofu* (peach charms) on the door. *Taofu* were boards made of peach wood, painted with charm inscriptions or with the pictures of the two gods, Shenshu and Yulü, and were hung on both sides of the door as an antidote against evil spirits. By the end of the Tang Dynasty some people started to write two auspicious antithetical lines on peach-wood boards to replace the pictures of the two gods. According to historical records the first *duilian* was written on peach-wood boards by Emperor Mengchang of the State of Later Shu of the Five Dynasties Period (907—960 A.D.). The *duilian* reads: "*Xin nian na yu qing, jia jie hao chang chun.*" (Everything will go on fine in the new year and the festival brings in eternal spring.) More than one thousand years have passed since then. Later people wrote *duilian* on red paper instead of peach-wood boards.

The auspicious *duilian* people put on the door during the Spring Festival is called *chunlian* (spring couplets). The word *chunlian* was first used in the Ming Dynasty (1368—1644 A.D.), Zhu Yuanzhang, Emperor Taizu of the Ming Dynasy, once issued an imperial decree on the eve of the Spring Festival ordering every family to put up *chunlian*. From then on the custom became more widespread.

Chunlian is usually used to fan up a festival atmosphere. *Duilian* serves other purposes as well. At scenic and historical places *yinglian* can be seen on the pillars of temples and palaces, which add much to the beauty of the scenery and the ancient architecture. Although most *yinglian* do not have many characters, there are indeed lengthy ones. There is one at Daguanlou (Grand View Tower) in Kunming which has as many as 180 characters, whose author was a Qing Dynasty (1644—1911 A.D.) poet named Sun Ranweng. This *duilian* has been commended as "the No.1 lengthy *duilian* in history". In fact there are even longer *duilian*, one of which was written by Zhang Zhidong, a leader of the Westernization Movement of the Qing Dynasty. Boasting of more than 400 characters, this *duilian* was written for a temple in honour of Qu Yuan (a great poet) and Xiang Fei.

In the past business *duilian* was also very common. Every trade had its own particular business *duilian*, from which one could tell what business it was engaged in. For examples, one *duilian* for a bookstore went like this: "If one wants to be acquainted with events of one thousand years, he must read five cart-loads of books"; a *duilian* for a hotel read, "Welcome visitors at all times and entertain guests from all directions."

People sometimes write *duilian* either for themselves or for other people, which may seve as an impellor or encouragement. "Diligent study is the path to knowledge and hard training is the carrier to great learning" is a *duilian* loved by many people as it encourages people to study hard.

Duilian often finds its use for many other purposes, such as offering congratulations, extending good wishes to people on their birthdays, expressing one's condolences to the family of the deceased, etc.

54. 什么是年画？年画的发展历史是怎样的？

年画是中国特有的一种绘画体裁，因为是在过年时张贴的，因此叫年画。

年画起源于先秦时期(公元前 221 年以前)。《战国策》里已有关于年画的简单记载。到了两汉(公元前 206 ~ 220 年)时期，人们爱在门的两旁张贴各种各样神的偶像，以期避凶纳福。这些偶像被称为“门神”。每逢过年，人们便张贴。这样，门神成了春节张贴的年画。雕版印刷在唐代(公元 618 ~ 907 年)发明以后，促进了年画的进一步发展。唐代以前，年画的内容多是神仙鬼怪，其含义大抵是避邪祟、取吉利。唐代以后，年画中有了直接反映现实的作品，这时的门神变成了秦琼、尉迟敬德两位将军。宋代(公元 960 ~ 1279 年)开始有了比较多的雕版年画。到了明代(公元 1368 ~ 1644 年)，以宗教为题材的木刻年画也逐渐发展起来。明清两代是木版年画的发展高峰。随着木版年画的发展，年画进入了普通百姓的家庭。在清代(公元 1644 ~ 1911 年)，全国大多数省都有生产年画的作坊。年画的集中产地有：苏州桃花坞、天津杨柳青、山东潍坊、广东佛山、四川绵竹、河北武强、河南朱仙镇、浙江绍兴等。

从年画的发展来看，年画可分为南北两大流派。北方年画的代表流派是著名的天津杨柳青年画和山东潍坊年画。杨柳青年画创于明代末年，清代最为兴盛。其题材多为戏曲人物、胖娃娃和家庭过年场景。形象构图丰满，笔法精细整洁。潍坊年画的题材多是神话传说、吉祥图案等，风格朴实，线条粗犷，色彩鲜艳。南方年画最著名的是苏州桃花坞年画和广东佛山年画。两地的年画生产都始于明代，在清代雍正、乾隆年间(公元 1723 ~ 1796 年)达到了鼎盛时期。在风格上既有传统木版画的影响，又有一些欧洲铜版画的特点。在石印和胶印技术传入中国后，木版年画大都受到冲击而濒于衰落。1949 年以后，传统的木版年画才得以新生，出现了许多内容、形式俱佳的新年画。在内容上主要是表现现实生活的题材。随着印刷技术的不断更新，一些新材料的年画也越来越多，年画这一古老的艺术形式更充满了活力，受到人们的喜爱。

54. What Is *Nianhua* (*Spring Festival Picture*)? How Did It Develop?

Nianhua is a special type of painting in China. It is used during the Spring

Festival.

It originated in the Pre-Qin Period (before 221 B.C.), a brief record of which can be found in *Zhanguo Ce* (*Strategies of the Warring States Period*). As late as in the Western and Eastern Han Dynasties (206B.C.—220 A.D.), people liked to paste the images of various gods on both sides of the door, expecting them to ward off the evils and usher in good luck. These images are called "the door-gods". Since people pasted them up during the Spring Festival, these pictures gained a special significance for the Spring Festival occasion. The art of printing from engraved plates, which was invented in the Tang Dynasty (618—907 A.D.), brought about further development of *nianhua*. Beforethe Tang Dynasty, *nianhna* in most cases were images of deities and spirits. After the Tang Dynasty, some works came to reflect the reality, and the images of the door-gods turned into two generals: Qin Qiong and Yuchi Jingde. There were more *nianhua* produced in this fashion in the Song Dynasty (960—1279 A.D.), and xylographic *nianhua* of religious themes developed gradually in the Ming Dynasty (1368—1644 A.D.). In the Ming and Qing dynasties, xylographic *nianhua* reached a new height of development and *nianhua* came into the homes of the ordinary people. In the Qing Dynasty, most of the provinces had their own workshops for making *nianhua*. The main producers included Taohuawu of Suzhou, Yangliuqing of Tianjin, Weifang of Shandong, Foshan of Guangdong, Mianzhu of Sichuan, Wuqiang of Hebei, Zhuxianzhen of Henan, Shaoxing of Zhejiang, and so on.

Judging from their development, there are two schools of *nianhua*: the southern school and the northern school. The representatives of the northern school are those from Yangliu-qing of Tianjin and Weifang of Shandong. *Nianhua* produced in Yangliuqing originated in the late Ming Dynasty and reached its peak in the Qing Dynasty. The subjects were mainly images from traditional operas, fat and healthy babies and fairy New-Year celebrations. A rich composition and refined drawing style showed its artistic characteristics. *Nianhua* produced in Weifang mainly dealt with fairy tales, legends and auspicious designs. A style of simplicity, with bold and vigorous lines and bright colors, showed its characteristics. The most famous *nianhua* of the southern school were those from Taohuawu of Suzhou and Foshan of Guangdong. Both originated in the Ming Dynasty and reached their peak in the reigns of Emperor Yongzheng and

Emperor Qianlong of the Qing Dynasty (1723—1796 A.D.). While influenced by traditional styles, it also reflected certain features of European copper-plate printing. After the introduction of lithographic and offset printing into China, xylographic *nianhua* was under great pressure and almost on the brink of decline. However, after the founding of the P.R. China in 1949, traditional xylographic *nianhua* was reborn. Many new *nianhua* that were excellent in both content and form were produced and the theme focused mainly on the real life of the people. Along with the improvement of printing technology, there are more and more new materials for *nianhua*. This traditional artistic form of *nianhua* is full of vigor now and widely loved by the people.

55. 风筝是谁发明的？它的发展演变情况如何？

风筝现在是一种民间玩具，也是一种工艺品。它是用细竹扎成骨架，再糊上薄纸、系上长线而成。玩时利用风力使其升至空中。

但是，最早的风筝不是今天人们看到的样子，发明风筝的目的也不在于娱乐。相传，鲁班是风筝的发明者。他是春秋时期（公元前770～前476年）的人，他看到鹞鹰在空中盘旋飞翔便受到启发，削竹为鹞，称为“竹鹞”，据说“上天三日不下”。这就是最早的风筝。后来发明了纸，就用纸代替竹子，形成了轻便的风筝，史称“纸鸢”。据史书记载，南北朝（公元420～589年）时，梁武帝被侯景围困于台城（今南京鸡鸣山南），就是通过风筝把求援信送出城外的。宋代（公元960～1279年），人们为了突袭敌人，便在风筝上装上火药，导火线上缚上一段燃着的香火，将风筝放到敌营上空，燃烧爆炸，造成混乱，然后趁机出击，打败敌军。可见，风筝一开始是用于军事目的的。

大约在唐代（公元618～907年）以后，风筝才逐渐变为娱乐的玩具。但当时玩风筝的还只限于一些皇宫贵族和有钱人家的子弟。他们不满足风筝鸦雀无声地在空中飞行，就在风筝上系上一个竹哨。在空中，风入竹哨，发出像古筝鸣响那样的声音，十分动听，人们从此形象地称之为“风筝”。

纸料的风筝直至北宋（公元960～1127年）以后才逐渐增多，从此它才从有钱人玩的玩具，变成一种大众化的普遍流行的玩具。

中国是风筝的故乡，有很多制造风筝的能工巧匠。1903年美国纽约博览会上，中国著名的风筝艺人哈长英制作的风筝受到人们普遍的欢迎。1914年在巴拿马世界博览会上，天津魏元泰制作的风筝获得了金质奖章。近几年来，中国的风筝制造技术又有了进一步的提高，制作的风筝远销日本、东南亚和欧美各国。中国山东潍坊已经举办过几次国际风筝大会，中国的风筝也已名扬四海。

55. Who Invented *Fengzheng* (Kite)? How Did It Evolve?

Fengzheng is a kind of folk toy as well as a handicraft. It is made from slender slips of bamboo as the frame with thin paper plastered and a long thread to fly with. It flies into the sky with the wind.

However, *fengzheng* in its earliest stage did not look like what we see today, and it was not invented for amusement. It was said that Lu Ban was the inventor, who lived in the Spring and Autumn Period (770—476 B.C.). Enlightened from the sparrow hawk spiraling in the sky, Lu Ban made one with bamboo and called it "bamboo sparrow", which was said to have remained "flying in the air for three days". This was actually the earliest *fengzheng*. When paper was invented, it replaced bamboo to make a lighter *fengzheng*, which was named "paper bird" at that time. According to historical records, emperor Liangwu of the Northern and Southern Dynasties (420—589 A.D.) used a *fengzheng* to send his message for help when he was besieged in a city. In the Song Dynasty(960—1279 A.D.), people loaded fire powder on *fengzheng* to assault the enemies by tying a piece of kindling incense on the fuse and flying it into the sky above the enemy camp, where it exploded and caused chaos. Then they took the advantage to launch an attack and defeated the enemy. It is thus evident that *fengzheng* was originally made for military use.

It was from the Tang Dynasty (618—907 A.D.) on that *fengzheng* gradually became a toy for entertainment. But at that time, this entertainment was limited to the children of nobility and the rich. Getting bored with the silent *fengzheng*, they tied a bamboo whistle on it. When they flew *fengzheng* in the air, the wind blew the whistle and made a sound much like that produced by *zheng* (an ancient musical instrument), which was very pleasant to the ear. People then vividly named it *fengzheng* (wind musical instrument).

Only after the Northern Song Dynasty (960—1127 A.D.) was paper *fengzheng* increasingly made, and from then on it turned from the entertainment for the rich into a popular one among the ordinary people.

China as the birthplace of *fengzheng* has many skillful craftsmen. On the 1903 New York International Fair, kites made by Ha Changying, a famous Chinese kite craftsman, received an enthusiastic welcome. At the 1914 Panama International Fair, Wei Yuantai from Tianjin won the gold medal for his kites. In recent years, the technology for making kites has further improved. *Fengzheng* made in China have been exported to Japan, Southeast Asia, the United States and Europe. Weifang, a city in Shandong Province, has hosted several international kite festivals, and Chinese kites have become world-famous.

56. 中国一些大建筑物门前都摆放一对石狮子，它有什么含义？

狮子不是中国产的动物。据史书记载：汉朝（公元前 206～220 年）时安息国（今伊朗）等国家曾赠送狮子给中国。从此，中国开始有了狮子。

中国民间对狮子的喜爱和尊崇，除了由于狮子生相威猛、威镇百兽以外，也与佛教有关。佛教传说释迦牟尼降生时，一手指天，一手指地，作狮子吼。也就是说，声音极大，震动天地。佛教经籍中，把佛喻为“人中狮子 ”。象征智慧的文殊师利菩萨的坐骑也是狮子。可见佛教把狮子作为威猛和出类拔萃的象征。

随着佛教影响的扩大，中国人民越来越把狮子作为镇恶避邪的“灵兽”。自东汉（公元 25～220 年）起，中国就有石雕狮子出现。如四川雅安高颐墓和江苏句容梁朝墓前，都有石狮子。这些石狮距今已有 1400 多年。陕西省咸阳顺陵（武则天的母亲杨氏陵墓）前的石狮，造型威武生动，是现存石狮中的杰作。除了石狮子外，五代后周广顺三年（公元 953 年）在河北沧州铸有一个大铁狮子，身高 5.48 米，重约 40 吨，是中国现存最大的铁狮子。在故宫，还有鎏金铜狮。

据传，自明朝开始，在宫殿和王公府第门前摆放石狮，以显示威势并镇压邪恶。后来，一些民间住宅门前，也有摆放石狮子的。一般来说，一对狮子中，有一只前爪下按球，是雄狮；前爪下有一只小狮子的是雌狮。

狮子与绣球有什么关系呢？过去民间相传，雌、雄两只狮子嬉戏时，它们的毛缠在一起，成为一个球，小狮子就从这个球中生出来。所以流传下“狮子滚绣球”的吉祥图。民间舞狮子时，也常有一个人执球在前边行走。

56. There Are Always a Pair of Stone Lions before Some Big Architectures in China. What Does This Imply?

China is not the hometown of lions. According to historical books, in the Han Dynasty (206 B.C.—220 A.D.), Parthia (present Iran) and some other countries gave some lions to China as presents. Thereafter, lions began to live in China.

Lions look awe-inspiring and fierce and are known among all animals for their prowess. However, this is not the only reason that lions have won favour and respect from the Chinese people. Buddhism has also contributed to the status of lions in China. It is said that when he was born, Sakyamuni, with one hand pointing to the sky and the other to the earth, roared like a lion. That is to say that his voice was so loud that it shook the sky and the earth. In Buddhism manuscripts, Buddha is described as "a lion among human beings". What Manjusri (Bodhisattva of wisdom) rides on is also a lion. We can see that lions are regarded as a symbol of power and mightiness in Buddhism.

Along with the spreading of the influence of Buddhism in China, the Chinese people gradually took lions as intelligent beasts to keep away the evil. Stone lion sculptures first appeared in China during the East Han Dynasty (25—220 A.D.). For instance, stone lion sculptures were found in front of the tomb of Gao Yi in Ya'an, Sichuan Province and the tomb of Gou Rong in Jiangsu Province. These stone lion sculptures have existed for over 1400 years. The stone lion sculpture in front of the tomb of the mother of Wu Zetian in Xianyang, Shaanxi Province is so bravely and vividly shaped that it is regarded as a masterpiece among all the preserved stone lion sculptures in China. In addition to stone lions, a large iron lion of 5.48 m. in height and 40 tons in weight was cast in Cangzhou, Hebei Province in 953 A.D., which is the largest of all the extant iron lions in China. In the Palace Museum, there are also some gilded bronze lions.

It is said that from the Ming Dynasty (1368—1644 A.D.) on, stone lions were put before the palaces and residences of the nobility to show power and significance and to keep away the evil. Later on, stone lions were also put before the gates of the ordinary households. Normally, out of a pair of stone lions, the one having a ball under one of its front paws is the male lion while the other with a baby lion under one of its front paws the lioness.

As to the relationship between the lions and the ball made of strips of silk, legendary stories say that when a pair of lions play together, their hair would tangle into the form of a ball. And, the baby lion would be born from this ball. Therefore, the picture of a lion rolling a ball made of strips of silk has been handed down as an auspicious symbol. In lion dances, there is often a person with a ball.

57. 民间吉祥画中有《松鹤延年》和《岁寒三友》，这些是什么意思？来源如何？

“松鹤延年”是祈求或祝愿人长寿的意思。几千年来，中国人民因松树常青耐寒和寿命长的特点，而特别喜爱它。两千多年前，孔子就说过：“岁寒，然后知松柏之后凋也。”（《论语·子罕》）《史记》也说：“松柏为百木之长也。”因为松树常年葱郁，寿命长久，所以人们常以松树为坚韧和长寿的象征。史籍记载，秦始皇在泰山遇到雷雨，在一棵大松树下避雨，后来就封这棵松树为“五大夫”（是秦时爵位的第九级），后来人们也称松树为大夫。《太平御览》中引《礼斗威仪》说：“其政平，则松为常生。”则将松树与政治清明联系到一起了。还有一些古籍称松树所产的松脂能使人寿至百岁。有的书还记载了这样一个故事：晋代荥阳郡有一石室，室后有千丈孤松。曾有夫妇二人在石室隐居，活了几百岁。死后化为双鹤，绕松飞翔。也许因为这一传说，画家们常以松、鹤为主题，寓意长寿吉祥。松树在冬天也呈现一片苍绿，所以与经冬不凋的竹和严冬开花的梅被古人称为“岁寒三友”。宋朝林景熙在《霁山集》中，即称这三种植物为“岁寒友”。

岁寒三友中的竹，在过去的国画中也成为重要的题材。旧时文人称竹为“君子”，竹除了在外观上亭亭玉立、婆娑有致、清秀素洁、值霜雪而不凋、历四时而常茂外，主要取它本固（竹质坚固）象征君子德性坚固不拔，性直（竹杆直而不曲）象征君子立身中正不偏，心空（竹干中空）象征君子虚心学习，节贞（竹有节）象征君子有气节。自晋朝的王徽之、唐朝的白居易、宋朝的苏轼以至清朝的郑板桥（郑燮）等著名文人，都喜爱竹。在中国民间吉祥图画中，还有“竹报平安”一种。据唐朝段成式《酉阳杂俎》中所载，是李德裕（唐武宗时曾为宰相）说：北都只有童子寺有一丛竹，只有几尺高。传说寺内的纲维（就是知客僧）每天报告竹子平安。由此留下“竹报平安”的说法。

梅树因为寒冬开花，也是“岁寒三友”之一。自古以来，梅花以其香气清雅、开在百花凋谢的早春而为文人墨客所喜爱。宋朝诗人林逋隐居在杭州西湖孤山，种梅养鹤，终身不娶，人称他“梅妻鹤子”。由于梅花五瓣，人们又称梅花有“五福”，就是快乐、幸福、长寿、顺利与和平。所以民间吉祥图案中有“梅开五福，竹报平安”。

57. There Are *Song He Yan Nian* and *Sui Han San You* Among Chinese Auspicious Pictures. What Do They Mean? What Are Their Backgrounds?

The picture *Song He Yan Nian* is to wish longevity. For thousands of years, the Chinese people have been fond of pine because it is evergreen, cold-resistant and long-lived. Even two thousand years ago, Confucius said that pine withers later than others in cold winter. In *Shi Ji* (*Records of the Historian*), one finds such words: "Pine lives longer than any other trees." Since it is evergreen and lives a long life, pine is always regarded as a symbol of toughness and longevity. It was recorded in *Shi Ji* that when the first emperor of the Qin Dynasty was caught in a thunder storm on Mount Tai, he sheltered himself under a pine tree. Afterwards, he granted this pine tree the title *wudafu* (one of the titles in the Qin Dynasty). Thus, pine trees are also called *dafu*. In *Taiping Yulan* (*Imperial Digest of the Taiping Period*), there were the following words: Pine trees will be ever green when there is clean and wise politics. Other books say that pine resin can make people enjoy longevity. We can also find the following story in some books: In the Jin Dynasty, behind a stone house grew a lonely pine of one thousand *zhang* (about 33.3m.) high. There was once a couple who had lived there and enjoyed longevity of several hundred years. After their death, they turned into a pair of cranes and flew around the pine tree. Probably this is why painters take such a fancy to painting pine trees and cranes in their pictures to wish longevity. Pine trees are green in winter, bamboo never withers in winter and plum flower blossoms even in winter. For this reason, these three plants are called *sui han san you* (three friends in winter) by ancient people.

Bamboo used to serve as an important subject in Chinese painting. Bamboo is tall and erect, delicate and simple and evergreen in all the four seasons. However, bamboo is called a "gentleman" for still more reasons beside these characteristics. Being firm, straight, and hollow inside, bamboo may well be used to refer to a gentleman's characters: firm, moral, upright, modest, etc. And it has found favour in many well-known scholars such as Wang Huizhi in the Jin Dynasty (265—420 A.D.), Bai Juyi in the

Tang Dynasty (618—907 A.D.), Su Shi in the Song Dynasty (960—1279 A.D.) and Zheng Banqiao in the Qing Dynasty (1644—1911 A.D.). *Zhu bao ping'an* (bamboo reporting peace and safety) is another kind of auspicious pictures. It is said that in the north capital, only in Tongzi Temple could people find a clump of bamboo of several feet high. The monks in the temple reported on the safety of these precious plants every day and therefore the saying of *zhu bao ping'an* came into being.

Since it blossoms in winter, plum is one of the so-called *sui han san you* . Throughout the history in China, plum has always taken the fancy of Chinese scholars because of its clear fragrance and blossom in early spring when other flowers are still withered. A poet of the Song Dynasty who lived in seclusion in the West Lake of Hangzhou of Zhejiang Province for his whole life was called a person with *mei qi he zi* (with plum as his wife and cranes as his children), because he planted plum and raised cranes and remained single for his whole life. Since it has five petals, plum is also called *wufu* (five happinesses)—pleasantness, happiness, longevity, smoothness and peace.

58. 过去吉祥话中有"三阳开泰",它的来源如何?

"三阳开泰"或"三阳交泰"是旧时人们在旧历年的吉祥用语,也出现在年画和贺年片上。常见的图是:三只姿态不同的羊沐浴在晴和的阳光下,并衬以松柏、小草和山坡,给人以和平幸福、生机盎然的感觉。三阳开泰这种说法来源于《易经》。《易经》把由阳爻(—)和阴爻(- -)组成的图形重合,共有 64 种图形,用以卜筮,称做 64 卦。这种卦既可象征吉凶,又与四时月令相对应。据《易经》说,每年旧历十月与由六个阴爻组成的坤卦相对应,为纯阴之象,也就是说气候寒冷,万木凋零;旧历十一月的卦叫复卦,上面是坤,下面是两个阴爻覆盖着一个阳爻的震,这象征着虽然气候严寒,但是已有阳气从下产生,俗话说:"冬至一阳生",指的就是这个;旧历十二月为临卦,下面是两个阳爻;旧历正月是泰卦,卦象是上面为坤,下面为乾,三个阳爻在下面,所以称做"三阳","泰"指的是泰卦。农历正月冬去春来,阴消阳长,大地春回,万象更新。从卦象上看,有吉亨之义。所以"三阳开泰"为新春祝颂的吉祥话。因为羊与阳谐音,所以画三只羊来表示"三阳开泰"。还有一种说法是:明清时期民间曾用青阳、红阳和白阳代表过去、现在和未来。三阳开泰表示诸事顺遂,无往不利。

58. What Is the Origin of "*San Yang Kai Tai*", One of the Auspicious Expressions in Chinese?

San yang kai tai (or *san yang jiao tai*) used to be an auspicious expression used during the Spring Festival in the Chinese lunar calendar. The idea also appears on pictures and congratulation cards for the Spring Festival: three sheep in different posters bathe in the warm sunshine with a setting of pine, grass and hill slopes, out of which comes a peaceful, happy, lively and prosperous feeling. The term *san yang kai tai* originated from *Yi Jing* (*The Book of Changes*). In this book, the blends of *yin* (- -) and *yang* (—) or vice verse make up 64 designs which are known as 64 hexagrams. These divinatory symbols not only symbolize good or bad luck, but also correspond with the climatic changes of the four seasons. According to *Yi Jing*, the tenth moon in the Chinese lunar calendar corresponds to the feminine trigrams composed of six *yin*. This is pure *yin*, representing cold weather and withered plants. The trigrams in the eleventh moon is called duplicate trigrams: its upper part is *kun* (receptive, resting in firmness) and its lower part *zhen* (thunder)—a *yang* covered by two *yin*. This means that although it is still rather cold, there is an air of *yang*. Just as the proverb goes: at the Winter Solstice, an air of *yang* has already come out. In the twelfth moon, the trigrams is called *lin* (approach symbol of advance), in which there are two *yang* in the lower part. In the first moon, the trigrams is called *tai* (peace) consisting of *kun* at the upper part and *qian* (creative) at the lower part. Since there are three *yang* at the lower part, it is called *san yang*. The first moon is the turn of winter and spring. At this time, *yin* is declining while *yang* is on the rise, and everything on the earth starts to revive. In the point of view of the trigrams, it implies suspiciousness and good luck. For this sake, *san yang kai tai* has turned into an auspicious expression for greeting during the Spring Festival period. Since sheep and the sun share the same pronunciation "*yang*" in Chinese, three sheep were usually painted in the pictures to symbolize the term *san yang kai tai*. Another story goes that in the Ming and Qing dynasties (1368—1911 A.D.), a blue sun, a red sun and a white sun were once used to represent the past, the present and the future respectively. *San yang kai tai* indicates that everything goes on smoothly and successfully.

59."中国"这个名称是怎么产生的？为什么又称作"中华"？

"中国"这个词最早出现在周朝文献。在此以前，甲骨文已经出现了"中"字，字形像是一杆旗。当时商王在旗下召集开会，人们围着旗子听商王命令。因此引申为中央的意思。在《诗经》和《礼记》中都出现了"中国"这个词，当时有两个意思，一是指京师，也就是首都；另一个是指当时华夏族(即汉族)所居住的区域和所建立的国家。当时华夏族活动范围主要在黄河中游一带，建都也多在今陕西、河南，以及在"四夷"(指羌、戎、狄、蛮等民族)之中，或"九州"(指冀、兖、青、幽、并、扬、荆、豫、雍州)之中，所以称为中国。秦、汉以后，中国这个词已超越了民族与中原地域的界限，成为政权的代称。19世纪中叶以后，"中国"一词专指中国全部领土。可见，那些认为中国自以为是全世界的"中央王国"的说法，是不准确的。

中华的"华"字，是汉民族的祖先自称"华夏"，华有光彩的意思，夏有大的意思。孔颖达为《尚书》作的疏称："中国有礼仪之大故称夏，有服装之美谓之华。"实际上，早期华夏族已经是汉族与羌、夷、狄、戎、苗等民族融合而成。秦、汉时期，这一称谓为秦人、汉人所代替，唐朝时称唐人。近代出现的"中华民族"这一概念，即作为中国各民族的总称。

59. How Did the Term *Zhongguo* (China) Come into Use? Why Is China Also Called *Zhonghua*?

The term *Zhongguo* appeared for the first time in some historic records of the Zhou Dynasty (c.1100—221 B.C.). In *jiaguwen* (oracle bone inscriptions), which was found in the ruins of the Shang Dynasty (c.1600—1100 B.C.), the form of the character *zhong* looks like a flag. At that time, the emperors would call on meetings under a flag and the participants would stand around the flag listening to orders. For this reason, the character *zhong* also referred to the centre. In *Shi Jing* (*The Book of Songs*) and *Li Ji* (*The Book of Rites*), the term *Zhongguo* means, first, capital of the state; and second, the territory where the Han nationality lived and their state. At that time, the Han nationality mainly lived in the area of the middle reaches of the Yellow River, with their capitals in Shaanxi and Henan. Since the Han people were surrounded by the minority nationalities, and their territory also covered the central part with the other nine regions around, the state of the Han nationality was also called *Zhongguo* (the Central State). After the Qin and Han dynasties (221 B.C.—220 A.D.), the meaning of the term *Zhongguo* expanded. It was not just used to refer to the Han nationality and the central part of China, but was also used to refer to the regime. Since the mid 19th century, the term *Zhongguo* has become a special term referring to the whole territory of China. Thus, we can see that it is not correct to think that China has always regarded itself as the "central kingdom" of the world.

The character *hua* in *Zhonghua* originated from the term *Huaxia*, which the Han nationality calls themselves. *Hua* means splendor, and *xia* means greatness. In his notes to *Li Ji*, Kong Yingda wrote that China is called *Xia* for its perfect etiquette; and *Hua* for its splendid clothes. Actually, in the far early period, the Huaxia nationality had already been a nationality fused by the Han nationality and other minority nationalities such as Qiang, Yi, Di, Miao, etc. During the Qin and Han dynasties, the term *Huaxia* was once replaced by *Qinren* (people of the Qin Dynasty) and *Hanren* (people of the Han Dynasty). During the Tang Dynasty (618—907 A.D.), it was once again replaced by *Tangren* (people of the Tang Dynasty). In modern times, the term *Zhonghua Minzu* serves as a general name for all the nationalities in China.

60. 中国古代皇帝都有哪些称号?

中国古代皇帝的称号主要有三种,即谥号、庙号和年号。

谥号是在皇帝死后,根据他的生平事迹和品德,按照谥法规定所给予他的称号。一般认为谥法产生在西周(约公元前1100~前771年),在周共王、周懿王之后。谥号在秦代(公元前221~206年)曾被废除,到汉代(公元前206~220年)又恢复了。西汉第一个皇帝刘邦(公元前206~前195年)史称汉高帝,“高”就是他的谥号。帝王的谥号通常由礼官议上,由新继位的皇帝裁定。谥号含有褒贬善恶的意思,分为褒、贬、怜三类,即表扬的、批评的和表示同情的三种。属表扬的谥号常用“文”、“武”、“明”、“昭”等字,如汉朝的汉文帝刘恒(公元前179~前157年)、汉武帝刘彻(公元前140~前87年)和汉明帝刘庄(公元58~75年)。属批评的谥号常用“厉”、“灵”、“炀”等字,如周代的周厉王姬胡(? ~公元前828年)、汉代的汉灵帝刘宏(公元168~189年)和隋朝的隋炀帝杨广(公元605~617年)。表示同情的谥号常用“哀”、“怀”、“愍”、“悼”等字,常给那些短命的,或国家遭到不幸的值得同情的皇帝。如汉代的汉哀帝刘欣(公元前6~前1年)、晋代的晋怀帝司马炽(公元307~312年)和晋愍帝司马邺(公元313~316年)。唐代以前的谥号仅为一个字或两个字。自唐代始谥号的字数开始增多。唐代第一个皇帝李渊(公元618~626年)的谥号有9个字,而清代的清太祖努尔哈赤(公元1616~1626年)的谥号竟长达26个字之多。在古代谥号也赐予高官大臣。南宋爱国名将岳飞死后被赐予武穆的谥号,因此后人也称岳飞为岳武穆。另外,从东汉(公元25~220年)开始还有私谥,通常是有名望的学者死后,他的亲友或弟子为之取谥。

自唐代起谥号的字数逐渐增多,用谥号称古代帝王很不方便,因此对唐代以后的皇帝多称其庙号。如唐太宗、宋太祖都是称的庙号。在古代有作为的皇帝死后,在祖宗的太庙里为之设一庙室供奉。每个庙室有一个名称,这一名称即是该皇帝的庙号。庙号早在殷周时就有了,但从殷周到汉代,不是每个皇帝都有庙号,只是那些生前有功德的皇帝才有庙号。到南北朝时有庙号的皇帝就多了,尽管有的皇帝并没有什么功德可言。自唐代起差不多每个皇帝都有庙号了。开国皇帝的庙号一般都称太祖、高祖或世祖,以后的皇帝或称太宗,或称世宗、仁宗等。因此许多不同朝代的皇帝却有相同的庙号。

年号实际上并不是皇帝的称号,而是一种记年的方法。中国以年号记年始自汉武帝刘彻。汉武帝在位的第19年(即公元前122年)首创年号记年,并把该年称为“元狩”元年。但汉武帝又为前18年追补了3个年号,即建元、元光和元朔。这样汉武帝即位的第一年(公元前140年)就是建元元年,也是中国用年号记年的开始。一个新皇帝即位即建立新的年号，而一个皇帝也可以有几个年号。汉武帝就是每隔6年改元一次，在位期间共建了11个年号。唐高宗李治则有14个年号。但明、清两代的皇帝大都只有1个年号。因此也常用年号来称这些帝王。如明代永乐皇帝的“永乐”就是明代第三位皇帝朱棣的年号。还有清代的“康熙”、“乾隆”以及末代皇帝的“宣统”都是这些皇帝的年号。

60. What Titles Have Been Used for Ancient Chinese Emperors?

The titles for ancient Chinese emperors are mainly *shihao* (posthumous title), *miaohao* (ancestral temple title) and *nianhao* (reign title).

Shihao is a title conferred on an emperor after his death and was chosen in accordance with a special code following an evaluation of his lifetime achievements and errors as well as his moral character. It is believed that such practice went back as far as the Western Zhou Dynasty (c. 1100—771 B.C.), after King Gong and King Yi. The conferment of *shihao* was once abrogated in the Qin Dynasty (221—206 B.C.), but was later resumed in the Han Dynasty (206 B.C.—220 A.D.). The first emperor of the Western Han Dynasty, Liu Bang (206—195 B.C.), was known in history as Emperor Gao of the Han Dynasty. *Gao* was his *shihao*. *Shihao* as a rule was chosen by officials from the board of rites and submitted to the newly-enthroned emperor for approval. *Shihao* could have commendatory or derogatory connotations, or show sympathy for the deceased emperors. The words *wen* (literary), *wu* (military), *ming* (wise), *zhao* (brilliant), etc. were often used as *shihao* of commendation. Liu Heng (179—157 B.C.)—Emperor Wen of the Han Dynasty, Liu Che (140—87 B.C.)—Emperor Wu of the Han Dynasty, and Liu Zhuang (58—75 A.D.)—Emperor Ming of the Han Dynasty were such examples. *Li* (tyrannical), *ling* (wizard), *yang* (cruel), etc. were usually chosen as critical *shihao*, which were given to Ji Hu (? —828 B.C.)—King Li of the Zhou Dynasty, Liu Hong(168—189 A.D.)—Emperor Ling of the Han Dynasty, and Yang Guang(605—617 A.D.)—Emperor Yang of the Sui Dynasty. On emperors who either died young or whose states suffered from great misfortunes during their reigns, sympathetic *shihao* were conferred, which often included such words as *ai* (grievous), *huai* (memorable), *min* (pitiful), *dao* (mourning), etc. Emperors with such *shihao* included Liu Xin (6—1 B.C.)—Emperor Ai of the Han Dynasty, Sima Chi (307—312 A.D.)—Emperor Huai of the Jin Dynasty, and Sima Ye(313—316 A.D.)—Emperor Min of the Jin Dynasty. Before the Tang Dynasty (618—907 A.D.), *shihao* consisted of only one or two characters. However, more characters were used in *shihao* later. Li Yuan(618—626 A.D.), the first emperor of the Tang Dynasty, was conferred a *shihao* of 9 characters and the *shihao* for Nurhachi(1616—1626 A.D.), Emperor Taizu of the Qing Dynasty, had as many as 26 characters. In ancient China, *shihao* was also granted to high-ranking officials. Yue Fei, a famous patriotic general of the Southern Song Dynasty (1127—1279 A.D.) was granted the *shihao* "Wumu", hence he was also known as Yue Wumu in later times. Another practice started in the Eastern Han Dynasty (25—220 A.D.), i.e. when an eminent scholar died, a *shihao* was often conferred on him by his relatives, friends or disciples.

As more characters were used in *shihao* after the Tang Dynasty, it became quite inconvenient to use such a title to refer to the kings and emperors of the ancient times, and therefore *miaohao* came into use when emperors after the Tang Dynasty were mentioned. Emperor Taizong of the Tang Dynasty and Emperor Taizu of the Song Dynasty were cases in point. In ancient times, when an emperor died, a shrine was set up in his honour in the ancestral temple and the name of the shrine would be the emperor's *miaohao*. *Miaohao* can be traced back to as early as the Shang and Zhou dynasties. However, *miaohao* was not given to every emperor at that time—it was only given to emperors who had great merits and virtues. In the Northern and Southern Dynasties (420—589 A.D.) more emperors had *miaohao*, even though some of them had hardly any achievements or moral character to be mentioned. Since the Tang Dynasty nearly every emperor had a *miaohao*. *Taizu*, *gaozu* and *shizu* were *miaohao* for dynastic founders and the succeeding emperors usually took *taizong*, *shizong*, *renzong* and so on. That was why some emperors of different dynasties shared the same *miaohao*.

Nianhao was in fact not a title for an emperor but was used to designate the years in a dynasty. The naming of the years with *nianhao* started from Liu Che, Emperor Wu of the Han Dynasty. In 122 B.C., the 19th year of the reign of Emperor Wu of the Han Dynasty, "*Yuanshou*" was chosen to mark the reign of his majesty and the year

122 B.C. was then the "first year of Yuanshou." Another three *nianhao*, Jianyuan, Yuanguang and Yuanshuo, were used subsequently to name the previous 18 years of his reign, so that the year 140 B.C., the year when he was enthroned, was the first year of Jianyuan. And it was also the year when this method of designating the years was adopted. When an emperor came to the throne, a new *nianhao* would be named. And it was commom for an emperor to have more than one *nianhao*. Emperor Wu of the Han Dynasty, who changed his *nianhao* every six years during his rule, had 11 *nianhao*. Li Zhi, Emperor Gaozong of the Tang Dynasty, had as many as 14 *nianhao*. But most of the emperors in the Ming and Qing dynasties had only one *nianhao*, and that was why *nianhao* was used as titles when those emperors were referred to. For instance, Yongle was the *nianhao* for Zhu Di, the third emperor of the Ming Dynasty, who in most cases was known as Emperor Yongle. Other examples were Emperor Kangxi and Emperor Qianlong of the Qing Dynasty as well as the last emperor, Aisin Gioro Pu Yi, whose *nianhao* was Xuantong.

61. 皇帝有其他的称呼吗?

在传统戏曲中,皇帝被称作“万岁爷”,人们见了皇帝要三呼“万岁”。那么,“万岁”只是皇帝专用的吗?皇帝还有其他的叫法吗?

“万岁”这个词本意是祝人长寿的意思。古代生活条件艰苦,不少儿童夭折,青壮年因病和饥饿死亡的现象也很普遍。因此,长寿是人们最大的愿望。每当喜庆日子,大家欢聚时,人们常以“万岁”一词互相祝愿长寿。这样,“万岁”一词逐渐成为欢呼用语。中国最早的诗集《诗经》在记载人们庆祝丰收时就使用了“称彼兕觥,万寿无疆”的诗句。另据《战国策》记载,冯谖在薛地(今山东滕县南)召集欠孟尝君债的人,当场烧毁债券时,“民称万岁”。秦汉(公元前 221 ~ 公元 220 年)时人们取名字,也有不少人以千秋、万岁、万寿为名。秦汉以后,臣下朝见国君便开始呼“万岁”。自宋代(公元 960 ~ 1279 年)开始,万岁一词逐渐被皇帝垄断。人们只能对皇帝祝贺万岁,禁止对其他人祝万岁。明代(公元 1368 ~ 1644 年)规定只有皇帝才能称万岁。皇后、皇子或其他的王只能称作千岁。清代沿袭明代的制度。到公元 1911 年辛亥革命后,由于封建王朝被推翻,才结束了皇帝垄断“万岁”一词的历史。

在古代,对皇帝的称呼除了“万岁”以外,还有以下几种称呼:

天子:春秋时期,由于吴国、楚国等国的国君相继称“王”,各国便称周王为周天子,以区别于其他诸侯王。从此,天子便成了皇帝的一种代称。所谓“天子”,即为“上天之子”。周王室为了巩固自己的统治,制造了“君权神授”的理论,宣扬周王是上天之子,以使各诸侯听从他的命令。

足下:据史书记载,春秋时期,晋公子重耳逃亡在外 19 年,后来到了晋国,当了国君,就是晋文公。晋文公在封赏功臣时,曾经和晋文公同甘苦、共患难的介子推,却携带老母跑到绵山隐居去了。晋文公派人到绵山找他,他躲在山里不肯出来。晋文公就用烧山的办法迫使他出山,但最后介子推宁被烧死也不下山,就抱树被烧死了。晋文公非常悲痛,让人砍下这棵树,做成木屐,穿在脚下,平时总是看着脚下的木屐说:“悲乎,足下!”表达了晋文公对介子推的怀念。由于“足下”一词最初代表了一个为晋文公所敬重的人,因此,后来这个词就变成了对人的一种尊称。皇帝的权力是至高无上的,以后又用来称呼皇帝,成为皇帝的一种代称。

除此之外,陛下、阁下、殿下也曾用来称呼皇帝。

61. Are There Any Other Forms of Address for Emperors?

In traditional Chinese opera, the emperor is called "*wansuiye*" and people have to exclaim "*wansui*" (ten thousand years old) three times when they meet the emperor. Is *wansui* a special address only for the emperor? Are there any other forms of address for the emperor?

The original meaning of *wansui* is to wish people longevity. As the living conditions were poor in ancient times, many children died very young, and it was also very common for young people and adults to die of hunger and disease. Therefore, to live a long life was the greatest wish of all people. On days of jubilation, people get together happily and wished longevity to each other. Thus, *wansui* came to be a word for "cheers!". The earliest poetry anthology in China, *Shi Jing* (*The Book of Songs*), contains a line describing the celebration of a good harvest. Another account from *Zhanguo Ce* (*Strategies of the Warring States Period*) recorded that when Feng Yuan called for the debtors of Meng Changjun and burnt the debentures at the spot, "people exclaimed '*wansui*'". In the Qin and Han dynasties (221 B.C.—220 A.D.) many people liked to take names which were similar to *wansui*, for example, *qianqiu* and *wanshou*. Thereafter, the ministers began to exclaim "*wansui*" when they had an audience with the emperor. Ever since the Song Dynasty (960—1279 A.D.), *wansui* was gradually monopolized by the emperor. People were forbidden to use *wansui* to wish a long life to any others but the emperor himself. In the Ming Dynasty (1368—1644 A.D.), it was stipulated that only the emperor could be called *wansui*. The empress, princes and other dukes could only be called *qiansui* (one thousand years old), and this system was carried on to the Qing Dynasty (1644—1911 A.D.). Only as late as in 1911, when feudalism was overthrown by the revolution led by Dr. Sun Yat-sen, was the address of *wansui* brought to an end.

In ancient times, apart from *wansui*, there were some other forms of address for the emperor as listed below:

Tianzi: In the Spring and Autumn Period (770—476 B.C.), as the rulers of the State of Wu, the State of Chu, and some other states called themselves *wang* (king) one after another, in order to differentiate the king of the Zhou Dynasty from others, "*tianzi* of the Zhou Dynasty" was used to refer to the king of the Zhou Dynasty. Ever since then, *tianzi* became another address for the emperor, which means "the son of the heaven". In order to solidify their rule, the rulers molded the theory that "the monarchical power was given by the heaven" and the king of the Zhou Dynasty was the son of the heaven, so as to enable all the dukes to be at his order obediently.

Zuxia: In the Spring and Autumn Period, the prince of the State of Jin, Chong'er, went into exile for 19 years and finally came back to the State of Jin and became the ruler. When he began to grant titles and territories to the nobles, Jie Zitui, who had once shared weal and woe with him, went to Mount Mian with his mother and lived in seclusion. The ruler sent someone to look for him, but he refused to come out. Then a fire was set in the mountain in an attempt to force him out, but Jie Zitui would rather die than come out, so he was burnt to death, hugging a tree. The ruler was so deeply grieved that he had this tree cut and a pair of clogs made from it. Whenever he saw the clogs under his feet, for they would cherish the memory of Jie Zitui, he would exclaim: "How mournful! *Zuxia* (meaning under my feet)!" As *zuxia* originally represented a man that the ruler paid great respect to, it gradually evolved into a respectful form of address. The emperor held absolute power, therefore people used this to address the emperor later.

Beside these, *bixia* (your majesty), *gexia* (your excellency), *dianxia* (your highness) were also used to address the emperor.

62. 清代宗室的爵位分几等？爵位名称有哪些？

清代皇室成员都有皇帝加封的爵位。这些爵位共分为12个等级。

封爵第一级称为和硕亲王，主要是封皇子，蒙古贵族亦有封亲王的，如科尔沁亲王。第二级为多罗郡王，第三级为多罗贝勒，第四级为固山贝子，简称贝子。以上四级都属“王”的范围。第五级到第八级均称“公”，其顺序是：奉恩镇国公、奉恩辅国公、不入八分镇国公、不入八分辅国公。从第九级到第十二级都称“将军”，他们的顺序是：镇国将军、辅国将军、奉国将军和奉恩将军。

爵位的继承办法，一般是每差一代，爵位就降一级。比如郡王的儿子要世袭爵位，就是贝勒，郡王的孙子所世袭的爵位就变成贝子，依次顺延，直到没有爵位为止。但也有例外，八大王（俗称“铁帽子王”）的后代在继承爵位时，没有降一级的问题，他们都享有和其先辈一样的爵位，被皇帝封为亲王或郡王。除此之外，清朝后期，终身爵位还封给其他一些人，如人们熟知的恭亲王、庆亲王和醇亲王。

62. What Were the Ranks of the Imperial Nobility of the Qing Dynasty?

In the Qing Dynasty, all members of the imperial family had titles ganted by the emperor. The titles were divided into twelve ranks. The first was *heshuo qinwang*. It was mainly for the princes. The second was *duoluo junwang* (also known as *junwang*). The third was *duoluo beile* (also known as *beile*). The fourth was *gushan beizi* (also known as *beizi*). The first four all belonged to "*wang*". From the fifth to the eighth, were "*gong*": *feng'en zhenguo gong*, *feng'en fuguo gong*, *burubafen zhenguo gong* and *burubafen fuguo gong*. From the ninth to the twelfth, were "*jiangjun*": *zhenguo jiangjun*, *fuguo jiangjun*, *fengguo jiangjun*, and *feng'en jiangjun*.

The rank would be one level lower when it was inherited. For example, the son of *junwang* got the title of *beile*, the grandson got *beizi*, etc. until there was no title left. But there were also exceptions to this rule. Some titles were given with the right of inheritance for ever. This was the case with the "iron-capped princes" (*tiemaozi wang*), descendants of the eight minority princes who helped in the establishment of the dynasty. They were all, by right of perpetual inheritance, *qinwang* or *junwang*. Besides, the honour of a perpetual title was given to others, for example, to Gong Qinwang, Qing Qinwang and Chun Qinwang in the late years of the Qing Dynasty.

63. 中国古代官吏的“休沐”和“休致”指的是什么？

“休沐”指的是古代官吏休假。“休致”又叫“致仕”，指把官位还给皇帝，也就是人们今天说的退休。中国历代对官吏休假和退休规定并不一致。

周朝（约公元前 1100 ~ 前 256 年）时，每年有春祭和秋祭两次祭祀活动，春祭是祈求农业丰收，秋祭则是庆贺丰收。两次祭祀活动时，杀牛宰羊，人人庆贺，官府也停止办公，这可能是中国最早的休假日。

汉朝（公元前 206 ~ 公元 220 年）时，除了规定元旦、腊日、夏至、冬至休假以外，朝官“五日一下里舍，休沐”。意思是在朝做官的人每五天可以回家沐浴、休息一天。

唐朝（公元 618 ~ 907 年）对官吏休假又有新的规定，除了传统节令休假以外，官吏每十天可以休假一天。唐初诗人王勃在他所写的《滕王阁诗序》中写道：“十旬休暇，胜友如云；千里逢迎，高朋满座。”就是描写官吏利用每十天一次的休假，宴集宾朋的情景。唐玄宗把自己的生日定为千秋节，让官吏休假三天。玄宗以后，唐朝不少皇帝都把自己的生日定为千秋节，让官吏休假。

到宋朝（公元 960 ~ 1279 年），官吏休假较多。当时规定元旦、寒食（清明前一天）、冬至各休假七天，夏至和腊日各休三天，三伏天也有休假。此外，立春、春分、立夏、立秋、立冬和重阳等节令日都休假。总计一年有七十多天假。

明、清（公元 1368 ~ 1911 年）时休假没有宋朝多，可是有比较集中的假期。一般官府除端午、中秋节休假外，从腊月二十日封印到正月二十日开印，年假一个月。

对于官吏致仕的年龄，自周朝起，一般规定为 70 岁，明、清两朝改为 60 岁。汉朝规定，官员到一定级别致仕后，可享受原俸禄的三分之一。唐朝规定，五品以上官员致仕后，享受原俸禄的一半；五品以下虽然不享受俸禄，但是可拥有“永业田”。宋朝对官员致仕的规定更加严密，一般文官年满 70、武臣年满 80 都应该自行申请致仕，被批准后，颁给告、敕（证明文件）。一般在致仕时加官阶一级，享受一半俸禄。当时对四品以上文官和六品以上武臣，致仕时还可以授给他们的几名近亲和子弟以较低官衔。对那些年老体弱而又不申请致仕的，则由朝廷勒令致仕，或采取降官等惩罚措施。

明朝自洪武十三年（公元 1380 年）起，命令文、武官员满 60 岁的致仕，致仕后给其原俸，并免除徭役。同时也规定了年老有病不能胜任官职而又不申请致仕的，勒令致仕。清朝对于四品以下官员到致仕年龄的，给予“原品休致”。对于休致以后的，或升官级，或享受原俸，或给予子弟官职，都出自皇帝特恩，没有固定制度。

63. What Did the Terms *Xiumu* and *Xiuzhi* Stand for?

Xiumu referred to furlough granted to officials in the past; *xiuzhi* referred to retirement of officials. The regulations on furlough and retirement in different dynasties varied.

During the Zhou Dynasty (c. 1100—256 B.C.), there were spring worship and autumn worship every year. The spring worship was to pray for good harvests while the autumn worship was to celebrate bumper harvests. During each of these two periods, pigs and sheep were slaughtered for celebrations and officials also had several days off. This might be the earliest holidays in China.

During the Han Dynasty (206 B.C.—220 A.D.), beside New Year's Day, *Lari*, the Summer Solstice and the Winter Solstice, government officials could also go home to have baths and rest for one day every five working days.

During the Tang Dynasty (618—907 A.D.), there were new regulations on furlough. Beside the traditional holidays, officials could rest for one day every ten days. This was mentioned in *Tengwang' ge Shi Xu* (the preface to the poem for the Tengwang Pavilion) written by Wang Bo, a poet of the Tang Dynasty. Officials were also granted three days to rest at the time when Emperor Xuanzong of the Tang Dynasty celebrated his birthday. From Emperor Xuanzong on, many emperors granted officials holidays during their birthday celebration periods.

During the Song Dynasty (960—1279 A.D.), officials had more holidays. Officials were given seven days off at each of the following festivals: New Year's Day, the Cold Food Festival (the day before *Qingming*) and the Winter Solstice. Beside the above holidays, three days were also granted at both the Summer Solstice and *Lari*. Officials also had extra days off at dog days in summer. Beside all these, officials were granted several days to rest at the Beginning of Spring, the Spring Equinox, the Beginning of Summer, the Beginning of Autumn, the Beginning of Winter and the Double Ninth Festival, (the 9th day of the 9th lunar month). Altogether, there were more than 70 holidays every year.

During the Ming and Qing dynasties (1368—1911 A.D.), though fewer, holidays were put together. Usually, beside the traditional holidays at the Dragon-boat Festival and the Mid-autumn Festival, government offices closed for a month from the twentieth of the twelfth lunar month to the twentieth of the first lunar month.

As to the age for officials' retirement, from the Zhou Dynasty on, officials would retire at the age of seventy. However, during the Ming and Qing dynasties, the age for retirement was lowered to sixty. During the Han Dynasty, there were regulations that officials at and above a certain rank could still be entitled to one-third of his previous salary after retirement. During the Tang Dynasty, officials above the fifth rank (inclusive) were entitled to half of his previous salary after retirement, and those below the fifth rank were given a piece of "permanent land", though they would no longer get any salary after retirement. During the Song Dynasty, regulations on retirement of government officials were much stricter. Civil officials at the age of seventy and military officials at the age of eighty should automatically apply for retirement. When applications were approved, some certificates would be issued. Usually, the officials would be promoted by one rank at the time he applied for retirement and would get half of his previous salary after retirement. For civil officials above the fourth rank and military officers above the sixth rank, some of their close relatives or children could be offered low-rank official positions. As to those who were old and frail but did not apply for retirement, the government would request them to retire or lower their rank as punishment.

From the 13th year in the reign of Emperor Hongwu (1380 A.D.) of the Ming Dynasty, it was decreed that all civil and military officials at the age of sixty should apply for retirement and would get full salaries and would be exempted from taxes and corvee. It was also decreed that those who were old and frail but did not apply for retirement be requested to retire. During the Qing Dynasty, it was regulated that officials below the fourth rank were entitled to the same treatment as before after their retirement. There were no written regulations on the post-retirement treatment such as promotion, receiving the same salary, offering official positions to their children, etc., which were usually given at the whim of the emperors.

64. 中国最早的户籍制度是从何时开始的?

户籍制度是国家对全国人口实行的登记造册制度。中国户籍制度最早萌芽于春秋战国(公元前770~前221年)时期。其时,掌管户籍的官吏称之为"司民",其职责是,"掌登万民之数目,自生齿以上,皆书于版,辩其国中,与其都鄙,及于郊野,异其男女,岁登下其死生。"即:男孩、女孩出生后七八个月,都要登记到户口簿上,并且户分城乡,人分男女,每年统计出生和死亡。

在户籍制度中,秦国尤为重视。秦献公十年(公元前375年)乃"为户籍相伍"。具体实行情况如《商君书·境内篇》所载:"四境之内,丈夫女子皆有名于上,生者著,死有削。"即全国男女,都要在官府的户籍上注册,出生的要登记,死去的要注销。

对于户籍制度,秦国还有各种法律规定,如禁止隐匿户口和假报残疾,否则予以严惩。《传律》规定:隐匿成童,申报废疫不确实,里典、伍老处以赎耐(两年以上的刑罚)。百姓不应免老,或免老不加申报;敢弄虚作假,罚两副铠甲;里典、伍老不告发,各罚一副铠甲,同伍的人每罚一盾,都迁至边远地区。

秦法律还规定了户口迁移制度。居民迁居,必须"谒史更籍",即向官府申请办理迁移户口手续。擅自脱离户籍而逃亡,叫做"亡命",抓住后即予治罪。同时,对于不及时给户口迁移者办理迁移手续的官吏,视后果轻重的不同,分别给予惩罚。《法律答问》有:"甲迁居,请求办理迁移户籍,吏拖延不予迁移。以后甲犯了应处耐刑和罚款以上的罪,问吏应如何论处? 甲罪在耐刑以上,应罚吏两副铠甲。"

至汉代(公元前206~公元220年),户籍制度得到进一步完善。汉朝每年要统计一次户口,称作"案比",并具体定在八月进行,故又称"八月案比"。汉代,从中央到地方皆设有管理户籍的职官,汉初称为"计相",后改称"大司"。当时的户籍册叫作"版"或"户版"。在户籍册上,所有居民要详细登记年龄、性别、籍贯、社会关系、社会地位、财产状况、以及身高和肤色等个人特征。汉代的户籍制度已达到相当完备的程度。

户籍制度的实行,一方面有利于统治者征发徭役、征收赋税,另一方面对社会的安定也有着不可低估的作用。

64. When Did Household Registration Start in China?

Household registration is the system carried out by the state to register the population of the whole nation. In China, this system originated in the Spring and Autumn and the Warring States periods (770—221 B.C.). At that time, officials in charge of household registration were called *simin* and their responsibilities were to enter boys and girls on the household booklet within seven or eight months after their births, to keep the record in separate categories of urban and rural areas, male and female, and then to calculate the annual births and deaths.

The State of Qin paid special attention to household registration. As early as in 375 B.C., they carried out the system. As recorded in books, men and women all over the state had to register on the governmental household booklets, births must be entered and deaths must be removed. There were various laws and regulations concerning this system. For example, to hide anyone from registration or to register feigned disablement were forbidden, and one would be severely punished for violation. The law also stipulated on household transfer system. If the resident wanted to transfer to another place, he must apply and go through the procedures involved. Those who just fled without doing this were called *wangming*. Once caught, they would be regarded as criminals and be punished. In the same way, officials who didn't conduct the procedures in a timely fashion would also be punished accordingly.

This system was further developed in the Han Dynasty (206 B.C.—220 A.D.). Household registration, known as *anbi*, must be done once a year, and, since it was always in August according to the rule, it was therefore also called "August *anbi*". In the Han Dynasty, there were household officials at all levels from the central government to the local ones. They were first called *jixiang* in earlier times, and then changed to *dasi*. The household booklets were called *ban* or *huban*, in which detailed information from age, sex, hometown, relationships, social position, property to such individual characteristics as height and complexion, etc. of all the residents should be entered. This system was rather complete in the Han Dynasty.

The implementation of household registration was convenient for the ruling class to collect taxes on the one hand, and also beneficial to the stability of the society on the other hand.

65. 中国的科举制度是什么时候开始的？它有什么内容？

中国的科举制度是封建社会从读书人中选拔官员的一种制度，是从隋朝（公元 581 ~ 618 年）开始的。隋朝以前，历代选拔官员的办法不尽一样。如：汉朝（公元前 206 ~ 公元 220 年）曾让郡国每年选孝（孝子）、廉（廉洁的人）、贤良方正（能直言进谏的人）和秀才（才华优秀的人，又称茂才）各若干名，经过一定的考试手续，任用为官员。魏晋（公元 220 ~ 420 年）时，曾实行九品中正制。就是任用地方能识别人才的官兼任中正官，由他把同籍的士人评列为上上到下下共九品，每十万人推举一人，供吏部任用官员时参考。实际上所举荐的人大都是豪门望族，贫寒的知识分子很难被推举上去。隋文帝（杨坚）废除九品中正制，于开皇七年（公元 587 年）设志行修谨（有德）、清平干济（有才）两科。隋炀帝（杨广，公元 605 ~ 617 年）于大业二年（公元 606 年）正式设置进士科。这就是科举制度的开始。因为分设各科，又是由地方考取后举至京城参加殿试，所以叫科举。

唐朝（公元 618 ~ 907 年）在继承隋朝科举的基础上，分科举为常举（每年考试）和制举（由皇帝决定临时设置），科目设有秀才、明经、进士、明法、明书、明算等。各种考试的内容和录取标准并不一样。武则天（公元 684 ~ 704 年）曾亲自主持殿试，并增设武举。由于科举是通过知识性的考试而录取人才，对德行的要求就不太严格了。

宋朝（公元 960 ~ 1279 年）对科举更加重视，宋太祖（赵匡胤，公元 960 ~ 975 年）对考中进士的人亲自进行殿试，并从此形成制度。宋太宗（赵光义，公元 976 ~ 997 年）时，规定进士按三甲发榜，第一甲由皇帝赐进士及第，第二甲赐进士出身，第三甲赐同进士出身。被录取的进士由皇帝宣布名次，并在琼林苑赐宴，称为琼林宴。凡是被录取的都有资格做官。南宋（公元 1127 ~ 1279 年）规定，一甲第一名称为状元。考中状元会得到优厚待遇和极大的荣耀。因此，大多数读书人把参加科举作为自己进身求荣的惟一途径。

明清（公元 1368 ~ 1911 年）时期，科举的科目只有进士一科，试题的内容限定在“四书”（《大学》、《中庸》、《论语》、《孟子》）和“五经”（《诗经》、《尚书》》、《礼记》、《周易》、《春秋》）之内，应考的考生必须按照一定的格式写一篇解释经义的文章，就是“八股文”。全篇文章分八股，实际是六段，开始要用两句话说出题目的要义，叫“破题”，下面再用几句话阐明“破题”的意思，叫“承题”，其他几段用排比对照的形式，围绕主题发议论。八股文形式规定得很严，内容必须符合宋朝朱熹的《四书章句集注》等书，不许自由发挥。考试的时间定为三年一次，正式考试分乡试（在省城考）、会试（在京城贡院考）、殿试（在皇宫考）三级，因为为取得乡试资格而举行的郡试（清朝叫童试）也可以算一级，实际是四级。参加郡试的人不论年龄大小都叫童生，郡试被录取的叫秀才，乡试被录取的叫举人，会试被录取的叫贡士,殿试被录取的叫进士。除进士第一名称状元外,第二名叫榜眼,第三名叫探花。凡是得中进士的,都在特设的石碑上刻名。现在北京孔庙院子里的石碑上,还刻有元、明、清三朝进士的姓名。

清朝光绪三十一年(公元 1905 年)推行学校,废除了科举制度。

65. When Did the Imperial Examination System Start? What Did It Test?

The imperial examination system was applied in the fedual society to select officials from intellectuals. It started from the Sui Dynasty (581—618 A.D.). A variety of ways were used to select officials in the previous dynasties, e.g. in the Han Dynasty (206 B.C.—220 A.D.), the local administration would select *xiao* (filial sons), *lian* (honest people), *xianliang fangzheng* (frank demonstrators) and *xiucai* (talented intellectuals) to take part in a certain examination and appoint them as officials. In the Three Kingdoms Period as well as in the Jin Dynasty, *jiu pin zhongzheng zhi* (the nine-rank judging system) was introduced. Local officials who were good at finding talents would be assigned to the posts of *zhongzheng*, whose job was to give appraisals to the candidates, score them by nine ranks and recommend them to the Board of Civil Office. Only one out of a hundred thousand was recommended and most of them were from rich and powerful families. Poor intellectuals could hardly get any chance. This system was abolished by Emperor Wen of the Sui Dynasty in 587 A.D. He set up two branches to be tested: moral character and knowledge. In 606 A.D., Emperor Yang (605—617 A.D.) set up another branch called *jinshi*, which was the formal start of the imperial examination system. The Chinese word for this system is *keju*.

In the Tang Dynasty (618—907 A.D.), the imperial examination system further developed into *changju* (annual examination) and *zhiju* (temporarily decided by the emperor). The content tested and the criterion for each branch were all different. Empress Wu Zetian (684—704 A.D.) once presided over the final examination. She also added a new branch: *wuju*. Since the imperial examinaion mainly tested on knowledge, its demands on moral character were not very high.

In the Song Dynasty (960—1279 A.D.) more importance was attached to the examination. Emperor Taizu(960—975 A.D.) presided over the final examination for one branch personally and thus established it as a system thereafter. During the reign of Emperor Taizong (976—997 A.D.), a regulation was made, according to which successful candidates were divided into three groups and titles were conferred to them by the emperor. The emperor would announce the names in order of their scores, and bestow them a banquet. All the successful candidates were qualified for a post. In the Southern Song Dynasty (1127—1279 A.D.), it was stipulated that the person who got the highest score in the first group would be granted the title of *zhuangyuan* , who was entitled to liberal benefits and high honour. Therefore, most intellectuals took the imperial examination as the only access to official ranks and glory.

In the Ming and Qing dynasties (1368—1911 A.D.), the branches tested were reduced to only one and the contents tested were also limited to "the four books", namely *Daxue* (*The Great Learning*), *Zhongyong* (*The Doctrine of the Mean*), *Lunyu* (*The Analects of Confucius*), and *Mengzi* (*Mencius*), and "the five classics", namely *Shi Jing* (*The Book of Songs*), *Shang Shu* (*The Book of History*), *Zhou Yi* (*The Book of Changes*), *Li Ji* (*The Book of Rites*) and *Chunqiu* (*The Spring and Autumn Annuals*). All the candidates had to write a composition explaining ideas from these books in a rigid form and structure. This composition was called *baguwen* (eight-part essay). To start with, two sentences should be used to tell the main idea of the title. This was called "to clear the topic". Then it should be followed by several sentences to clarify the meaning of the topic. This was called "to continue the topic". The remaining part had to carry on discussions on the topic in the form of parallelism and antithesis, which was rigidly restricted. The ideas must be in keeping with *Si Shu Zhangju Jizhu* (*A Variorum of the Four Books*) by Zhu Xi. Liberal ideas and free rein were not accepted. The examination was held once every three years. It had four levels: the county examination, the provincial examination, the academy examination and the palace examination. Only when one passed a lower-level examination, was he qualified to sit for one of a higher level. All the candidates for the county examination were called *tongsheng*. Those who passed were called *xiucai*. Those who passed the provincial, the academy and the palace examinations were called *juren*, *gongshi* and *jinshi* respectively. The first three of *jinshi* were ranked *zhuangyuan*, *bangyan* and *tanhua* respectively. All those who passed the palace examination and obtained the title of *jinshi* were entitled to have their names carved on a special tablet. On a tablet in the Confucius Temple in Beijing, we can still find the names of those *jinshi* in the Yuan, Ming and Qing dynasties.

The imperial examination system was terminated in 1905.

66. 中国最早的警察何时产生？行使什么职能？

警察作为维护国家统治秩序和社会治安的武装人员，早在奴隶制夏代（约公元前2100～约前1600年）就产生了。当时，行使警察职能的职官有：处理民事的警察“司徒”、具有武装警察和边防警察职能的“司马”，以及刑侦和管理监狱方面的警察“士”。

商周（约公元前1600～前256年）时代，基本上延续了夏代的制度，其警察职能仍寓于行政、军事和司法三种职官之中。如西周（约公元前1100～前771年）执行警察职能的官员就包括“司徒”、“司马”和“司寇”。“司寇”掌管刑狱和纠察等事，比夏代“士”的权力更大。夏代的“士”在西周为“司寇”，帮助司马在宫中、官府、城中、乡下、军中五种范围内处理刑罚。

至春秋战国（公元前770～前221年），具有警察性质的职官已相当繁多，而且职能也有了很大发展。这主要反映在《周礼》中。

第一，民事管理。执行该方面警察职能的官吏有“司民”，犹如今天的户籍管理，所谓“掌登万民之数目”。另外有“司市”，管理市场。

第二，治安管理。包括“司暴”，负责维持治安和秩序，制止暴动；“司稽”，主管巡市，司察犯禁者及拘捕盗贼；“司寤氏”，为掌禁夜之官；“禁暴民”和“禁杀戮”是对那些敢于暴乱、触犯禁令及敢于相斩杀的吏民给以严厉制裁，并可诛杀的官职。

第三，消防管理。主要有“司烜(huǐ)氏”和“司爟(guàn)”。

第四，交通管理。主要有类似今天交通警察的“野庐氏”。即“掌通达道路，使之往来顺畅”。

第五，刑徒管理。有“司马”、“司录”、“司圜”、“掌囚”、“掌戮”等，相当于今天的司法警察。如“司圜”负责“收教罢民，凡害人者弗使冠饰，而加明刑焉，任之以事而教之”。又如“掌囚”，则是看守未决与已决罪犯的司法警察。

第六，城门与关口检查，包括“司门”，掌管京城诸门、稽查走私。“司关”负责检查出入关门的货物并收税、接待过关的四方宾客、检查关口的符节凭信。

第七，边防警戒，主要是“司险”，其职能为开路架桥。一旦国家遇外敌入侵和国内发生非常事件，则负责设立路障，类似今天的边防警察。

综上所述，可见中国警察形成的历史已有4000余年。到奴隶社会末和封建社会初，在各个领域，警察的设置已相当普遍，其职能也已相当完备了。

66. Who Were the Earliest Policemen in China and What Were Their Functions?

Policemen, acting as the armed personnel to safeguard the ruling order and public security of a nation, emerged as early as the Xia Dynasty (c.2100—c.1600 B.C.) in the slave society. At that time, officials who performed the functions of policemen were called *situ* (handling civil lawsuits), *sima* (acting as military policemen and frontier policemen) and *shi* (dealing with criminal offenses and executing prison administration).

This system continued into the Shang and Zhou dynasties (c.1600—256 B.C.). The function of police still resided in the three posts of executive, military and judiciary. For example, in the Western Zhou Dynasty (c. 1100—971 B.C.), the officials performing the function of policemen included *situ*, *sima* and *sikou*. *Sikou* was in charge of criminal cases and picketing, holding greater power than *shi* of the Xia Dynasty, and *shi* became a subordinate official of *sikou* in the Western Zhou Dynasty, helping *sima* in handling criminal cases and meting out punishments in the five areas of the imperial palace, official circles, cities, countryside and the army.

As late as in the Spring and Autumn and the Warring States periods (770—221 B.C.), there were a great many posts of policemen and their functions were also further developed. It was mainly reflected in *Zhou Li* (*Ritual of Zhou*).

The first function was civil administration. The officials in charge of this aspect were *simin*. They were like the policemen today and were in charge of household registration. Besides, there was *sishi* to command the market.

The second function was maintaining public order. The officials included *sibao*, who were in charge of maintaining social order and public security and preventing rebellions; *siji*, who were in charge of patrolling, scrutinizing and arresting bandits; *siwushi*, who were in charge of imposing a curfew; and *jinbaomin*, whose duty was to punish or put to death those who dared to revolt, violate the rules and regulations or kill others.

The third function was fire fighting. Officials in charge of this mainly included *sihuishi* and *siguan*.

The fourth function was traffic controlling. Officials in charge of this aspect were called *yelushi*. Like traffic police today, they took care of the traffic, ensuring a smooth coming and going.

The fifth function was prisoner administration. Officials in charge of this included *sima*, *silu*, *sihuan*, *zhangqiu* and *zhanglu*, etc. analogous to the judiciary police today. For example, *zhangqiu* was the police in charge of guarding convicted and unconvicted prisoners.

The sixth function was city gate and pass inspection. Officials in charge of this included *simen*, who were in charge of checking the passers-by at city gates to prevent smuggling, and *siguan*, who were in charge of inspecting goods, collecting duties, receiving guests and examining tallies and letters at the customs.

The seventh function was frontier defending. Such officials included *sixian*, who were in charge of making roads and building bridges. If there was foreign invasion or domestic disturbances, they were in charge of setting up roadblocks.

To sum up, the history of policemen in China was well over 4000 years. And in the slave society and the beginning of the feudal society, policemen could be seen in various fields and their functions were also well developed already.

67. 中国古代的驿路是怎样发展起来的?

根据史书记载,中国从周朝(约公元前1100~前221年)开始,就已经建立了比较完整的邮驿制度。邮驿主要是传递官方文书,后来还担负迎送来往官员的任务。开始时有以车传递和由人跑步传递两种,沿驿路设置了“委”、“馆”等休息站。当时邮驿还仅限于周朝统治的中心地区,边陲地区交通还很不方便。春秋战国(公元前770~前221年)时期,由于生产发展和频繁战事的需要,出现了单骑通信和接力车传,速度进一步提高。据《左传》记载,鲁昭公元年(公元前541年)秦晋之间就修了一条驿路,每十里设置一舍,邮传车每到一舍就把文书交给另一辆车,经过一百舍就由秦国都城雍(今陕西凤翔)到达晋国都城绛(今山西绛县)。秦始皇(公元前221~前210年)时,以都城咸阳(今陕西咸阳东北)为中心,修筑了两条路面宽阔的“驰道”,一条通向现在的河北、山东,直到海边;另一条通向现在的江苏、浙江等地。“驰道”两旁种有松树,很是讲究。除了“驰道”以外,还在其他地区修了“新道”和“五尺道”。为了保证文书及时传递,秦朝用《行书律》规定如果耽搁了紧急文书要以法律处置。

到隋唐(公元581~907年)时期,邮驿有了很大发展。驿的任务除了传递公文和军事情报外,还兼管遣送官员、追捕罪犯、押送犯人和灾区抚慰等事务。盛唐时,全国有陆驿1297个,水驿260个,水陆兼驿86个,形成遍布全国的交通通信网。全国驿夫有17000人。对于递送文书的速度,朝廷都有明文规定:一般快马递送日行180里,紧急的文书要求日行300到500里。公元755年,安禄山在范阳(今北京大兴)起兵反唐,当时唐玄宗在距范阳几千里外的陕西华清宫,他在六天之内就得到了报告。可见当时驿递组织的严密了。驿路的发展,给交通、通信带来了很大方便。当然,也为统治者骄奢淫逸的生活服务。唐朝诗人杜牧在《过华清宫》诗中写出了为满足杨贵妃吃新鲜荔枝的需要,通过驿路飞骑传送鲜荔枝,驿差中暑而死的很多。诗是这样的:“长安回望绣成堆,山顶千门次第开。一骑红尘妃子笑,无人知是荔枝来。”

清朝末年,办起了新式邮政,驿路逐渐被代替。到1913年,北洋政府宣布将驿站全部撤消,从此结束了驿路的历史。

67. How Did Ancient Post Roads Develop in China?

According to historical records, postal system was well-developed in the Zhou

Dynasty (c.1100—221 B.C.) in China. It was mainly used for the delivery of official documents, as well as for ushering in and out the officials . At the beginning, official documents were deliverel by post chaises or running postmen, so there were places for them to take a rest along the post road, which was then concentrated in the center of the ruling area, without reaching into the remote regions. In the Spring and Autumn and the Warring States periods (770—221 B.C.), owing to the rapid development of production and frequent warfares, relays were used to speed up the delivery. It was recorded in the book *Zuo Zhuan* that a post road was built between the state of Qin and the state of Jin in 541 B.C., with a stop every five kilometers, where the documents were shifted from one post chaise to the next. The road covered a full distance of 100 stops. During the reign of Emperor Qinshihuang(221—210 B.C.) two express ways were built, one from the capital Xianyang via Hebei and Shandong to the sea, the other from Xianyang to Jiangsu and Zhejiang. The express ways were lined with exquisite pinetrees. In addition, some other roads were also built in other areas. There were even laws to stipulate punishment on the delay of urgent documents.

Postal system advanced greatly in the Sui and Tang dynasties(581—907 A.D.). The range of its mission expanded from delivery of documents and military information to sending off officials, pursuing and escorting criminals, and consoling the peplpe in the afflicted areas. A network was formed in the Tang Dynasty, which covered 1297 land posts, 260 water posts and 86 incorporate ones. There were 17000 postmen all over the country. Regulations were made by the imperial court on the speed of delivery. An ordinary mail required a speed of 90 kilometers per day and an urgent one, 150 to 250 kilometers per day. In 755 A.D., when a rebellion arose, the emperor got the message from a distance of thousands of kilometers within six days, from which we can see how well the system worked. The development of post roads brought great conveniences to traffic and correspondence, while on the other hand, it also provided an extravagant life for the ruling class. There was a famous poem describing the hardships of the delivery of fresh lychee for the spoiled imperial concubine Yang Guifei. Many postmen died of heat-stroke on their way in order to deliver lychee.

Post roads were gradually replaced by new postal systems in the Qing Dynasty and were formally abolished in 1913.

68. 中国古代的书籍是什么样子的?

书籍是有一定内容的文字按照一定形式编排在一起的。中国在3000多年前的商朝已经有刻、写在龟甲或兽骨上的甲骨文。稍晚一些时候,又有铸在铜器上的金文。这些文字内容大部分是占卜的卜辞或记事的铭文,还不能叫做书籍。

中国最古老的书籍应该是竹简,据说从商朝(约公元前1600~约前1100年)晚期或西周(约公元前1100~前771年)开始,中国就有了竹简编成的书籍。人们把青竹剖开,削成竹片,在上面书写。然后用丝、麻或牛皮绳把写好的竹简编缀起来,就成为册,这就是中国最早的书籍。在制作竹简的过程中,为了便于书写和保存,人们把削好的竹片在火上炙烤,去掉竹中汁液,这道工序叫"杀青",也叫"汗青"。中国宋代民族英雄文天祥在《过零丁洋》诗中写的:"人生自古谁无死,留取丹心照汗青。"正是指的用竹简做的书。中国最早的历史《竹书纪年》就是用竹简书写的,所以文天祥用"汗青"指历史。这种竹简编缀的书搬运、翻阅都很费事。据说孔子晚年喜欢读《周易》,因为翻阅次数多,把编竹简的牛皮绳子磨断了很多次。古人把熟制的皮革叫"韦",所以留下"韦编三绝"这个成语。

在用竹简的同时,人们也用木片写书。这种木片叫札或牍。直到汉朝(公元前206~公元220年),人们还在用竹简和木牍。

与竹简、木牍同时,中国另一种写在丝织品上的"帛书"也在使用。由于中国养蚕缫丝的历史很长,所以使用帛书的时间也比较早。在春秋战国(公元前770~前221年)时期,已经有关于帛书的记载。与竹、木相比较,帛书轻便,易于携带,而且幅面宽,可以在上面画图。但是丝织品比竹、木价格昂贵,所以帛书比竹简、木牍要少。另外,由于帛书不易保存,所以出土的帛书也比竹简、木牍少。中国现有的帛书时间最早的,是在马王堆三号汉墓中发现的。这批帛书是用生丝织成细绢,用烟墨书写的。书写的年代距今已经2000多年了。

西汉时,中国发明了"麻纸",到东汉时纸的使用已经比较普遍。以后纸逐渐取代竹、木和丝织品,成为书籍的材料。

68. What Do the Ancient Chinese Books Look like?

Books are characters with a certain content compiled together in a certain way. In the Shang Dynasty over 3000 years ago, there were already characters carved or written on tortoise shells and animal bones in China. Some time later, characters were molded on bronze vessels. Since most of these inscriptions were divination scripts or records of events, they could not be seriously regarded as books.

The oldest books in China were made of bamboo slips. It was said that bamboo slips appeared in the late Shang Dynasty(c.1600— c. 1100 B.C.) or in the Western Zhou Dynasty (c. 1100—771 B.C.). Bamboo was made into slips for writing. Then the written slips would be strung together with silk, linen or ox hide thread. This was the earliest book in China. To make them suitable for writing and preservation, bamboo slips must first be dried by fire. This process was called *hanqing* in Chinese, namely, removing the moisture from the green bamboo slips. It was on bamboo slips that the earliest historical records were written. The disadvantage of these books was that they were not convenient for either carrying or reading. It was said that Confucius broke the strings threading *Zhou Yi* (*The Book of Changes*) several times because he read the book repeatedly in his late years.

Wood slips were in use simultaneously with bamboo slips. Bamboo slips and wood slips were still in use even in the Han Dynasty (206 B.C.—220 A.D.).

Silk fabric was another kind of writing material used at that time. The early use of silk as writing material should be attributed to the long history of Chinese silk production. Early in the Spring and Autumn and the Warring States periods (770—221 B.C.), there were records on using silk as writing material. Compared with bamboo and wood, silk is lighter, easier to carry and more suitable for painting due to its width. However, it was expensive and few people could afford it. Furthermore, because it is hard to preserve, the unearthed pieces of silk writing are much fewer than bamboo and wooden ones. So far, the earliest silk writing available in China is the one unearthed in the third tomb of Mawangdui in Changsha, Hunan Province, which has a history of over 2000 years.

During the Western Han Dynasty, paper was invented. It was used widely in the Eastern Han Dynasty. Gradually, paper replaced bamboo, wood and silk as writing material.

69.《孙子兵法》是中国第一部兵法书吗？它的主要内容是什么？

《孙子兵法》是春秋末期军事家孙武的著作。它不仅在中国，而且在世界上也是最早的军事著作。

孙武，字长卿，春秋（公元前770～前256年）末期齐国（今山东北部）人，他到吴国（今江苏、安徽一部）后，吴王阖闾采用他的兵法，任孙武为将。以3万人破楚国20万众，攻入楚国都城。据《史记》说，吴国后来还战败过齐国。这与孙武用谋略是分不开的。

《孙子兵法》有：计、作战、谋攻、虚实、行军、地形、火攻、用间等13篇，在当时条件下，从主观和客观上全面论述了作战的道理和取胜的方法。《孙子兵法》说："兵者，国之大事，死生之地，存亡之道，不可不察也。"意思是：战争是国家的大事，关系到军民的生死、国家的存亡，不可不认真研究。孙子认为，决定战争胜负的基本因素，要看五种情况和七条优劣。五种情况就是：道（即政治，就是说民众与君主的愿望一致）、天（天时，就是阴晴、寒暑等气候与季节情况）、地（就是地形条件）、将（指挥官的才智、品质）、法（军队的组织与制度等）。七条优劣（后人称为"七计"）要看：主孰有道（哪一方政治开明）；将孰有能（哪一方将帅指挥高明）；天地孰得（哪一方天时地利有利）；法令孰行（哪一方法令能贯彻执行）；兵众孰强（哪一方军事实力比较强大）；士卒孰练（哪一方兵卒较有训练）；赏罚孰明（哪一方赏罚比较严明）。考察了以上情况以后，战争的胜败就大体可以判断了。

在全书的论述中，贯穿了朴素的辨证法与唯物主义。孙武强调对敌我双方情况的掌握，除了上面所说的内容外，还有一句名言："知彼知己，百战不殆"。他主张"攻其无备，出其不意"；主张集中优势兵力打击敌人；主张将帅思考问题要兼顾有利和不利两个方面：要在不利的情况下看到有利的条件，在顺利的情况下看到危害的可能，才能解除祸患。他说：作战方式有些像水，水避高处而往下流，用兵就要避实而击虚；水流动没有定形，作战也没有固定的方式，能根据敌情变化而取胜的，叫用兵如神。此外，对如何瓦解敌人，如何利用地形，如何爱护士兵以及进行火攻、利用间谍等，都有精辟的论述。

对《孙子兵法》，历代都有人作注。最著名的作注者为曹操等。现代有郭化若的《孙子今译》。《孙子兵法》也受到国外的重视，日、英、法、俄、德国等都出版了译本。

69. Is *Sunzi Bingfa* the First Book on the Art of War in China? What Are the Main Ideas in the Book?

Sunzi Bingfa (*The Art of War* by Sunzi) is a book written by strategist Sun Wu in the late Spring and Autumn Period(770—256 B.C.). It is the first book on the art of war not only in China, but also in the world.

Sun Wu was from the State of Qi (north of present Shandong Province) in the Spring and Autumn Period. When he moved to live in the State of Wu (part of present Jiangsu and Anhui), the King adopted his military strategies and appointed him the general. In 506 B.C., 30000 soldiers from the State of Wu went to attack the State of Chu (part of present Hubei and Hunan). They not only defeated the Chu troops of 200000 soldiers, but also occupied the capital of the State of Chu. It was recorded in *Shi Ji* (*Records of the Historian*) that the State of Wu also defeated the State of Qi afterwards. All these victories should largely be attributed to Sun Wu's strategies.

There are 13 chapters in *Sunzi Bingfa* which expounded, both subjectively and objectively, the reasons to fight and ways to win. According to *Sunzi Bingfa*, since it is important state affairs and has a lot to do with the lives of the soldiers and subjects and the existence of the state, war should be carefully studied. Sun Wu believed that the fundamental determinant factors in wars included five kinds of situations and seven favorable and unfavorable elements. The five kinds of situations are: *dao*, namely political situations; weather and climate; topography; wit and personality of the generals; and laws. The seven favorable and unfavorable elements, which are called *qi ji* (seven stratagems) by later generations, are: who has the *dao* (who has better political situations); whose generals are more capable; who has taken the advantage of better weather and topography; whose orders can be carried out more effectively; whose troops are better equipped and organized; whose soldiers are better trained; and who is stricter and fairer in meting out rewards and punishments. When the above are studied, it will be clear which side will win.

Naive dialectics and materialism run through the exposition of the whole book. Another well-known saying of Sun Wu is: Know the enemy and know yourself, and you will fight a hundred battles without defeat. He also advocated attacking the enemy unaware and unprepared. His thought also includes: to attack with a troop which greatly outnumbers your enemy; generals should take both advantages and disadvantages into consideration; advantages should be kept in mind under unfavorable situations while possible dangers should not be ignored under favorable circumstances. Only in this way can disasters be avoided. He also likened the art of war to the nature of water: Like water flowing from higher places to lower places, in war, the weak and unprepared enemy ought to be attacked while the stronger and better-prepared enemies avoided; just as water has no permanent form, the strategies of war are also not unchangeable, and a man who can deploy his army in light of changeable arrangements of the enemy is a superb military commander. Apart from all these, he also expounded such issues as how to disintegrate enemy forces, how to make use of different topography, how to protect the soldiers, how to launch fire attacks, how to use spies, etc.

Many persons have written notes to *Sunzi Bingfa* . The most well-known one is Cao Cao, a strategist in the Three Kingdoms Period. *Sunzi Today* is a book written in modern times. *Sunzi Bingfa* has also drawn attention abroad and has been translated into Japanese, English, French, Russian, German, and other languages.

70. 中国古代最早的有关农业的书是哪些？内容如何？

中国古代最早有关农业生产方面的书要算西汉(公元前206~公元24年)时期氾(fán)胜之所著的《氾胜之书》。氾胜之曾在汉成帝(刘骜,公元前32~前7年)时担任过议郎(掌顾问应对,为郎官之一),并且以轻车使者名义到三辅(今陕西关中平原)去劝说农民种麦,获得丰收。后升迁为御史(当时为史官)。《氾胜之书》成书约在公元前1世纪后期,后失散多年。据后人辑录流传下来的内容,可以看出这本书在总结关中农业生产的经验上有过贡献。包括区田法、溲种法(在种子表面粘上一层粪肥壳作为种肥)和调节稻田水温法、种麦法、种瓜法等。

中国现在完整保存下来的有关农业生产方面的书,是贾思勰著的《齐民要术》。贾思勰是南北朝(公元420~589年)时北魏的人,他的家乡是山东益都(今青州市),生卒年月已不可考。他曾任北魏高阳郡(今河北保定市、高阳、清苑一带)太守。《齐民要术》一书大约写成于公元533~544年之间。全书共10卷,92篇,分门别类地论述了各种农作物、蔬菜、果树、竹木的栽培,家畜、家禽的饲养,农产品加工和副业等。这本书比较系统地总结了6世纪时中国黄河中、下游地区劳动人民丰富的农业生产经验。其中有些在当时是居于世界前列的。

书中对耕地绿肥轮作制进行了研究与总结。大约在两三千年前,中国人民已经开始翻压青草作为绿肥。到公元6世纪时,用绿肥轮作制代替休闲地轮作制已经逐渐推广。贾思勰研究了这方面的经验,肯定了绿肥在增加土地肥力上的作用,并且鉴定了不同植物作为绿肥的效果。书中指出:“凡美田之法,绿豆为上,小豆、胡麻次之。”肯定了豆科植物的肥效。在欧洲,这种绿肥轮作制据说是18世纪30年代在英国开始实行的,比《齐民要术》晚1200多年。

在农作物和家畜、家禽选留良种方面,《齐民要术》也做出了贡献。贾思勰研究了当时作物品种和选育良种的经验,提出选种和良种繁育的原则及方法。他从当时农家培育的优良品种中,仅粟(谷)就研究了80多个品种。并提出早熟、晚熟、高杆、矮杆与产量的关系。指出谷类良种应该进行穗选,单收单藏;对瓜果“食瓜时把好瓜子留下作种”。提出家畜“母良畜好”的选优留种原则。

书中关于测定韭菜种子发芽能力的简便方法、对大麻雌雄异株的观察以及在林业上关于阔叶树育种的详细记载等,在当时是居于世界农、林业科学前列的。

19世纪英国博物学家达尔文在他的著作《物种起源》中写道:“在一部古代的中国百科全书中,已有关于选择原理的明确记载。”达尔文这里所指的,很可能就是《齐民要术》中关于选育良种的部分。

70. What Are the Earliest Works on Agriculture in Ancient China? What Are Their Contents?

The first book on agriculture in ancient China is generally considered to be *Fan Shengzhi Shu* by Fan Shengzhi in the Western Han Dynasty (206 B.C.—24 A.D.). Fan Shenzhi once was a governmental official in the reign of Empeor Cheng (32—7 B.C.) and was sent to Sanfu (present Guanzhong Plain, Shaanxi Province) as envoy of the emperor to encourage farmers there to grow wheat. There was a bumper harvest there and then he was promoted to the position of attorney general.

Fan Shengzhi Shu was compiled approximately in the late part of the first century B.C., and then it was scattered around and left unused for many years. Based on what have been kept by later generations, we know that he made great contributions to the summing up of farming experiences in Guanzhong Plain, Shaanxi Province, such as field compost-making method, seedsoaking method, water temperature-adjusting method in paddy fields, wheat cultivating methods and melon cultivating methods.

The best preserved book on farming is *Qimin Yaoshu* (*Important Arts for the People's Welfare*) written by Jia Sixie, who lived in Northern Wei of the Northern and Southern Dynasties (420—589 A.D.). He was from Yidu, Shandong but no record on his birthday or the date of his death can be found. He once was the magistrate of Gaoyang Prefecture (present Baoding, Gaoyang and Qingyuan of Hebei Province). Between 533 and 534 A.D., he completed *Qimin Yaoshu*, which consisted of 10 volumes, 92 articles. The book contained expositions on the planting of various crops, vegetables and fruit trees, the raising of farm animals and poultry, as well as on agricultural produce, sideline production, etc. In this book, he systematically summed up the farming experiences in the middle and lower reaches of the Yellow River in the 6th century. Some of these experiences were among the most advanced in the world at that time.

The book included research on and summing-up of field ploughing and the system of rotating with green manure crops. About two or three thousand years ago, the Chinese people started to make manure by covering over grass with the soil turned up in the fields. From the 6th century, the system of rotating with green manure crops gradually replaced the fallow land system and was adopted extensively. Jia Sixie did research in this aspect and further confirmed the fact that green manure could increase soil fertility. Furthermore, he identified the effects of green manure of different crops. In his book, Jia pointed out: to make land fertile, green bean is the best, and the next come red bean and sesame. This statement affirmed the effect of leguminous plants as green manure. It was said that the system of rotating with green manure crops was adopted in the 1830's in Europe, more than 1200 years after *Qimin Yaoshu* was written.

Qimin Yaoshu has also made great contributions to the improvement of crop varieties and breed improvement of livestocks and poultry. Jia Sixie made research on the crop varieties and breeding experience at that time and put forward principles and ways for seed selection and variety improvement. By comparing good varieties bred by farmers, for instance, he studied more than 80 varieties of millets and analysed the differences between the early variety and the late variety, and between the high stalk and short stalk, and their relationships with the yields. He also put forward the following principles in seed selection: select good ears of grain and keep them in separate storage; reserve good seeds while eating melons; and select good female animals to ensure the breeding of good baby animals.

In his book, Jia pointed out the simple ways of checking the ability of seed germination of Chinese chives, made observations on dioecism of hemp and also made notes on variety improvement of broadleave trees. All these were among the best in the world science of agriculture and forestry.

Charles Darwin, an English naturalist of the 19th century, mentioned in his *Origin of Species* that in one of the ancient Chinese encyclopedias, there were explicit statements on principles for selection. It is most likely that what Charles Darwin referred to was the part on seed selection in *Qimin Yaoshu*.

71.《天工开物》是一部什么著作？它的影响如何？

《天工开物》出版于明崇祯十年（公元 1637 年），是一部关于中国古代农业和手工业生产技术经验的著作。分上、中、下三编，上编内容包括谷类和棉麻栽培、养蚕、缫丝、染料、食品加工、制盐、制糖等；中编包括制造砖瓦、陶瓷、铜铁器具、建造舟车、采炼石灰、煤炭、硫磺、榨油、制烛、造纸等；下编包括五金开采及冶炼、兵器、火药、朱墨、颜料、曲药的制造和珠玉采琢等。全书附有 200 多幅插图，生动地展示了当时生产技术的情景。全书内容几乎涉及从生产到生活的各行各业，其中有些技术不仅在中国，而且在世界当时也是先进的。如：不同品种的蚕蛾杂交后，能生产优良蚕种。书中说："今寒家有将早雄配晚雌者，幻出嘉种，一异也！"这是生物杂交优势较早的记录。关于煤炭部分，作者根据煤的硬度和挥发性对煤分类，是世界上最早提出来的。对各种生产技术的介绍也很详细。如介绍小麦加工成面粉，不仅叙述了打麦、去秕、淘晒、上磨、罗面的各道工序，并且介绍了各地磨石质地不同而影响面粉的成色的情况。

对于过去一些不合科学的传说，如"珍珠出于蛇腹、龙颔"、"砂金产自鸭屎"等，书中一一做了订正。

《天工开物》的作者宋应星是江西奉新（今江西奉新县）人，万历（公元 1573 ~ 1620 年）年间的举人。曾在江西、福建等地做官。他在各地十分注意考察农业和手工业生产技术，并加以比较，最后归纳成书。这本书的书名，意思是大自然（天）和人为（工）创造了世上万物。

这本书出版后，流传很广。17 世纪末传到日本，1869 年被译成英文，以后又被译成其他文字。很多外国学者在自己的著作中广泛引用这本书，并给予高度赞扬。英国的科学史专家李约瑟博士将宋应星与法国《百科全书》主编狄德罗相提并论，称他为"中国的狄德罗"。

71. What Kind of Book Is *Tian Gong Kai Wu* and What Was Its Influence?

Tian Gong Kai Wu (*The Exposition of Works of Nature*), published in the tenth year of the reign of Emperor Chongzhen (1637) of the Ming Dynasty, is a book on the experience of ancient Chinese farming and handcraft industry. The book consists of three parts. The first part includes cultivation of grains and hemp, silkworm breeding, silk reeling, dyestuff manufacturing, food processing, salt production and sugar extraction, etc. The second part includes brick making, the making of pottery and porcelain and bronze and iron utensils, boat and cart manufacturing, the mining of lime, coal and sulphur, oil extraction, and candle and paper making. The third part includes the mining and smelting of metals, the making of weaponry, gunpowder, red ink and pigment, and pearl processing. There are more than two hundred illustrations in the book, which vividly illustrate the production skills at that time. This book covers almost everything from production skills to everyday life. Among them, some were advanced not only in China, but also in the world at that time. For instance, about the hybridization of different silk moths to produce better silkworm seeds, it is recorded in the book: "This winter, some farmers hybridized early male silk moths with later female silk moths and then got better seeds." This is the first record of this kind. As for coal, the author put forward the way to grade coal according to its hardness and evaporation, which was also the first of its kind in the world. There is also very detailed record on production skills. For instance, in the section about wheat flour processing, the book not only recorded the process in threshing, washing and drying, grinding and sifting, but also pointed out the effect of different mill stones on the quality of the flour.

In this book, the author also corrected some wrong statements, such as the one that said pearls came out of snake bellies and dragon jaws, and placer came out of duck droppings, etc.

Song Yingxing, author of the book, was from Fengxin, Jiangxi Province. He was once an official in Jiangxi and Fujian. While he was in office at different places, he paid much attention to observing agrotechnigue and handcraft skills, made comparisons and then compiled them into the book. The title of this book means that all things on the earth are the creations of nature and human beings.

This book was widely spread after its publication. In the late 17th century, it was introduced into Japan and in 1869, translated into English. Later on, it was gradually translated into many other foreign languages. Many writers once quoted something from this book and spoke highly of it. Dr. Joseph Needham, a British expert of science history, mentioned Song Yingxing and compared him with the editor general of the French *Encyclopedia*.

72.《永乐大典》和《四库全书》是什么样的书？各有什么特点？

《永乐大典》是中国明朝所编的一部类书（类书就是采辑群书，将各种材料分类汇编，以供检查资料用的书）。因为它内容丰富、卷帙浩繁，被称为世界最大的百科全书。这部书编成于16世纪，在当时的确可以称为世界第一。即使与今天世界上的百科全书相比，在篇幅与内容上也可名列前茅。

明永乐元年（公元1403年）7月，明成祖朱棣命令翰林院学士解缙主持纂修此书，到永乐二年12月完成，当时名为《文献大成》。但是朱棣觉得书的内容太简略，故又下令重修，并特派太子少师姚广孝为监修。参加编修和誊写的有2000多人，到永乐六年（公元1408年）年底，全书完成。朱棣亲自写了序言，并命名为《永乐大典》。全书按韵目分列单字，按单字依次辑入与这个字有关的文史记载。为了编修这部书，除了采用当时皇家图书馆——文渊阁的藏书以外，还派人到各地采购了各类图书共七八千种。《永乐大典》全书包括目录、凡例共22937卷，分装为11095册，总字数约3.7亿。这部书收集自先秦至明初的大量书籍，许多佚文秘籍由于《永乐大典》得以流传。

明朝嘉靖、隆庆年间，依照永乐年缮写的正本又摹写了一份副本。明朝灭亡时，文渊阁被烧毁，《永乐大典》正本可能毁于此时。副本到清朝咸丰年间已逐渐散失，八国联军侵入北京后，焚毁了大部分，其余几乎全被劫走。1960年，中华书局将搜集到的730卷影印出版，1984年增补重印，共797卷。

清朝乾隆年间编成的《四库全书》是中国古代最大的一部丛书（丛书是把很多种书籍汇集在一起印行的书）。为什么叫《四库全书》呢？是因为中国古代把图书分成经、史、子、集四类，而在唐朝初年，皇家图书馆按上述四类分四个库藏书。《四库全书》对这四类书籍的包容量非常大，可称全书。所以这部书的命名是确切的。从乾隆三十七年（公元1772年）清高宗下诏征集图书起，十年期间共征集了各种书籍约33000种。书的总裁由三位皇子和于敏中担任，总纂官是纪昀。到乾隆四十六年（公元1781年）完成了第一部《四库全书》。接着又用了三年时间，抄录了三部。到乾隆五十二年（公元1787年），另外又抄出了三部。经过100多年，现在仅存四部了。

《四库全书》收录著作3500多种，共79000多卷，比《永乐大典》的卷数多出三倍半。对中国古代有关政治、经济、哲学和文学方面的文献起到了整理保存的作用。

72. What Kind of Books Are *Yongle Dadian* and *Siku Quanshu*?

Yongle Dadian (*Yongle Canon*) is a reference book of materials taken from various sources and compiled according to subjects for reference use. When it was finished in the 16th century, it was known as the biggest encyclopedia in the world for its rich content and vast collection. Even today, compared with the updated encyclopaedia of the world, it still wins first place as far as its contents and size are concerned.

In July 1403, Emperor Chengzu of the Ming Dynasty asked *Xie Jin*, a scholar of the Imperial Academy, to be in charge of the compiling of the book. When it was finished in December 1404, it was initially entitled *Wenxian Dacheng* (*A Vast Collection of Documents*). But the emperor was not satisfied with its brief content so he ordered it to be recompiled and sent the prince's tutor, Yao Guangxiao, to supervise the project. More than 2000 people were involved in the compilation. By the end of 1408, the whole book was finished, prefaced by the emperor himself and renamed as *Yongle Dadian*, in which Chinese characters were listed in order of their rhymes, and all relevant historical and literary documents were listed under each character. Apart from the collection of books of the Imperial Library, another seven to eight thousand books were bought from all parts of China for the compilation. The whole book, including contents and notes, were in 22937 volumes bound into 11095 booklets, covered 3.7 hundred million Chinese characters, and collected enormous materials from the Pre-Qin Period (before 221 B.C.) to the Ming Dynasty (1368—1644 A.D.). Many ancient works were collected in *Yongle Dadian* and were hence preserved. A transcript of the book was made during the reigns of Emperors Jiajing and Longqing of the Ming Dynasty. When the Ming Dynasty was overthrown, the Imperial Library was destroyed, and the original *Yongle Dadian* was burned. The transcript was partially lost during the reign of Emperor Xianfeng of the Qing Dynasty. When the aggressive troops of the Eight-power Allied Forces came to Beijing, much of the transcript was burnt, and almost all the rest was plundered. In 1960, a photo-offset copy in 730 volumes was published by Zhonghua Book Company. In 1984, an enlarged edition was reprinted in 797 volumes.

Siku Quanshu (*The Complete Collection of the Four Storerooms*) finished during the reign of Emperor Qianlong of the Qing Dynasty is the biggest book series in ancient Chinese history. It was so named because in the old times, Chinese books were divided into four categories: classics, history, philosophy and belles-letters. In the early Tang Dynasty (618—907 A.D.) the four categories of books in the Imperial Library were kept in storage in four separate storerooms. *Siku Quanshu* was such a comprehensive collection that it really deserved the title. Ever since 1772, when Emperor Gaozong of the Qing Dynasty issued an imperial edict to collect books, 33000 books of various kinds had been collected wthin ten years. In 1781, the initial book was finished. And three copies were made in the following three years. In 1787, another three copies were made. Now, over a hundred years later, there are only four copies existing.

Siku Quanshu includes a total of over 3500 kinds of books in over 79000 volumes, which is 3.5 times the size of *Yongle Dadian*. It has served as a good preservation and sorting of those ancient Chinese works concerning politics, economy, philosophy and literature.

73. 天安门是谁设计的?

天安门是明、清两代皇城的正门,最初叫承天门。承天门建成于明永乐十八年(公元1420年)。它的设计者是明代杰出的建筑师蒯祥。

蒯祥是江苏吴县(今江苏吴县)人,生于明洪武(公元1368~1398年)年间,木工出身。他后来成为吴县香山一带专门从事营造事业的香山帮的一代宗师。在明代营建皇宫的工作中,他功绩卓著,官至工部侍郎。

明太祖朱元璋在南京建都后,曾征召几十万工匠民伕,用了几十年的时间大规模营造南京。燕王朱棣用武力夺取皇位后迁都北京。在营造北京时,明成祖朱棣为标榜自己的正统,完全依照南京旧制建设皇城。除外朝三大殿之外,也按南京旧制在午门前设端门,端门前设承天门。此工程历时三年,于永乐十八年完成。

据说蒯祥年轻时曾参加过南京皇宫的营建工作。由于他技艺出众、经验丰富,被征召到北京,参加了北京皇城的建设工作,并被任命为"营缮所丞",负责工程的设计与施工。蒯祥有很高的艺术修养和审美能力,善于领会和贯彻皇帝的意图,因而很得皇帝的赏识,后来升任工部侍郎。

承天门后来曾遭到破坏,因此于成化元年(公元1465年)又进行了第二次营建。此时的蒯祥已是80多岁高龄,但他仍参加了这一工作,起了技术顾问的作用。为此明宪宗还接见了他。在天顺(公元1457~1464年)年间,蒯祥还参与了规划营建裕陵,即明英宗朱祁镇的陵墓。

清顺治八年(公元1651年),清世祖爱新觉罗·福临将承天门改名为天安门,这个名字一直沿用至今。

73. Who Was the Architect of Tian'anmen?

Tian'anmen (the Gate of Heavenly Peace), originaly known as Chengtianmen, was the front gateway to the imperial palace during the Ming and Qing dynasties. Chengtianmen was constructed in 1420, the 18th year of the reign of Emperor Yongle of the Ming Dynasty, by Kuai Xiang, an outstanding architect of that time.

Kuai Xiang was born in the reign of Emperor Hongwu (1368—1398 A.D.) of the Ming Dynasty in Wu County, Jiangsu Province. He began his livelihood as a carpenter and later became a great respected master of the Xiangshan Guild of Architects in Wu County. He was promoted to the minister of Public Works for his meritorious contribution in building the imperial palace for the Ming rulers.

Zhu Yuanzhang (Emperor Taizu) of the Ming Dynasty conscripted in dozens of years several hundred thousand workers and artisans in a large scale construction of the imperial city after he had made Nanjing the capital. When Zhu Di (Prince Yan) seized the throne by force and became the emperor, who was known as Emperor Chengzu of the Ming Dynasty with Yongle as his reign title, to display his legal status, he built his imperial palace in Beijing by fully adopting the imperial palace of Nanjing as the model. This was not only manifested in the building of the three main halls in the front court of the Forbidden City, but also in the construction of Chengtianmen to the south of Duanmen, which was likewise to the south of Wumen. It took three years to complete this project.

It is said that Kuai Xiang also participated in the construction of the Nanjing imperial palace. Owing to his superb skill and experience, he was summoned to Beijing and was appointed chief of the Construction Bureau in charge of both the designing and construction of the whole project. His high artistic attainments, aesthetic judgment and full comprehension of the emperor's intentions won him praise from the emperor and he was later promoted to minister of Public Works.

As Chengtianmen was destroyed later, it was rebuilt in 1465 (the first year of the reign of Emperor Chenghua of the Ming Dynasty). Kuai Xiang was then already over eighty. So he took part in the construction as a technical advisor. Emperor Xianzong of the Ming Dynasty granted him an audience for his service.

In 1651, Emperor Shizu of the Qing Dynasty, Aisin Gioro Fulin, changed the name of Chengtianmen to Tian'anmen, which has since been used till today.

74. 北京的四合院是何时兴建的?

四合院是北京传统的院落式住宅形式。这种独特的艺术建筑以其古朴、典雅著称于世。四合院是以正房、倒座和东、西厢房四面合围并用卡子墙连接起来的封闭式院落,整个建筑呈“□”形,因此称为四合院。四合院这种建筑形式已经有数百年的历史了。金代(公元1115~1234年)末年,中都城遭到严重破坏,残破不堪。到了元代(公元1271~1368年),在中都城东北另建新城,即元大都城。四合院这种建筑形式就是与元大都的兴建同时发展起来的。对中国古代劳动人民独创的这种住宅形式,意大利著名旅行家马可·波罗曾写道:“设计的精巧和美观,简直非语言所能描述。”

由于年代久远,元代所建四合院现在大多不复存在了。北京现存的四合院大都建于明、清和民国时期。

四合院在建筑的种类和规模上各不相同,但基本格局则是一致的。四合院的房屋是沿着纵向的轴线对称地建造的。朝南的四合院大门要建在东南角;朝北的四合院大门则开在西北角。这是因为中国古代用八卦代表八个方位,而以这两个方位为吉利。一所坐北朝南的四合院,走进大门,正对的是一面影壁(亦称照壁)。影壁可以起到隔断视线和美化庭院的作用,上边多饰有内容吉祥的石雕或砖雕,并以阴文刻上诗文或联句。再向左转即进入前院(或外院),前院只有朝北的几间房屋(或称倒座)。从前院穿过建在中轴线上的一座二道门即进入内院(或正院)。这里是四合院的主体建筑。房屋较前院的高大、宽敞、明亮。北面是一排正房,东、西两边建有厢房,三面的房屋以回廊相连。正房的两头又有耳房 ,正房的背后建有一排罩房,作为整个院落的尽头。四合院这种建筑形式十分适合中国北方冬、春季节多风的地区,而且院中可以种植花木,夏季搭上凉棚,自成天地。

四合院有大有小,有单院落的,也有多重院落的。四合院的规模和建筑的设计不仅因主人的经济地位不同而不同,更因主人的社会地位而异。中国古代是一个等级森严的封建社会,这一特征在四合院这种住宅建筑上也充分体现了出来。在清代,皇族中亲王、郡王的住宅称“王府”,其他皇族成员如贝子、贝勒等的住宅则称为“府”。“王府”的建筑规模较大,正房称为殿,殿顶以绿琉璃瓦覆盖,大门和墙为朱红色。而“府”在规模上要小于“王府”,正房不能称殿,上边也不能用琉璃瓦。除此之外,在房屋的间数、油饰彩画、台基高低、门钉多少上,“王府”和“府”也各有规定,不能逾制。至于一般人的住宅只能称作“宅”、“第”了,房顶和墙只能涂青灰色。另外,在四合院里房屋的使用上也体现着上下、尊卑之分。最好的正房为长辈居住,东、西厢房由晚辈儿孙居住。佣人则只能住在外院的倒座房里了。

现在北京城区保存完好的典型的四合院有些已被列入文物保护单位。有的四合院，如西城区的恭王府还对外开放,吸引了不少中外游客。

74. When Did Beijing's *Siheyuan* Begin to Be Constructed?

Siheyuan is the traditional courtyard-style residence of Beijing. This architectural style is world-famous for its unsophisticatedness and elegance as well as its unique artistic attainment. It is called *siheyuan* because the houses in it are constructed in such a way that *zhengfang* (the main house), *xiangfang* (the wing houses) and *daozuo* (house facing the main house) are connected with walls and that the whole complex creates an enclosed square courtyard. It has been several hundred years since this kind of architectural form took shape. In the late years of the Jin Dynasty (1115—1234 A.D.), Zhongdu (then the capital) suffered from severe damages and became desolate. The new capital city Dadu of the Yuan Dynasty (1271—1368 A.D.) was constructed to the northeast of Zhongdu and in the meantime *siheyuan*, a new style of residential houses, shaped and developed. The great Italian traveller, Marco Polo, once praised the ingenious and elegant design of this highly original house style created by ancient Chinese people as beyond description of any language.

Most of the *siheyuan* which were built during the Yuan Dynasty no longer exist because of old age. The existing ones are mostly from the Ming and Qing dynasties (1368—1911 A.D.) and the time of the Republic of China (1912—1949 A.D.).

The construction of *siheyuan* may vary in type and size but is identical in general pattern. The houses in a *siheyuan* are symmetrically built along a south-north axis. A *siheyuan* that faces the south has its entrance at the southeast corner while the entrance of one facing the north is at the northwest corner. This is in conformity with the ancient Chinese customs under which the eight diagrams were used to stand for the eight directions and the above two directions were considered the lucky ones. When entering a southerly *siheyuan*, one faces a *yingbi* (screen wall). *Yingbi* functions as a screen to protect the inner courtyard from public view and as a decorative element, on which auspicious stone or brick carvings as well as poems or couplets are engraved. Turning left, one will reach the front courtyard and see the house facing the north which is called *daozuo*. From another entrance on the axis one enters from the front courtyard into the main courtyard (or the inner courtyard) where the important buildings catch the eye. The houses in the main courtyard are taller than those in the front courtyard and the rooms are more spacious and bright. On the north side are the main house called *zhengfang* and on the east and west sides are the wing houses called *xiangfang*. The houses on the three sides are normally connected with a winding corridor. The main house on the north side is supported by two small rooms on both sides which are called *erfang* (ear rooms—flanking the principal rooms). *Zhaofang* (the back house) is built behind the main house and is at the rear of the whole complex. *Siheyuan* is an ideal house style in north China where it is windy in winter and spring and the complex creates a unique style of its own especially when different kinds of plants are grown in the courtyard and a mat shelter is put up to screen off the sunshine in summer.

Siheyuan may be big or small, or varied in the number of courtyards. In the construction of a *siheyuan* its magnitude and design were based not only on the owner's economic situation but also on his social status. Ancient China as a feudal society honoured strict hierarchical principles which found its expression also in the construction of *siheyuan*. During the Qing Dynasty the residences of the princes were called *wangfu* while those of other royal family members could only be called *fu*. *Wangfu* was of great magnitude. Its main house was called *dian* (hall), its roofs were covered with green glazed tiles and its gates and walls were painted red. *Fu* was normally smaller in size than *wangfu*, its main house could not be called *dian* and it was not roofed with glazed tiles. Apart from these there were also rules in connection with the number of rooms, decorative paintings, the height of the foundations as well as the number of decorative nails on the gate and all these allowed no breach. The residences for commoners were called *zhai* or *di* and the roofs and walls were of grey colour. The allotment of the houses in a *siheyuan* also called for separation of the old from the young and of master from servants. *Zhengfang* was for the elder generation while *xiangfang* for their children. The servants had no choice but to live in *daozuo* in the front courtyard.

So far some of the well-preserved model *siheyuan* in the urban district have been on the list of preserved cultural relics. Some *siheyuan*, like that of Prince Gong's, have been opened to the public and have attracted numerous tourists.

75. 浮屠和宝塔是不是一回事？中国不同类型的名塔有哪些？

中国的塔最初是随佛教传入中国而开始兴建的。梵文中塔的名称译作窣(sū)堵波，又译作浮图或浮屠。佛教中浮屠原是为藏置佛祖的舍利或遗物而建造的，后来演变成为佛教信徒顶礼膜拜的纪念性建筑。佛教传入中国以后，早期修建的寺庙是以塔为主体建造的。晋(公元265～420年)、唐(公元618～907年)以后，寺内专门建造了供奉佛像的大殿，塔逐渐退居次要地位，多建在大殿之后了。塔的形制早期受到印度影响，多为木制方形。隋、唐(公元581～907年)以后，多结合中国传统高层建筑的特点，由方形而发展为六角形、八角形或圆形；塔的内部也由实心改为有扶梯的高塔，既供奉佛像，又可以登高远眺。由于佛教徒用"七宝"(金、银、琉璃、砗磲、珍珠、玫瑰、玛瑙)装饰塔，所以塔又称"宝塔"。塔的层数多用单数，一般为七层。

除了佛教以外，中国的道教和传入中国的伊斯兰教也有建塔的习惯。还有一些地方，由官员或名士以振兴文风或镇压"邪物"为名建造的塔，这些与佛教就没有什么关系了。

按塔的建造材料分，有木塔、石塔、砖塔和铁塔等；按建造的形式来分，有楼阁式、密檐式和金刚宝座式，还有喇嘛塔。楼阁式塔的特点是层与层之间距离较大，有楼梯可以攀登，每层有门窗可供人们远眺。中国现存最大的楼阁式木塔是山西应县木塔，建于辽代清宁二年(公元1056年)，外观为5层，塔总高67.13米。密檐式塔的特点是塔身第一层比较高大，内供佛龛或佛像，其他各层距离较近，都是实心，没有门窗或设小假窗。中国现存最早的密檐式塔是河南登封县嵩岳寺塔，建于北魏正光元年(公元520年)，是15层砖塔，高约40米。而云南大理县崇圣寺三塔之一的千寻塔是16层密檐式砖塔，高59.6米。金刚宝座式塔的特点是，在一座较高的平台基座上，建造五座小塔，以供奉"金刚界五佛"。北京西直门外明代成化九年(公元1473年)修建的真觉寺塔，就是金刚宝座式。喇嘛塔是藏传佛教修建的塔，形式类似印度的窣堵波，塔身为圆形，状如覆钵。北京西城妙应寺(俗称白塔寺)的塔就是这类塔中较早的一座。元代至元八年(公元1271年)在来自邻邦尼泊尔的工匠阿尼哥参与设计与建造下，历时八年才建成。中国其他名塔还有湖北当阳县玉泉寺的铁塔，共13层，建于宋代嘉祐六年(公元1061年)；四川省峨嵋山报国寺14层铜塔，高7米，为明代所建；河南开封市祐国寺13层琉璃塔(因为用褐色琉璃砖，民间俗称"铁塔")等。

75. Do Stupa and Buddhist Pagoda Stand for the Same Thing? What Are the Well-known Pagodas of Different Styles in China?

The first pagodas were built along with the introduction of Buddhism into China from India. Pagoda was translated as *stupa* in Sanskrit. At first, stupas were built to lay Buddhist sarira and other things left behind by the Buddhas. As time passed on, they evolved into memorial buildings for devotees to prostrate themselves in worship. Buddhist temples came into China together with Buddhist doctrines. Pagodas were usually the dominant parts of the temples built in the very early period. From the Jin (265—420 A.D.) and the Tang(618—907 A.D.) dynasties on, however, big halls were built inside temples specially for consecrating Buddha figures, and gradually, pagodas became less important and were built behind big halls. Influenced by India, those early-built pagodas were mainly of quadrangular wood constructions. After the Sui and the Tang dynasties(581—907 A.D.), because the characteristics of traditional Chinese high-storeyed architecture were incorporated into the construction of pagodas, quadrangular pagodas gradually evolved into hexagonal, octagonal, or circular pagodas, and the solid inside was also replaced by staircases. With these changes, pagodas could not only serve as a place to consecrate Buddhist figures, but also provide a panoramic view with their height. Since the so-called "seven treasures" (gold, silver, colored glaze, agate, etc.) were used to decorate pagodas, pagodas were also called treasure pagodas. The storey of pagodas was usually odd-numbered, and in most cases, seven storeys.

Beside Buddhist, it was also the custom of Taoism and Islamism to build pagodas. Pagodas that were built under the pretext of promoting styles of writing or suppressing evils in some places can also be found. However, these pagodas have nothing to do with Buddhism.

According to building materials, pagodas can be classified into wooden pagodas, stone pagodas, brick pagodas and iron pagodas; according to architectural styles, attic, close-eaved, diamond-throne pagodas, and Lamaist pagodas. The characteristics of attic style pagodas include: excessive height of every storey, staircases for climbing up and down and windows on each storey for a panoramic view. The largest well-preserved wood-structure pagoda of attic style in China is the wooden pagoda in Ying County, Shanxi Province. This five-storey pagoda with a height of 67.13 meters was built in 1056 A.D. The characteristics of close-eaved style pagodas are that the first storey is rather high and large to enshrine the statues of Buddhas while the other storeys are short and solid with no windows, some with small fake ones. The earliest pagoda of this style in China now is the pagoda in Songyue Temple in Dengfeng County, Henan Province. The fifteen-storeyed brick pagoda of some 40 meters high was built in 520 A.D. Qianxun Pagoda, one of the three pagodas in Saint Temple in Dali County, Yunnan Province, is a 16-storeyed brick pagoda of close-eaved style with a height of 59.60 meters. The characteristic of diamond-throne pagodas is that five small pagodas were built on a fairly high terrace to enshrine the "Five Buddhas in Vairadhatu". The pagoda in Zhenjue Temple, west of Xizhimen of Beijing, is a diamond-throne pagoda built in 1473 in the Ming Dynasty. The Lamaist pagoda with a circular body looks like an Indian stupa. The White Pagoda in Miaoying Temple in Beijing is one of this kind. It took eight years to build it with the help of a Nepalese craftsman. Other well-known pagodas include the 13-storeyed iron pagoda in Yuquan Temple in Hubei Province built in A.D. 1062, the 14-storeyed bronze pagoda of 7 meters high in Baoguo Temple in Sichuan Province built in the Ming Dynasty, the 13-storeyed glazed pagoda in Youguo Temple in Kaifeng, Henan Province, etc.

76. 中国著名龙壁有多少?

中国是龙的故乡,龙不仅出现于各种建筑装饰和物品装饰上,而且还出现 了专门的巨形龙壁。较著名的龙壁如下:

襄樊99条巨龙壁。位于湖北省襄樊市襄阳城东南侧。壁为明襄藩王府的照壁,1436年建造。壁围用汉白玉石镶边,上刻神态各异、栩栩如生的99条纹龙,下衬以扬涛海水。

五台山89条石龙壁。位于山西五台县五台山龙泉寺前,是座牌坊式巨壁。寺前平台上四根雕龙巨柱后面,有一庞大的汉白玉巨壁,巨壁上85条飞龙各呈其态。龙围雕有各种鸟兽、花草,形成一幅天然的洁玉图画。据载,此壁成于1926年。五台山菩萨顶另有一座九龙壁。

大同九龙壁。位于山西省大同市城区东街。为中国最大龙壁,长45.5米,高8米,厚2米。9条金黄色巨龙合嵌于426块硕大的五彩琉璃构件上,龙与龙之间衬以水草山石图案,成一幅流云碧涛飞龙之景。此壁建于1598年,为中国现存最早的一座龙壁。

北京北海九龙壁。位于北海公园。建于1756年。壁系一仿木结构彩色琉璃砖照壁。该壁前后两面各雕9条飞龙,在9条大龙的周围又雕刻6条小飞龙,形成一个共计30条飞龙的琉璃砖建筑,壁体由424块琉璃砖构成,围衬雕以云水图案。

北京故宫九龙壁。位于故宫皇极门前两院夹峙间。壁同大同和北海九龙壁样式略同。单面九龙飞跃,有较高的艺术价值。

北京故宫保和殿九龙壁。位于故宫保和殿后。壁体斜放于保和殿后门外路阶正中。长16.57米,宽3.07米,厚1.7米,重20多吨。上刻浮雕飞跃九龙,瑞云、寿山、福海纹饰于龙周围。

陕西蒲城六龙壁。位于陕西省蒲城县文庙门前。建于1618年。高约5米,长约10米。正面塑“六龙飞舞图”,背面塑“龙狮舞蹈图”,造型生动。在六龙壁两边,各竖一石牌坊,石柱高耸壁上,称为“云冠”,使龙壁更显奇美壮观。

大同善化寺五龙壁。位于山西省大同善化寺西院。长19.9米,高7米,厚1.48米。宽大的壁面上浮雕5条四爪金龙,盘旋回绕,上下翻腾,形象活泼,制作精巧。

大同文庙五龙壁,位于山西省大同文庙门前。长28.5米,高5.7米,为砖雕壁体。壁面高浮雕5条团龙,直径各2.2米。在龙壁两旁分立的八字墙上,又砖雕两幅巨画。一幅为鲤鱼跃龙门;一幅为鲤鱼跃龙门后所变成龙的形象。

大同三龙壁。位于山西省大同市城西观音堂前,为观音堂门前琉璃照壁。壁为明代建筑。长12米,高6米,厚1.2米。两面分雕3条高达3米多的黄色琉璃巨龙(共6条)。

巨龙遨游在蔚蓝色天空中,下衬涌泉雕刻。

中国的巨形龙壁多为庭院照壁。始造于明代,精构于清代,绵延接续到近、现代。以山西大同最为集中,北京、五台山次之。龙壁以琉璃砖雕为最精彩,艺术价值最高;以汉白玉石体为最珍贵。这一庞大的艺术群,构成了中国雕刻艺术中的一朵奇葩。

76. How Many Famous Dragon Screens Are There in China?

China is the homeland of the dragon. Its image appears not only on various ornaments of architecture and articles, but also on huge dragon screens. The following are the most famous dragon screens.

The 99-dragon screen in Xiangfan, Hubei Province, is located to the southeast of the city of Xiangyang. It is the screen wall of a prince's mansion of the Ming Dynasty. Built in 1436, it is edged with white marble, with 99 dragons vividly romping in the sea in different postures.

The 89-dragon screen in Mount Wutai is located in front of the Dragon Spring Temple. It is a huge stone screen in the form of an archway. In front of the temple, there are four pillars with dragons carved on them. On a platform behind the pillars, there is a huge marble screen, on which 85 flying dragons are carved in different postures. There are also various birds, beasts, flowers and plants on the rim, forming a natural scenery in white. It is recorded that this screen was built in the year of 1926. There is also a 9-dragon screen on the top of Pusading of Mount Wutai.

The largest dragon screen in China is the 9-dragon one at East Avenue in the city of Datong, Shanxi Proince. It is 45.5 meters long, 8 meters high and 2 meters thick. On the background made of 426 pieces of glazed tiles, there are nine golden dragons. Between the dragons, there are designs of water, plants, mountains and stones, forming a scenery of flying dragons amongst flowing clouds and green waves. It was erected in 1598, and is the earliest dragon screen of all the existing ones in China.

The 9-dragon screen at Beihai Park in Beijing was erected in 1756. It is a screen wall built of 424 pieces of glazed tiles. On each side of the screen, there are nine flying dragons, with six little ones around them. Therefore, altogether the screen shows 30 dragons playing in the waves, which are carved at the edges.

The 9-dragon screen in the Palace Museum is located in front of the Gate of Imperial Zenith. It is similar to the ones in Datong and Beihai, but has nine flying dragons on one side only. It is of great artistic merit.

Another one in the Palace Museum is placed at the steps leading to the back gate of the Hall of Perfect Harmony. It is 16.57 meters long, 3.07 meters wide and 1.7 meters thick ,and weighs over 20 tons. It shows nine flying dragons edged with clouds, mountain of longevity and sea of happiness.

The 6-dragon screen of Shaanxi Province is located in front of Wen Temple in the County of Pucheng. It was erected in 1618. It is 8 meters high and 10 meters long. On the front of the screen, there is a carved picture of six flying dragons. On the back, there is a picture of a dragon dancing with a lion. There are two stone archways standing on both sides of this screen. High stone pillars called "cloud cap" make the dragon screen an even more magnificent sight.

The 5-dragon screen of Datong is located in the west yard of Shanhua Temple. It is 19.9 meters long, 7 meters high and 1.48 meters thick. On the wide screen, there are five four-claw dragons, winding and twisting, all in vivid postures.

There is another 5-dragon screen in Datong. It stands in front of the gate of Wen Temple. It is 28.5 meters long and 5.7 meters high, and is made of bricks. On the screen, there are carved five round dragons, with a diameter of 2.2 meters each. At the two sides of the screen, there are two walls in the shape of "八", on which there are two huge pictures. One is *A Carp Jumps Over the Dragon Gate*. The other is the image of a dragon that the carp turns into after jumping over the Dragon Gate.

The 3-dragon screen in Datong is located in front of the Temple of Guanyin. It is a glazed screen wall built in the Ming Dynasty. It is 12 meters long, 6 meters high and 1.2 meters thick. On each side, there carved three huge dragons of more than three meters in height. (Altogether there are six dragons.) The yellow glazed dragons are playing in the blue sky, with spring water carved at the bottom.

Most of the huge dragon screens in China are screen walls for courtyards. Dragon screens were first built in the Ming Dynasty, developed to a higher standard in the Qing Dynasty and continued into the modern times. They are mostly centered in Datong, Beijing and Mount Wutai. Those carved on glazed tiles are the most beautiful ones with the greatest artistic merits, while those carved on white marble are the most precious. This huge artistic group composed an exotic branch of the art of carving in China.

77. 华表象征着什么?

华表也叫华表柱,是中国古建筑中一种形象非常优美的建筑,常常设在桥梁、宫殿、城垣或陵墓等前面作为标志和装饰。

华表有着一段古老的历史演变过程。它在原始社会的后期就出现了。那时人们在交通要道竖立木柱,作为识别道路的标志,因此叫它"华表木"或"桓表",相当于现在的指路标;另外,也让人们在木柱上刻写意见,是统治者用来采纳民众意见的标志,因此又叫"诽谤木"。诽谤这个词在古代是指议论是非、指责过失,即现代的提意见,并不是指造谣污蔑。随着历史的发展,华表的作用和形式也有所改变和发展。秦朝(公元前 221 ~ 前 206 年)曾将它废除。汉代(公元前 206 ~ 公元 220 年)虽然予以恢复,但是讷谏的作用逐渐消失,而作为路标和装饰的作用逐渐增加。以后在帝王宫殿、陵墓、坛庙之前,常常采用这种标志性装饰;在大路通衢、关津渡口、桥头市井以及王公大臣及平民墓地等处都建立华表以作标志。为了更加坚固以长久保存,人们逐渐用石头代替了木头。到明清(公元 1368 ~ 1911 年)时期,华表已基本定型,为石制,下面是一个雕刻精细的须弥座,座上置八角形或圆形柱身,帝王用者刻升降盘龙,一般的或刻花纹或是素面。柱身上部贯以华版,顶上置圆盘,饰以珠串,圆盘上立石刻望天犼(hǒu)。天安门前后都有一对华表,为明朝永乐(公元 1403 ~ 1422 年)年间雕造。外面两个华表顶上的犼头向外,称之为"望君归",是希望帝王不要耽恋山水、废弃政事。后面的华表顶上的犼头向内,名为"望帝出",是希望帝王不要沉湎于纸醉金迷的宫廷生活,经常出来看望臣民。

在一些古画上,常常看到华表柱顶站立一个仙鹤之类的鸟,如宋代《清明上河图》、元代《卢沟运筏图》等。关于这鸟有一个传说:汉朝时一位名叫丁令威的辽东人,在灵虚山学仙,成道后化作仙鹤归来,落在城门华表柱上,有少年想射它,鹤飞起用人语说道:"有鸟有鸟丁令威,去家千年今始归;城郭如故人民非,何不学仙冢垒垒。"(见陶潜《搜神后记》)。画家们便把这一故事画在华表柱上了。

此外,还有用石柱作为纪念的。河北正定有一个北齐时期(公元 550 ~ 577 年)的义慈惠石柱,是为纪念在一次农民起义中大批死亡战士而建立的。这一石柱建于北齐太宁二年(公元 562 年),柱上有 3000 余字的颂文,记叙了战争的经过。柱下有一个巨大的莲瓣柱础,雕刻质朴有力。最为珍贵的是柱顶上刻有石屋三间,屋顶为单檐庑殿式,刻出屋脊、瓦陇、角梁、斗拱、柱子等结构,是研究唐代以前建筑的重要形象资料。

77. What Does *Huabiao* Signify?

Huabiao (ornamental pillar), also called *huabiaozhu*, is an exquisite structure in ancient Chinese architecture. It is mostly erected in front of bridges, palaces, city walls and tombs as symbols and ornaments.

Huabiao emerged in the late period of the primitive society and experienced a long historical evolution. At that time, people set up wooden posts at major crossroads as street signs and called them "*huabiao* wood" or "*huanbiao*". People could also write their criticisms on them. This was a symbol that shows the monarch's willingness to accept the views of the common people. Thus it was also called *feibangmu* (slander wood). The word *feibang*, translated as "slander" in English, just meant to put forward suggestions and recommendations at that time. It did not mean to defame as it does now. With the on-going of history, the function and form of *huabiao* gradually changed and developed. It was once abolished during the Qin Dynasty (221—206 B.C.), and though restored in the Han Dynasty (206 B.C.—220 A.D.), its role as "slander wood" decreased while the function as street signs and ornaments gradually increased. It was frequently used in front of imperial palaces, tombs and temples as symbolic architectural ornaments, and as signs on roads, at hubs and ferries and in front of bridges and tombs of both the nobility and populace. In order to make it more enduring, wood was gradually replaced by stone. When it came to the Ming and Qing dynasties (1368—1911 A.D.), *huabiao* had fallen into a basic pattern: stone-made, with an exquisitely-carved Xumi base and an eight-angled or a round post on it. For emperors, the surface of the post would be carved with flying dragons up and down, and for others, with ordinary designs or just plain-surfaced. A decorative board was installed across the upper part of the post and a round plate with chains of pearls was placed on the board. At the top of the plate there stood a stone mythological animal called *hou*. Both in front of and behind Tian'anmen were erected a pair of *huabiao* made during the Yongle Period (1403—1422 A.D.) of the Ming Dynasty. The *hou* on the pair in front of Tian'anmen, facing south, were called "*wangjungui*", meaning "awaiting the emperor's return". It was supposed that their duty was to watch over the emperor's behavior when he went on an inspection tour, and to summon him back to attend to state affairs rather than be infatuated with beautiful sceneries. The *hou* on the pair behind Tian'anmen, facing north towards the Fobidden City, were called "*wangjunchu*", meaning "awaiting the emperor's emergence", which were a symbol to remind the emperor to often go out of the palace to see his people, and not indulge in the dissipated court life.

We can often see in some ancient paintings a red-crowned crane standing at the top of the *huabiao*, such as *A Fair in the Qingming Festival* of the Song Dynasty and *Go Rafting on the Lugou Channel* of the Yuan Dynasty, etc. There is a legend about this crane: A man named Ding Lingwei in the Han Dynasty tried to become a celestial in the bier. When he succeeded, he turned himself into a red-crowned crane, and flew back home and stayed at the top of the *huabiao* in front of the city gate. A youngster tried to shoot the crane. The crane flew to the sky and spoke in human language: "There is a crane named Ding Lingwei who left home for a thousand years and now has come back. The city is still as it was before but the people have changed. Why not go to be a celestial and leave piles of tombs hehind?" Later this legend was painted on the *huabiao*.

Huabiao was also used for commemoration. In Hebei Province there is a *Yicihui* column built in the Nothern Qi Period (550—577 A.D.) in memory of those who died in a peasant uprising. On the column there is a three-thousand-word eulogy describing the whole process of the war. The column has a huge lotus base which was sculptured simply and firmly. Most preciously is that there are three single-eaved stone houses at the top of the column with carved ridges, tiles, beams, arches and pillars. They provide important image data for the study of the architecture before the Tang Dynasty.

78. 过去皇帝的坟墓为什么叫陵？北京除了十三陵以外还有别的明陵吗？

陵本来是大土山的意思，用陵来称呼皇帝的坟墓，主要是形容其坟高大，同时也借以显示帝王的威严。

现在人们把土葬的坟墓说成一个词，实际在古代，葬人的地方称为墓，而高起的土堆称为坟。据记载，商朝（约公元前 1600～约前 1100 年）和商以前墓地不建坟，也不种树。周朝（约公元前 1100～前 256 年）起，王侯贵族墓才修坟、种树，而坟的高度也依照爵位高低而定。到春秋（公元前 770～前 476 年）时，墓上修坟已逐渐流行，且有些诸侯的坟墓称为陵。据说以战国赵肃侯的坟称寿陵为最早。秦始皇为营建自己的坟墓征调民工数十万人，工程浩大。他的坟称为郦山。自汉朝起，历代皇帝（元朝按蒙古族传统风俗下葬，不建坟墓）的坟都称为陵。

北京的十三陵是旅游胜地，人们都知道那儿埋葬着明朝十三个皇帝，但是人们却很少注意到在北京西山附近（海淀区金山口）的景泰陵。为什么这座明朝皇陵和十三陵不连在一起呢？原来在明英宗正统十四年（公元 1449 年）七月，蒙古瓦剌部首领也先率领军队南犯，年轻的英宗在宦官王振怂恿下，贸然亲征，结果兵败被俘，史称"土木之变"。英宗的弟弟朱祁钰即帝位，称为代宗，年号定为景泰。1450 年，也先送回英宗，代宗把英宗安置在南宫，与外界隔绝。1457 年代宗病危，英宗在宦官曹吉祥等拥戴下，恢复帝位。代宗死后，英宗将他以亲王礼葬于金山口。后来英宗的儿子宪宗朱见深为他的叔父朱祁钰恢复了帝号，把他的坟墓扩建为皇陵，这就是景泰陵。

78. Why Are Imperial Tombs Called *Ling*? Is There Any Other Ming Tomb in Beijing Apart from the Thirteen Noted Ming Tombs?

Ling referred to big earth dunes before. The term was used to stand for imperial tombs for two reasons: first, to describe the size of the tombs; second, to show the dignity of feudal emperors.

Nowadays, people usually take *fenmu* (tomb) as one term to stand for the place where the dead is buried. Actually, in ancient times, the place where the dead was buried was called *fen* (grave), while the earth dune was called *mu*. It was recorded that during the Shang Dynasty (c.1600—C.1100 B.C.) and before, no *mu* was built and no trees were planted in graveyards (*fen*). It was not until the Zhou Dynasty (c. 1100—256 B.C.) that *mu* was built and trees were planted in the graveyards of those nobilities. At that time, the height of a *mu* depended on the social status possessed by the dead during his life time. During the Spring and Autumn Period (770—476 B.C.) the building of *mu* became popular and the tombs (*fenmu*) of some nobilities began to be called *ling* (mausoleums). It was said that the *fen* for a marquis of the State of Zhao was the first to be called *ling*. The first emperor of the Qin Dynasty once recruited several hundred thousand laborers to build the mausoleum for him, which was so big that it was called Mount Li. Since the Han Dynasty, all the imperial tombs have been called *ling*.

It is well known that in the area of the thirteen noted Ming Tombs in Beijing, a famous place for tourism today, thirteen emperors of the Ming Dynasty were buried. But, few people have noticed the Jingtai Mausoleum of the Ming Dynasty, which is just located near the Western Hills. Why is this mausoleum not located in the same place as the other thirteen? The story goes as follows. In the seventh moon of the fourteenth year of the reign of Emperor Yingzong of the Ming Dynasty (1449), Yexian, head of a Mongolian tribe, led his army southward in a fight against the Ming rule. Instigated by an eunuch named Wang Zhen, the young and inexperienced emperor Yingzong decided that he would personally lead his army to wage a counterattack. Without careful preparation, he was defeated and caught alive by the Mongolian troops. Then, his brother, known as Emperor Daizong, succeeded to the throne, with Jingtai as the title for his reign. One year later, Emperor Yingzong was sent back by Yexian, but was placed in the South Palace in isolation by Emperor Daizong. In the year 1457, Emperor Yingzong was restored to the throne when his brother, Emperor Daizong, was severely sick. When Emperor Daizong died, he was buried as a prince. Later, when the son of Emperor Yingzong succeeded to the throne, he resumed the reign title Jingtai for his uncle and rebuilt the tomb for him, which is the Jingtai Mausoleum.

79. 牌楼是什么？它有什么作用？

牌楼又叫牌坊，或者简称坊，是古建筑中常见的一种类型。它不仅自身具有高度的艺术价值，而且还把它所在的建筑组群衬托得更加雄伟壮观。

牌楼属于大门一类的建筑物。根据历史文献和考古遗址推断，大约在原始社会后期，人类聚居的村落和其他群体建筑的入口处，就已经有了简单的过门了。形状大概是在两旁竖立的柱子之上加一横木。在《诗经·阵风·衡门》上有"衡门之下，可以栖迟"的诗句。衡门可能就是这种形式的门。在中国北方的农村，有时还可以看到这种两柱加一横木的简单大门。后来，牌坊的作用从大门转为表彰忠臣孝子、节妇义女以及圣贤人物的纪念性建筑物。这要溯源到中国古代的乡里制度上去。《周礼·天官·小宰》记载，周朝（约公元前1100～前256年）以25户为一闾。春秋战国（公元前770～前221年）及秦汉（公元前221～公元220年），城市中有闾里制度，隋唐（公元581～907年）时称作里坊。城市中有许多里坊，每个里坊就好像一座四四方方的小城，坊四面开门或两面开门，叫作坊门。这时的里坊之门较早期的两柱横一木之门要讲究得多。文献记载：一个里坊之内，如果出了好人好事，便把他的事迹和名字写下来，贴在坊门上。汉唐时期的里坊之门多为木造，贴上之后很快便坏了。后来人们为了能更长久地保存，便改用砖石来修筑，把受表彰的人和事刻在坊上，于是成了一种专门旌表的牌坊。现在能看到的许多牌坊大多是明清（公元1368～1911年）时期的。还有一种名叫"乌头门"的，也是坊门的一种，汉代称作"阀阅"。据记载，古代仕宦人家大门外，常立二柱，在左曰阀，在右曰阅，用来榜贴功状。宋朝《营造法式》（成书于公元1091年）一书上也专门有乌头门做法的图说。

牌坊种类很多。从修建位置来看，有街巷道路牌楼、坛庙寺观牌楼、陵墓祠堂牌楼、桥梁津渡牌楼、风景园林牌楼等；从建筑材料上看，有木牌楼、砖牌楼、石牌楼、琉璃牌楼等；从结构造型上看，有柱子不出头的牌楼和柱子出头的冲天式牌楼；从间数上看，有一间二柱一楼、一间二柱三楼、三间四柱五楼等。

现存牌楼中坛庙寺观牌楼保存得最多。北京的天坛、地坛、日坛、月坛、社稷坛均有牌楼。山东泰山岱庙前的石坊和曲阜孔庙、孔林的石坊雕刻均极精美。北京昌平十三陵牌楼，是现存石牌楼中规模最大、年代最早的一个，为五间六柱十一楼的形式，全部用汉白玉石修造，石上雕刻麒麟、狮子、各式龙和海兽，并间以云气波涛，神态生动。十三陵石象生以北还有一座三门并列的石坊，称为龙凤门，为冲天式牌坊，有横坊而无楼，在门上置石刻火焰宝珠，是石坊中重要实物。桥梁津渡牌楼不仅作为桥梁津渡的标志，而且也美化了环境。如北京北海的堆云、积翠牌楼，颐和园谐趣园的知鱼桥牌坊等等。名山胜景中的牌坊,不仅作为风景区的入口,在进山之后,每到一个转折之处也都设牌坊。如泰山的岱宗坊、一天门、二天门等等。

79. What Is *Pailou*? What Is Its Function?

Pailou, also known as *paifang*, or simply called *fang* for short, is a common type of ancient architecture—a decorated archway. Being of high artistic value by itself, it also serves as a foil for the group of architecture it belongs to, making it a grander and more magnificent sight.

Pailou is the kind of building under the category of gates. According to historical records and archaeological relics, it was inferred that as early as the later period of the primitive society, there were already simple gates at the entrances to villages or dwellings where people inhabited. It was simply a transverse wood over two upright pillars. In *Shi Jing* (*The Book of Songs*), there were these lines: "Under the Heng Gate, one can stay and have a rest." The *Heng Gate* here might possibly refer to the kind of gateway with a simple structure. In the countryside of north China, you may still find this kind of simple gate sometimes. With the passage of time, the function of *paifang* changed from being a gateway to a kind of memorial archway in honor of loyal officials, dutiful sons, women of virtue and men of letters and sages. This practice can be traced back to the *xiangli* system in ancient China. As was recorded in *Zhou Li* (*Ritual of Zhou*), in the Zhou Dynasty (c. 1100—256 B.C.), every 25 households formed a *lü*. In the Spring and Autumn and the Warring States periods (770—221 B.C.), as well as in the Qin and Han dynasties (221 B.C.—220 A.D.), there was the *lüli* system in urban areas, which was called *lifang* in the Sui and Tang dynasties (581—907 A.D.). There were many *lifang* in the city. A *lifang* was just like a square town, with gates on four or two sides named *fang* gates. They were much more exquisite than the original ones. It was recorded that if there were good people and good deeds in a *lifang*, their names and deeds would be written down and posted up on the *fang* gate. As most of the *fang* gates were made of wood in the Han to Tang dynasties, the posters would not last long. In order to preserve them for a long time, people began to build the gates with bricks and carve the names and deeds on them, changing the *fang* gate into a kind of archway in recognition of people's good deeds. Most of the *paifang* we see today are from the Ming and Qing dynasties (1368—1911 A.D.).

There was also another kind of *fang* gate known as "black head" and it was called *fayue* in the Han Dynasty. As it was recorded, in ancient times, there used to be two pillars outside the gates of the residences of government officials. The one on the left was called *fa* while the one on the right was called *yue*. They were for the purpose of putting up the account of the officials' meritorious services. In the book *Yingzao Fashi* (*Rules of Architecture*) of the Song Dynasty, there was a diagram illustrating how to make a "black head".

There are a great variety of *pailou*. If classified by their location, there are *pailou* in front of alleys and lanes, temples and altars, tombs and ancestral halls, bridges and ferries, and gardens and other scenic spots. If classified by the kind of materials, there are wood, brick, stone and glazed ones. If classified by their structural styles, there are those with the pillars' ends buried in the horizontal part, and those with the pillars getting through it. If classified by the number of arches, there are ones with one arch, two pillars, and one roof; ones with one arch, two pillars, and three roofs; and ones with three arches, four pilars and five roofs, and so on.

Most of the *pailou* in existence are those in front of temples and altars. For example, those in the Temple of Heaven, the Altar to the Sun, the Altar to the Earth and the Altar to the Moon, as well as the Altar to the God of Land and Grain in Beiing. And those in Mount Tai and the Confucius Temple are all extremely exquisite. Among all these *pailou*, the earliest and largest is the one at the Ming Tombs in Beijing. It has five arches, six pillars and eleven roofs, all made of white marble, with vividly carved kylin, lions, dragons and sea animals amidst clouds and waves. To the north of the Stone Sculptures at the Ming Tombs, there is another stone *fang* with three archways. It is called the Gate of the Dragon and Phoenix. On the marble pillars, there are carved pearls over flames, which are the most common and important ornaments on a stone *fang*. *Pailou* built in front of bridges and ferries not only are a symbol, but also make the surroundings more beautiful, such as the ones known as "Pile of Clouds" and "Heap of Green" in Beihai park, as well as the one in the Summer Palace. *Pailou* in the scenic spots serve the purpose of showing the entrances, as well as indicating the turning places in the mountains, like Daizongfang, Yitianmen and Ertianmen in Mount Tai.

80. 中国古代人有哪些称谓?

在中国古代,许多人除了姓、名之外还往往有别的称谓。这些称谓中主要有字和号。

名和字一般都是由长辈给取的。屈原是中国古代伟大的爱国诗人。他的名是“平”,字是“原”。他在《离骚》中写到:“皇览揆余初度兮,肇锡余以嘉名:名余曰正则兮,字余曰灵均。”这里的“正则”和“灵均”即暗指他的名、字“平”和“原”。名通常是在出生后不久取的,而字则是在长大之后才取。据《礼记》记载:“男子二十,冠而字,……女子许嫁,笄而字。”就是说男子在20岁成人举行冠礼时取字;女子到出嫁年龄举行笄礼时取字。

在相互交往中,名用于自称。称对方的名是不礼貌的。在朋友、平辈人或平级同事之间,用字相称。用字来称呼下级或晚辈人则是一种特殊的礼遇了。

字一般由两个字组成,其意义和名有关并往往是对名的意义的解释或补充,因此字也称为“表字”。在名和字的关系上,有不同的情况。有时字与名同义。如三国时蜀国丞相诸葛亮,名亮,字孔明;唐宋八大家之一的曾巩,名巩,字子固。在这里“亮”与“明”、“巩”与“固”都是同义词。字有时也取名的反义。如唐代著名古文学家韩愈,名愈,字退之;宋代著名理学家朱熹,名熹,字元晦。这里“愈”和“退”、“熹”和“晦”则意义相反。有些人的字是名的意义的引申。如唐代大诗人白居易,名居易,字乐天。因为一个人只有取“乐天”的生活态度大概才能“居易”吧。还有的人的字是对名的意义的解释。被尊为诗圣的唐代诗人杜甫,名甫,字子美。据《说文解字》,“甫者,男子之美称也。”因此,“子美”实际上是对杜甫的名“甫”的注解。

号不同于名和字。号是自己为自己取的。另外,一个人常常有不止一个号。号一般不用于相互称呼,而是多用于诗词书画的署名。号常表达一个人的志趣情操。宋代散文家欧阳修晚年曾自号“六一居士”,意为:“一万卷书、一千卷金石古文、一张琴、一局棋、一壶酒加上自己一老翁。”现代著名画家齐白石擅长篆刻,他曾以“三百石富翁”作为自己的别号之一。也有的人以自己的住地为自己取号。晋代的陶渊明,后人亦称他为“五柳先生”,因为在他的《五柳先生传》中有:“宅边有五柳,因以为号焉。”

除了字、号之外,古代一些名人还有一些别称流传于世。一种是称以官职。如书圣王羲之曾任右军将军,后人就称他为王右军。另一种是称以谥号。南宋爱国将领岳飞死后被谥为武穆,因此后人也称他为岳武穆。

古代人取字、号的习俗一直延续到解放前。现在取字和号的人已经很少了,只是一些文人、书画家还保留着这种习俗。

80. What Forms of Address Did Ancient Chinese Have?

In ancient China many people had other forms of address beside *xing* (surname) and *ming* (given name). *Zi* (name taken at the age of twenty) and *hao* (literary name) were the main ones.

A person's *ming* and *zi* were normally given by his or her elders. Qu Yuan, a great patriotic poet of ancient China, for example, was given "Ping" as his *ming* and "Yuan" as his *zi*. He wrote in his famous *Lisao* (a poetical work): "My father, having scrutinized me at my birth and consulted the oracle, granted me fair names: Zhengze being the *ming* and Lingjun the *zi*." "Zhengze" and "Lingjun" here imply respectively "Ping" and "Yuan", Qu's *ming* and *zi*. As a rule, *ming* was given shortly after one's birth, while *zi* was given only when one came of age. According to *Li Ji* (*The book of Rites*), a male was granted a *zi* at the age of twenty when he was capped at a ceremony, while a female was granted a *zi* at the time when she began to wear a pin to hold her hair, which was an indication of her coming of marriageable age.

Ming was used when one called oneself at social intercourse, and it was considered a breach of etiquette to address other people by *ming*. *Zi* was used by one's friends, people of the same generation or colleagues at the same level. It was regarded as a special favour to be called by *zi* by one's elders or superiors.

Zi, which was in normal cases composed of two characters, was related to *ming* in meaning and served as an explanation of or a complement to *ming*. The meanings of *ming* and *zi* might vary in the following ways. Firstly, *ming* and *zi* meant the same. For example, Zhuge Liang, prime minister of the Kingdom of Shu during the Three Kingdoms Period (220—280 A.D.), had "Liang" (bright) as *ming* and "Kongming" (bright) as *zi*; Zeng Gong, one of the well-known men of letters of the Song Dynasty (960—1279 A.D.), had "Gong" (solid) as *ming* and "Zigu" (solid) as *zi*. In the above two cases, "Liang" and "Ming", "Gong" and "Gu" are two pairs of synonyms. Secondly, *zi* was contrary in meaning to *ming*. Examples could be found in the following persons. Han Yu of the Tang Dynasty (618—907 A.D.) was a famous classical literary man. His *ming* was "Yu" (excel) and his *zi* was "Tuizhi" (retreat); Zhu Xi, a famous Neo-Confucian scholar of the Song Dynasty, had "Xi" (bright) as *ming* and "Yuanhui" (dark) as *zi*. Here "Yu" and "Tuizhi", "Xi" and "Yuanhui" are two pairs of antonyms. Thirdly, *zi* had the extended meaning from *ming*. The great poet of the Tang Dynasty Bai Juyi was given "Letian" as *zi*. Here his *zi* was chosen out of the logic that one could not have an easy life (*juyi*) unless he had an optimistic (*letian*) attitude. Fourthly, some people's *zi* served as an explanation of *ming*. Du Fu of the Tang Dynasty was honoured with the title of poet-sage. His *zi* was "Zimei" (handsome man). "Fu" means a handsome man according to *Shuo Wen Jie Zi* (*Explanation and Study of Principles of Composition of Characters*).

Hao was different from both *ming* and *zi*. *Hao* was chosen by oneself rather than by others. A person often had more than one *hao*. *Hao* was not used to address one another but as signature in one's poetic and artistic works. *Hao* usually revealed one's aspirations and moral values. Ouyang Xiu, a great writer of the Song Dynasty, named himself "Liu Yi Jushi" (six-one retired schodar) in his later years, which meant "an old man (one) who amuses himself with one ten-thousand volumes of books, one thousand volumes of ancient bronze and stone inscriptions, one *qin* (a musical instrument), one game of chess and one pot of wine". Qi Baishi, a great modern master of art who also excelled in stone seal carving, had many *hao*, one of which was "Sanbai Shi Fuweng" (a rich old man possessing three hundred pieces of precious stones). There were also people who chose *hao* for themselves out of inspiration from the places where they lived. For instance, Tao Yuanming of the Jin Dynasty (265—420 A.D.) was also known as "Wu Liu Xiansheng" (Mr. Five Willows). The origin of his *hao* could be found in his autobiography, which read: "Around my house there are five willow trees, hence my *hao*."

Apart from *zi* and *hao*, some noted Chinese of ancient times had other forms of address which were handed down to later generations. A person could be known to people by his official title. For instance, Wang Xizhi, the sage of calligraphy, who once held the post of *youjun jiangjun* (general of the right wing forces), was also known as Wang Youjun in later times. A person might as well be called by his posthumous title. Yue Fei, a patriotic general of the Southern Song Dynasty, was such a case. He was also known as Yue Wumu, "Wumu" being his posthumous title.

The practice of having other forms of address such as *zi* and *hao* in addition to *ming* had existed until the founding of the People's Republic of China (1949). Indeed some people today still have *zi* and *hao*, but such practice only remains in the literary and art circles.

81. 有关妻子的称谓有多少?

中国是个有着几千年文化的国家,语言丰富、地域辽阔,光是妻子的称谓就有很多种。下面我们简单介绍一下。

皇后:皇帝的妻子。

梓童:是皇帝对皇后的称呼。

夫人:古代诸侯的妻子才称为夫人;明清(公元1368~1911年)时候一、二品官的妻子封为夫人;近代和现代则用来称呼一般人的妻子;现在一般用于外交场合,有时也戏称自己朋友或者同事的妻子。

拙荆:是古代男人对自己妻子的谦称,现在很少用。

糟糠:糟糠之妻,形容贫穷时共患难的妻子。

内人:这是过去在别人面前对自己妻子的称呼,书面语也称"内子"、"内助"。尊称别人的妻子往往在"内助"前加上一个"贤"字,成为"贤内助",现在还经常使用这个词。

内掌柜的:过去有称男人为"掌柜的",妻子为"内掌柜的",后来恭维别人的妻子时也这样称呼。

太太:过去一般人称官吏的妻子为"太太"。有权势的富人对人也称自己的妻子为"太太"。

浑家:"浑家"也是丈夫对妻子的称呼,多见于早期白话小说。

妻子:当妻子的"子"读第三声时,妻子指的是妻子和儿女,早期的话中还有"妻小"的称呼;只有在"子"读轻声时,妻子才不包括儿女。妻子也称"妻室",或单称"妻"。

爱人:既可指妻子,也可指丈夫,现在普遍使用。

老伴儿:指老年夫妇的一方,一般多指女方。

从以上粗略介绍中可以看出,古代、过去和现在,由于时代不同,对妻子的称呼也不大相同。其实,就地方来讲,东西南北中对妻子的称呼也不一样。比如:

娘子:有些地方把妻子称为"娘子",还有的地方称为"婆娘"。

堂客:江南一些地方把妻子称为"堂客"。

媳妇儿:这种称法在河南农村最普遍,但在称平辈或晚辈亲属的妻子时,前边还得加上平辈或晚辈的称呼。如"王三媳妇"。

老婆:丈夫对妻子的这种称呼,过去在北方广大城乡尤其是乡村最普遍,现在南方年轻人特别喜欢这种称呼。这种称法多用于口头语言,往往再加上人称代词。

"家里"、"家里的"、"屋里人"、"做饭的",都是地方方言中对妻子的称呼。

81. How Many Forms of Address for a Wife Are There in Chinese?

China is a country with a civilization of long standing, a vast territory and a rich language. There are many forms of address for a wife. Here is a brief introduction.

Huanghou was used to address an empress.

Zitong was used by the emperor to address his empress.

Furen referred to the wives of the dukes and princes. In the Ming and Qing dynasties (1368—1911 A.D.), wives of those officials who held the first two senior ranks were honored by the title of *furen* . In modern times, it can also be used to refer to the wives of the common people, but now it is most commonly used in diplomatic communities. Sometimes, it is also used to refer to the wives of one's friends or colleagues in a casual atmosphere.

Zhuojing was a modest term referring to one's wife in ancient times. It is seldom used nowadays.

Zaokang refers to one's wife, espacially one who has shared his hard lot.

neiren was used by a husband to refer to his wife before his friends and colleagues. *Neizi* and *Neizhu* were also used in the written language. *Xianneizhu* was a polite term to refer to other people's wives. This term is still used today.

Neizhangguide was used to refer to the wife since the husband was called *zhangguide* in the past. It has become a flattery term for other people's wives.

Taitai was used by the common people in the old times to address the wives of governmental officials. Some rich men holding important positions also called their own wives *taitai* .

Hunjia was also a form used by the husbands to address their wives. It usually appeared in novels written in the vernacular in the old time.

Qizi includes both one's wife and children when *zi* is stressed and pronunced in the third tone. *Qixiao* was another term in old times. Only when *zi* is read in the neutral tone does *qizi* refer to the wife alone. *Qizi* can also be called *qishi* or simply *qi* .

Airen refers to either the husband or the wife. It is very commonly used nowadays.

Laobanr is used by old couples to address each other, but it is in most cases used to refer to the woman.

One may find from the brief introduction above that the forms of address for a wife have changed with the time. Actually, the forms of address vary from place to place. For example:

Niangzi in some places is used to call one's wife, while in other places the wife is called *poniang*.

Tangke is the form of address used in south China.

Xifur is most commonly used in the countryside of Henan Province. But when one addresses the wife of a man of his own generation or the wife of one's younger relatives, he should add the husband's name before it and call her "so-and-so's *xifur*".

Laopo is used by the husband to address his wife. It used to be the most popular address in north China, especialy in the countryside. However, it has become a popular address used among young people in south China, too. It is usually used in oral speech.

Jiali, *jialide*, *wulide* and *zuofande* are all forms of address for a wife in some local dialects.

82. 姓和氏一样吗?

中国汉族人的姓在古代是分为姓和氏的。姓产生在前,氏产生于后。姓的产生可以追溯到母系氏族社会。由于同一母系的后代不能通婚,为了区分不同的婚姻集团,便产生了姓。中国一些最古老的姓,在构字上大都有女字旁,如:姜、姬、姚、嬴、妫、姒等。这正是母系社会在姓上的遗迹。还有一些姓与动物有关,如:马、牛、鹿、熊、龙等,这反映了在原始社会中先民的图腾崇拜。

氏的产生要晚一些。由于人口的不断增加,同姓者越来越多,同一氏族往往分成若干支,散居在各地。为了表示区别,又产生了氏。氏的来源有很多种。主要有:以所封的国号或所封的地名为氏,如:周、夏、殷、齐、鲁、楚、赵、屈、解等;以先人的爵号或谥号为氏,如:王、侯、武、文、闵、穆等;以职业为氏,如:屠、陶、卜、巫、贾等。除此之外,还有以居住的地方为氏的,如:东郭、南郭、西门、柳下、柳、李等。

姓和氏是有区别的。除产生的时间先后不同之外,姓表示血统,氏则表示封地、职业等;姓是用来区别婚姻,而氏则表示社会地位。但是从秦代以后,姓和氏逐渐合而为一了。它们的区别也变得毫无意义了,从此姓代替了姓氏。

中国历史上就是一个多民族的国家,在长期的历史发展中,汉族和其他少数民族不断融合。这种融合在姓上也有所表现。如宇文、尉迟、慕容、贺兰等姓就是从少数民族的称呼转化而来的。有些少数民族也改用汉姓。如北魏孝文帝为推行汉化,命令鲜卑人改姓,皇族拓跋氏就改姓元。因此,今天同是姓元的人可能有着不同的祖先。

中国过去有一本为儿童识字用的通俗课本,叫《百家姓》,是宋代人编写的。因为宋代的皇帝姓赵,所以这本书以赵字开头。这本书虽叫百家姓,但所收的姓却不止 100 个,而且中国人的姓也远远超过 100 个。据统计,中国人的姓的总数超过 8000。但是最常见的姓只有 100 多个。这 100 多个姓中有 19 个最为常见。这 19 个姓就是:李、王、张、刘、陈、杨、赵、黄、周、吴、徐、孙、胡、朱、高、林、何、郭、马。

82. Does *Xing* and *Shi* Mean the Same?

Talking about the Han people's *xing* (surname) in ancient China, one should note the difference between *xing* and *shi*. The origin of *xing*, prior to that of *shi*, dated back to the matrilineal society. As marriage was forbidden between offsprings of the same matrilineal clan, *xing* came into use to differentiate one matrilineal clan from another for intermarriage. If we examine the composition of Chinese characters, we will find that the radical 女 (female) is used in some of the most ancient Chinese *xing*, e.g. 姜 (Jiang), 姚 (Yao), 姬 (Ji), 嬴 (Ying), 妫 (Gui), 姒 (Si), etc., which is a trace of the matrilineal society. Names of some animals such as *ma* (horse), *niu* (cattle), *lu* (deer) *xiong* (bear), and *long* (dragon) are also taken as *xing*, which reveals the totem worship of the people of the primitive society.

Shi was adopted sometime later. As the population grew, more and more people shared the same *xing* and one matrilineal clan was prone to be subdivided into several branches which lived apart from one another. This resulted in the use of *shi* which served to make distinctions between the different branches. *Shi* had varied origins, which stemmed mainly from: reign titles or place names of fiefs, e.g. Zhou, Xia, Yin, Qi, Lu, Chu, Zhao, Qu, Xie, etc.; peerage or posthumous titles of ancestors, e.g. Wang, Hou, Wu, Wen, Min, Mu, etc.; occupations, e.g. Tu (butcher), Tao (potter), Bu (fortune teller), Wu (wizard), Gu (merchant), etc.; and names of places where people used to live, e.g. Dongguo, Nanguo, Ximen, Liuxia, Liu, Li and so on.

The difference between *xing* and *shi* lay not only in the chronological order but also in the fact that *xing* showed the blood relationship by which marriages were arranged while *shi* indicated fiefs or professions which manifested people's social status. However, *xing* and *shi* gradually merged into one after the Qin Dynasty (221—206 B.C.) and their difference became meaningless. *Xing* alone has been used since then.

China has been a multi-racial country, and the merger of the Han people with other ethnic minorities has been a constant occurence in the long historical development. This merger found its expression in Chinese *xing* as well. For example, such *xing* as Yuwen, Yuchi, Murong and Helan, were taken from those of the minority nationalities. Some ethnic minorities also adopted *xing* from the Han people. Emperor Xiaowen of the Northern Wei (386—534 A.D.) once decreed that the Xianbei people should take the Han people's *xing* as part of his drive to push forward the Han culture. So people of the imperial family changed their *xing* from Tuoba to Yuan. Naturally people who share the same surname Yuan today might have descended from different forefathers.

There used to be a popular textbook for children to learn characters, which was entitled *Bai Jia Xing* (*A Hundred Chinese Surnames*). The book was written in the Song Dynasty (960—1279 A.D.), in which Zhao came first on the list as the surname of the emperors of the Song Dynasty was Zhao. Although the book is entitled *A Hundred Chinese Surnames*, the surnames listed in it are more than one hundred, and the total number of Chinese surnames well exceeds that number. According to statistics, the total number of Chinese surnames is more than 8000, of which only more than 100 are commonly used. 19 out of those 100 are the most common ones, and those who are surnamed one of these 19 constitute half of the Chinese population. These 19 surnames are: Li, Wang, Zhang, Liu, Chen, Yang, Zhao, Huang, Zhou, Wu, Xu, Sun, Hu, Zhu, Gao, Lin, He, Guo and Ma.

83. 避讳是怎么回事?

汉语里有一句谚语,是"只许州官放火,不许百姓点灯。"这句谚语是怎么来的呢?原来,宋朝(公元 960 ~ 1279 年)有一个州官,名叫田登。为了显示自己的尊严,他禁止人们说"登"字,也不许人们说与"登"同音的字。过灯节时,按例要放灯三日。为避与"登"同音的"灯"字,他叫有关的官吏在告示上写"本州依例放火三日"。因此出了大笑话并从此有了这句谚语。

这个故事就是有关避讳的一个例子。所谓"讳"就是古代帝王、圣人、长官及尊长的名字。避讳就是为了表示对这些人的尊敬,要设法避免直接说出或写出他们的名字。中国许多寺庙所供的观音菩萨,最初译为"观世音"。在唐代因为要避唐太宗李世民的"世"字讳,改为观音。

避讳制度早在春秋时期(公元前 770 ~ 前 476 年)就出现了,在秦代(公元前 221 ~ 前 206 年)正式形成,到了唐、宋时期(公元 618 ~ 1279 年)避讳之风大为盛行。避讳制度一直沿袭到清(公元 1644 ~ 1911 年)末,到辛亥革命(公元 1911 年)时才被废除。避讳是中国封建社会一种特殊的文化现象,是封建社会高低、贵贱、尊卑不可逾越的等级制度的反映。

避讳主要有"国讳"和"家讳"。国讳是指避皇帝及其父祖的名讳;家讳是指避父母及祖父母的名讳。此外还有"圣讳"和"宪讳"。圣讳是指避古代圣人如孔子、孟子、黄帝等的名讳;宪讳是指下级官员要避上级官员的名讳。

避讳在书写形式上主要有三种:即改字法、空字法和缺笔法。改字法是一种常用的方法,就是把帝王或尊长等的名讳用其他字来代替。例如,中国著名的古代神话"嫦娥奔月"中的嫦娥最初称"姮娥",到了汉代,为了避汉文帝刘恒的名讳,改"姮娥"为"嫦娥"。秦始皇姓嬴名政,为避其名讳,在秦代"正月"曾改为"端月"。空字法就是把应避讳的字空缺不写,或作"某"字,或作□,或直写为"讳"。中国第一部字书,东汉许慎所著的《说文解字》为避光武帝刘秀的"秀"字,在"秀"字处不写"秀"字,空一格,也没作任何解释,只写"上讳"。缺笔法大约起自唐代,就是把应避讳的字少写一笔。据宋代洪迈在《容斋随笔》卷三中记载:后蜀国君孟昶(公元 919 ~ 965 年)所刻《石九经》,其中渊、世、民三个字,因为避唐高祖、唐太宗讳,都写成缺笔字。

在中国封建时代,避讳不仅被认为是天经地义的事情,而且还有各种法律规定。若有违反,则被认为是大逆不道,要受到惩罚,而且不少人还为此送了命。

为了避讳而改字、空字或缺笔,造成了古籍文字上的混乱。尤其是人名、人姓、谥号、官名、地名、年号、书名等因避讳而更改,扰乱了历史事实,使后人在阅读古籍时遇到了极大的不便。但另一方面，通过对历代避讳的研究，不仅可以恢复历史的原貌，而且可以推断古书的著作年代，发现其中的差错，也是鉴定古籍真伪的一种重要手段。而研究避讳的学问也成了一门称为避讳学的学科。

83. What Is *Bihui*?

There is a saying in Chinese which goes like this: "The magistrates are free to set fire, while the common people are forbidden even to light a lantern." There is a story behind this saying, which goes back to the Song Dynasty (960—1279 A.D.). A magistrate named Tian Deng made it a taboo to say the word *deng* or its homonyms to show his dignity. At the time of the Lantern Festival, lanterns were lit for three successive days as a usual custom. In order to avoid using the word *deng* (lantern), a homonym of his name, he instructed the official concerned to use the word *fanghuo* (to set fire) instead of *fangdeng* (to light a lantern) in the official notice. Contrary to his wish, he made a fool of himself and hence came the saying.

The above story is an example about *bihui*. *Hui* referred to the names of ancient emperors, sages, one's superiors and elders. *Bihui* meant that one should avoid mentioning those names either in speech or in writing so as to show respect to them. Avalokitesvara, a bodhisattva, was first known in China as Guanshiyin. In the Tang Dynasty (618—960 A.D.), *shi* had to be avoided since Emperor Taizong had the word *shi* in his name Li Shimin and thus Guanshiyin became Guanyin.

It is believed that *bihui* originated in the Spring and Autumn Period (770—476 B.C.), took shape in the Qin Dynasty (221—206 B.C.) and was in full vogue in the Tang and Song dynasties (618—1279 A.D.). It existed till the end of the Qing Dynasty (1644—1911 A.D.) and was officially abolished only after the 1911 revolution. *Bihui* was a special cultural phenomenon of China's feudal society and a reflection of the hierarchical principle under which people's status was rigidly stratified.

There were mainly two kinds of *bihui*, namely *guohui* and *jiahui*. *Guohui* was one that concerned emperors and their forefathers while *jiahui* concerned that of one's parents and grandparents. Besides there were *shenghui* and *xianhui*. The former referred to evasion of using the names of such sages as Confucius, Mencius, the Yellow Emperor, etc. While the latter referred to evasion of using names of one's superiors.

In writing, *bihui* was applied mainly in three different ways. The first was to use another character to replace the one to be avoided. For instance, Chang'e, the moon goddess in the well-known legend *Chang'e Flew to the Moon*, was first known as Heng'e. In the Han Dynasty (206 B.C.—220 A.D.), her name was changed to Chang'e because the name of Emperor Wen of the Han Dynasty was Liu Heng and those names with *heng* had to be avoided. The first emperor of the Qin Dynasty was named Ying Zheng. For the same reason, *Duanyue* came into used in replacement of *Zhengyue* to stand for the first lunar month. The second way was either to leave a blank space for the character to be avoided, or to put the character *mou* (a certain character), or use a square block like □, or straightforwardly write the character *hui* in place of the character to be avoided. For instance, in *Shuo Wen Jie Zi*, the first book on Chinese characters written in the Han Dynasty, *shanghui* was written in place where the character *xiu* should be given and no explanation was rendered to *xiu*, as *xiu* happened to be the name of Emperor Guangwu, whose name was Liu Xiu. The third way was to omit one particular stroke in writing the character. Such application started from the Tang Dynasty. According to a book of the Song Dynasty, a stone tablet of an article had the characters *yuan*, *shi* and *min* one stroke omitted became of the names of the emperors of the Tang Dynasty.

In China's feudal society *bihui*, was not only regarded as something perfectly right but also written into various laws and regulations. Violation of such rules was then considered the worst offence and would be punished accordingly. The most unfortunate people even lost their lives.

As a result of *bihui*, great confusion was caused in the use of characters in classical writings. The changes that resulted from *bihui* in people's names, surnames, posthumous titles, official titles, place names, reign titles and book titles confused some historical events and caused great inconveniences to people when reading ancient books. However, the study of *bihui* of different dynasties not only helps return history its original feature but also helps correctly infer the time when these ancient books were written, and find revelant mistakes, which serves as an important means to determine the authenticity of ancient books. The study of *bihui* has long become a special branch of learning known as *bihuixue*.

84. 中国古代有哪些年龄称谓?

中国古代对不同的年龄段都有一定的称谓。这些称谓有些一直沿用至今。如常常把30岁、60岁称为“而立之年”和“花甲之年”。这些称谓各有来历。有些是根据不同年龄的外在特征而命名,有些是由因袭古人之言而逐渐形成了固定的称谓。下边是一些常见的年龄称谓。

一个人的童年时代常用“总角”或“垂髫”来表示。总角和垂髫是古代儿童特有的发式,因此用它们代表童年。

“成童”是指长到一定年龄的儿童。对成童的具体年龄有不同的说法。一般认为成童是15岁以上的儿童,也有认为是8岁以上的。成童也常用“束发”代替。因为到一定年龄的男童要把头发梳成一个髻,以此作为成童的标志。

“及笄”代表女子已成年。古代女子15岁即到了可以出嫁的年龄,这时要把头发簪起,故称为及笄。

古代男子20岁称“弱冠”。男子20岁成年,要举行冠礼,戴上成年人戴的帽子。但由于还不到壮年,故称为弱冠。

30岁、40岁、50岁通常也称“而立”、“不惑”和“天命”。这些称谓出自《论语·为政》:“吾十有五而志于学,三十而立,四十而不惑,五十而知天命,六十而耳顺,七十而从心所欲,不逾矩。”50岁也常称为“半百”。

“花甲”常用来代表60岁。中国古代用干、支记年,以60年为一轮,如:甲子年出生的人,60岁时又遇上甲子年,因此用花甲来表示60岁。

70岁称为“古稀”。唐代大诗人杜甫的《曲江》诗中有“酒债寻常行处有,人生七十古来稀”。后人即用“古稀”表示70岁。

对80、90岁的老人常称“耄耋”。耄耋两字都意为老,而且都有“老”字作偏旁。老字在甲骨文中是拄杖的长发老人的象形。

对百岁老人的称谓是“期颐”。据《礼记》:“百年曰期、颐”。期意为已到百年,颐是养的意思,后来把期颐放在一起作为百岁代称。

至今,中国人还习惯用“而立”、“不惑”、“天命”、“花甲”、“古稀”、“耄耋”等这些表示年龄的词语。

84. What Were the Special Expressions Used to Name Different Age Periods for People in Ancient China?

Some special expressions were used beside numerals to stand for different age periods in ancient China, and some of them are still used today. For instance, *erli zhi nian* and *huajia zhi nian* are phrases respectively for thirty and sixty years of age. Usually there are stories behind these expressions. Some are descriptions of the outward appearance of people at a particular age while others are derived from sayings of the ancients. The following are some of the commonly seen expressions.

Zongjiao, or *chuitiao*, stood for childhood as it was a special hair style for children in ancient times.

Chengtong referred to children at a certain age. There were different arguments about the exact age of *chengtong*. Most people believed that *chengtong* were children of fifteen years old or over. But other people thought they were eight years of age or older. *Chengtong* was also termed *shufa*, which meant that the hair was fixed into a bun on the head.

Jiji represented a girl's coming of age. The marriageable age for a girl was fifteen in ancient times and at this age girls began to use a hairpin to clasp their hair. Thus the word *jiji* came into use.

Ruoguan was for a man of twenty years of age. A twenty-year-old man was considered an adult in ancient times and a ceremony was held to have an adult's hat put on his head.

Erli, *buhuo*, and *tianming* are respectively for thirty, forty and fifty years of age. These expressions all came from sayings of Confucius, who said: "At fifteen I set my heart upon learning. At thirty I took my stand (*erli*). At forty I came to be free from doubts (*buhuo*). At fifty I knew the will of Heaven (*tianming*). At sixty I was ready to listen to it. At seventy I could follow my heart's desire without violating the regulations." Age fifty is also known as *banbai* (half a hundred).

Huajia signifies sixty years of age. In ancient China years were recorded by the combinations of *tiangan* (heavenly stems) and *dizhi* (earthly branches). The sixty varied combinations of the ten *tiangan* and the twelve *dizhi* form a complete cycle of sixty years which is known as a *jiazi* or *huajia*. Thus a man of sixty years of age came back to the year when he was born.

Guxi was used to mean the age of seventy. The word came from *Qujiang*, a poem by Du Fu, a great poet of the Tang Dynasty, in which there were these Lines: "Common are indebted drinkers wherever one goes; hardly seen are those who live to be three score and ten since ancient time (*guxi*)". Later the word *guxi* was taken to refer to the age of seventy.

As for old people aged from eighty to ninety, the word *maodie* was often applied. Both the characters *mao* and *die* shared the same radical 老 (old) which, in *jiaguwen* (the oracle bone inscriptions), was a pictograph of a long-haired old man with a walking stick.

For a hundred-year-old man the term *qiyi* was used. According to *Li Ji* (*The Book of Rites*), *qi* meant a hundred years and *yi* meant taking good care. Therefore *qiyi* later became a substitute for a hundred years of age.

Some expressions like *erli*, *buhuo*, *tianming*, *huajia* and *guxi* are still used by the Chinese people.

85. 中国历法是根据月亮的盈亏而制订的吗？祖冲之在历法上有什么贡献？现存的农历是什么时候制订的？

中国在汉代（公元前206～公元220年）初期以前，曾经变更过几次历法。那时历法的制订并不完全根据月亮的盈亏。对于一年的划定，是古人对太阳在两个冬至日之间的运行进行测算来定的；对于一个月的划分，则以月亮圆而后亏，再由亏复圆的时间测定。春秋末年（公元前5世纪）中国开始实行四分历，也就是在天文观测的基础上，计算出每年是365.25天；每个月是29.53085天。因此，用每19年设置7个闰月来补足实际天数。这在当时是比较精确的算法。比古希腊类似的"伽利泼斯历"要早100多年。四分历的缺点是当时对天体运行的观测不够精确。如果太阳运动的出发点是冬至点，那么经过一年以后，太阳并没有回到原来的地方，而是在原定冬至点的西边一小段距离之处。这种现象叫岁差。中国从汉朝起已经发现了岁差的存在，但是并没有据此修改历法。

祖冲之（公元429～500年），范阳迺（今河北省涞水县）人，是南北朝时期南朝宋、齐两代杰出的科学家。他为了精确观测天文以修订历法，采取了在冬至前后二十三四天测定日影长度，取它的平均值，再求出冬至的日期与时刻。用新的观测方法算出每年的天数是365.2428天。比四分历更精确了。同时按照祖冲之的计算，原先19年置7个闰月也不精确，那样每200年就要差一天。祖冲之在他制订的《大明历》（因为制成于宋大明六年，即公元462年，故名）中，改为391年置144个闰月，这就更符合天象实际，和现代观测所得的数据只差十万分之一日。因此他所创制的《大明历》在当时及其后的几百年间，是一部很精确的历法。可惜当时受到宠臣戴法兴的反对，没有施行。在祖冲之死后才施行了80年。

祖冲之以后，中国历法又有过几次变动。其中较著名的有唐代名僧一行编制的《大衍历》，元代郭守敬等人编制的《授时历》等。明代崇祯年间，经过40多年实测，并采纳西洋方法和数据，编制成《崇祯历书》，未及颁布施行而明代灭亡。清代顺治年间，天主教耶稣会传教士德意志人汤若望把《崇祯历书》删改压缩后，呈给清政府。清政府根据书上的数据，编制历书，于顺治三年（公元1646年）颁布施行，叫《时宪历》。中国现在所称"农历"或"旧历"就是《时宪历》。现行的公历是从欧洲引进的历法，俗称"阳历"。

85. Was the Chinese Lunar Calendar Worked out According to the Waxing and Waning of the Moon? What Was the Contribution of Zu Chongzhi in This Field? When Did the Current Chinese Lunar Calendar Come into Being?

There were several lunar calendars before the Han Dynasty (206 B.C.—220 A.D.). At that time, not every calendar was worked out according to the waxing and waning of the moon. The length of a year was decided upon the calculation of the movement of the moon between two Winter Solstices. The length of a month was decided upon the time between the waning and the waxing of the moon. During the late Spring and Autumn Period (770—476 B.C.), the *Sifen* Calendar was introduced. The so-called *Sifen* Calendar meant that calculations based on astronomical observations provided that there should be 365.25 days every year and 29.53085 days every month. For this reason, 7 leap months were inserted in 19 lunar years to make up for the remainder days. This was the most precise calculation of the time, and was more than 100 years earlier than the Galipoth Calendar of ancient Greece. The disadvantage of this calendar was that the observation on the movement of the celestial bodies was not precise. As we know, the sun moves from the Winter Solstice, and, after one year, it does not move back to the starting point. Instead, it arrives at another point to the west of the starting point. This fact was discovered during the Han Dynasty, but the calendar was not corrected accordingly.

Zu Chongzhi (429—500 A.D.), born in Fanyangqiu, was an outstanding scientist in the Song and Qi of the Northern and Southern Dynasties (420—550 A.D.). In order to get precise astronomical observations and reformulate the calendar, he adopted the way of calculating the length of the sunshine shadow on the 23rd and 24th days before and after the Winter Solstice and then worked out the average length. With that, he then worked out the exact date and time of the Winter Solstice. With the new way, he reckoned that there were 365.2428 days a year, which was more precise than the *Sifen* Calendar. In accordance with the calculation by Zu Chongzhi, those former calendars with 7 leap months in 19 lunar years were not precise either, because, in that case, there would be one day less every 200 years. When he worked out the *Daming* Calendar, he inserted 144 leap months in 391 years, which conforms more to the astronomical observations and was only 1/100000 day less than the data obtained through modern observation. Thus, his *Daming* Calendar was a fairly precise calendar at his time and for several hundred years thenceforward. Unfortunately, owing to the opposition of an official favored by the emperor at that time, the Calendar was adopted after his death for only 80 years.

The Chinese lunar calendar, underwent several changes after Zu Chongzhi. Among them, the *Dayan* Calendar worked out by Monk Yixing in the Tang Dynasty (618—907 A.D.) and the *Shoushi* Calendar by Guo Shoujing in the Yuan Dynasty (1271—1368 A.D.) were two of the most famous ones. In the reign of Emperor Chongzhen of the Ming Dynasty (1368—1644 A.D.), after a forty-year long survey and research combined with Western ways, the *Chongzhen* Calendar was formulated. But, the Ming Dynasty had been overthrown before the calendar was put into effect. In the reign of Emperor Shunzhi of the Qing Dynasty (1644—1911A.D.), Johann Adam Schall von Bell, a German Christian missionary, revised the *Chongzhen* calendar and submitted the revised one to the emperor. According to the data he submitted, the Qing Government completed a new calendar, the *Shixian* Calendar, which was declared to come into use in 1646. It is this *Shixian* Calendar that is still in use now as the Chinese lunar calendar. The Gregorian Calendar was introduced from Europe, and is generally known as the "solar calendar".

86. 中国的养蚕技术是何时传往国外的?

众所周知,中国是丝绸的故乡。中国人首先发明了养蚕。据传说,黄帝的妻子嫘祖是第一个发明养蚕并传授抽丝、织绸技术的人。北京的北海公园内有先蚕坛,供奉的蚕神就是嫘祖。

其实,养蚕抽丝技术并不是由一个人完成的,嫘祖不过是千千万万中国古代妇女的象征。正是广大的妇女,经过多次实验和摸索才逐渐发明了养蚕技术。据中国史书记载,中国在商代就开始了养蚕。中国最古老的文字甲骨文中已经有“桑”这个字。

自从中国人发明了养蚕技术之后,对外国人一直保守秘密而不外传。这种状况一直持续到公元3世纪才开始改变。

中国的养蚕技术,首先往东传播,传到日本。据日本最早的史书记载,公元300年,日本派了一批朝鲜人到中国学习,他们找了一些能工巧匠,教给他们养蚕、织绸的技术。当这些人回国时,还带回去四个中国姑娘,向宫廷和老百姓传授这方面的技术。后来,为了纪念这四位中国姑娘,还专门建立了一座寺庙。

就在养蚕技术东传不久,这种技术也开始往西传播,传入印度。首先传入的地区是在布拉马普特拉河流域以及该河和恒河之间的广大区域。从恒河流域逐渐再往西传播,传到了波斯和中亚一带。

养蚕技术传往西欧,是在公元6世纪的事。据史书记载,有两个波斯僧人,长期住在中国,了解到了养蚕的所有秘密,并且学会了养蚕技术。公元550年,他们到了君士坦丁堡(今土耳其的伊斯坦布尔),把他们的这些知识透露给了当时君士坦丁堡的皇帝,这位皇帝诱使两位僧人再次返回中国,让他们把养蚕最必需的东西(蚕卵)带回去献给皇帝。

他们到中国后,就偷偷地把各种蚕卵藏在挖空的手杖里,然后把手杖带到君士坦丁堡。就是用这根手杖里的蚕卵,他们繁殖出了品种齐全的蚕,从此以后这里成了另一个养蚕中心,供应西方世界丝绸制品前后达1200多年。养蚕技术从这儿也传遍整个西欧,在公元16世纪(1522年)西班牙人还把养蚕的技术带到了墨西哥,在北美地区开始了养蚕业。

86. When Was Sericulture of China Spread into Other Countries?

As we all know China is the land of silk. According to the legend, Leizu, the wife of the Yellow Emperor who lived about 4500 years ago, was the first lady to introduce the culture of silkworms and the spinning of silk among the Chinese people. In Beihai Park in Beijing, there is the Altar of the Godess of Silkworms, and the goddess of silkworms enshrined there was Leizu.

In fact, the invention of sericulture in the remote past, of course, could not have been the job of one single person. Leizu was only taken as the symbol for the thousands of ancient Chinese women. According to historic records, China had sericulture in the Shang Dynasty (c.1600—1100 B.C.). The cultural relics unearthed show that in the Shang Dynasty the character *sang* (mulberry tree) already appeared.

The Chinese guarded the secrets of their valuable art with great vigilance until the 3rd century when sericulture began to spread beyond the country of its origin.

One of the most ancient books of Japanese history states that towards 300 A.D., some Koreans were sent from Japan to China to engage competent people to teach them how to rear silkworms and make silk. They even brought back four Chinese girls to Japan to instruct the court and the folk people in the art. And later, a temple was erected to the honor of these four Chinese girls. Shortly after that, the knowledge of silk travelled westward and the cultivation of silkworms was established in India. From the Ganges Valley the art was slowly carried westward and spread in Persia and the states of Central Asia.

According to historic records, two Persian monks who had long resided in China learned the whole art and mystery of silkworm rearing. In the 6th century, they arrived at Constantinople and imparted their knowledge to the emperor, by whom they were induced to return to China to get and bring back to the emperor the material necessary for the cultivation of silkworms. They concealed silkworm eggs in a hollow cane and brought them back. It was from these precious contents of that bamboo tube that, in the year 550 A.D., all the races and varieties of silkworms were bred in Constantinople, and thereafter, it grew into a sericulture center that stocked and supplied the Western world for more than 1200 years. From there the art of sericulture was spread to all parts of Europe. In 1522, Spain introduced sericulture into Mexico, and mulberry trees were then planted in North America.

87. 中国传统农学有哪些伟大成果?

除了众所周知的四大发明(指南针、火药、造纸、活字印刷)外,中国的传统农学对人类文明也做出过伟大贡献。

早在秦、汉时期(公元前221~公元220年),中国的传统农业科学技术体系已经初具规模,后来又在这个基础上不断创进、完善。与欧洲中世纪传统农业科学技术相比,中国古代农业科学技术当时是处在世界领先水平的。比如,当欧洲人还在使用木犁时,中国已经推广了铁犁。欧洲人18世纪才发明了条播机,中国却早在汉代(公元前206~公元220年)便有了这种农具。

中国是世界上最早的水稻生产国。相传在3000年前的周代,水稻开始从中国传到国外。1973年,考古学家在浙江省余姚县河姆渡村新石器时代遗址中,发掘出大量的炭化稻谷,经专家测定,距今已有6700多年。

中国是世界上首先饲养家蚕和织造丝绸的国家。早在四五千年前的新石器时代,中国人的祖先就在河北、河南一带养蚕缫丝。春秋(公元前770~前476年)至秦汉,丝绸生产已遍及全国。远在公元前2世纪的西汉时期,质地精美的中国丝绸就通过著名的“丝绸之路”输往西亚和欧洲各国。古希腊、罗马称中国为Seres,意为丝绸。Seres这个词显然是从中国的“丝”音转化过去的。

同丝绸相辉映,中国是世界上种茶、制茶和饮茶最早的国家。相传早在4000多年前中国就用茶叶来治病。秦汉以后饮茶之风逐渐传开。

公元5世纪时,中国茶叶输出到亚洲一些国家,16、17世纪时输往欧洲各国。中国不仅输出茶叶,而且向很多国家提供茶树或茶籽。公元9世纪初茶树传入日本,以后相继传入印尼、印度等国。茶在世界各国的传播和影响极为深远,英语单词tea和法语的thé都来自汉语的t'e,这是中国福建省方言中对茶的称呼。

中国蔬菜种类繁多,品种丰富,总数大约160种,其中一半是中国原有品种。有不少流传海外,深受各国人民欢迎。如营养丰富、利用价值高的大豆,约在1790年传入欧洲。在中国从春到冬都出产的大白菜和小白菜,因原产地是中国,所以它们的拉丁文和英文的名字都加上了“中国”或“北京”。日本从1875年开始由中国引种白菜,现在产量和种植面积都很大。

中国还是世界上不少品种的果树的原产地。如桃是中国古老的栽培果树之一,大约在公元前1到2世纪,桃由中国西北经由中亚传入伊朗,再由伊朗传到希腊,以后再传到欧洲各国。19世纪后半期,日本、美国等国又从中国引种水蜜桃和蟠桃,在此基础上培育了很多新的品种。原产于中国的柑橙也是在 1945 年第一次由葡萄牙人引种到里斯本的，在这以后西方各国才开始大量栽培，逐步传播到世界各地。

虽然中国有过以上的诸多贡献，但是，中国的传统农学局限于经验，农业基础理论科学始终未得到发展，因此无法完成自身体系的完整性。加之小农经济的封闭性，妨碍了农业科学技术的交流。而人口的激增既加大了农业的压力，也成了运用农业科学技术的限制因素，这些都导致了中国农学在近代落后于西方。

87. What Are the Great Achievements of Traditional Chinese Agriculture?

Apart from the four major well-known inventions—compass, paper-making, letter-press printing and gunpowder—traditional Chinese agriculture also made great contributions to the development of human civilization.

It was as early as in the Qin and Han dynasties (221 B.C.—220 A.D.) that the system of traditional Chinese agricultural science and technology began to take shape. As time went on, the system further developed and became more perfect on the basis. Compared with the agricultural technology in Europe at that time, traditional Chinese agricultural science and technology were in the forefront in the world. For instance, when wooden plows were used in Europe, iron plows were widely used throughout China. The Europeans had not invented drill seeders until the 18th century, while these tools had been widely used in China in the Han Dynasty (206 B.C.—220 A.D.).

China is also the first paddy rice producer in the world. It was said that rice was spread to other countries in the Zhou Dynasty, about 3000 years ago. In 1973, a large quantity of carbonized rice was discovered in a New Stone Age relics in Hemudu Village, Yuyao County, Zhejiang Province. It was determined by archeologists that the rice had a history of over 6700 years.

China also took the lead in silkworm raising and silk production. It was as early as in the New Stone Age about 4000 to 5000 years ago that the Chinese ancestors began to raise silkworms and produce silk in the present Hebei and Henan provinces. From the Spring and Autumn Period (770—476 B.C.) to the Qin Dynasty, silk production was spread out all over China. During the Western Han Dynasty, fine silk products were transported to the countries in Southwest Asia and Europe through the well-known "Silk Road". The ancient Greeks and Romans called China *Seres*, which means silk. *Seres* derived from the Chinese pronunciation *si* (silk).

China is also the world pioneer in growing, producing and drinking tea. Legend goes that tea was used as a medicine as early as over 4000 years ago. During the Qin and Han dynasties, drinking tea gradually became a fashion. China not only exported tea, but also provided tea trees and seeds to many other countries. In the 9th century, tea trees were transplanted in Japan, and in turn, in Indonesia, India, and some other countries. Tea has been so widely spread and has produced so great influences that the English word *tea* and French *thé* both derived from Chinese *t'e*, the pronunciation of tea in Fujian dialect.

There are many kinds and varieties of vegetables in China, totally 160. Half of them originated in China. Among these vegetables, many have been spread abroad and appreciated there. For instance, soybean of great nutrition and utility was spread to Europe in 1790. The scientific names of Chinese cabbage and pakchoi are respectively Brassica Chinensis and Brassica Peckinensis Japan began to transplant cabbage from China in 1875, and now it has a great output and growing field.

Quite a few fruit varieties also originated in China. For example, peach is one of the old fruit vavieties in China. Peach trees were spread to Iran through Middle Asia during the 1st and 2nd centuries B.C., and then to Greece through Iran, and further to some other European countries. In the second half of the 19th century, Japan and the United States introduced honey peach and flat peach from China and bred new varieties. Sweet orange was introduced from China to Lisbon, Portugal, in 1945, and then it was grown on a large scale in other Western countries. And now it has been spread all over the world.

Although it has made great contributions in many fields, traditional Chinese agricultural science and technology basically limited themselves to experience summarization, without further theoretical development. This has hindered its system from developing completely. The nature of small-scale farming economy has also discouraged the exchange of agricultural science and technology. The fast increasing population, as a hindrance factor, has put a big pressure on Chinese agriculture. All these combined have caused Chinese agriculture to fall behind Western agriculture.

88. 中国古代货币是如何发展和演变的?

中国货币史是一部饶有趣味的历史。在中国,最原始的货币是贝壳。从中国的汉字来看,与贸易、货物交易有关的字大部分都由一个“贝”字来组成,这也说明了古代贝壳是作为货币使用的。随着时间的推移,玉和丝绸也成了交易的媒介物,起着货币的作用。因为丝绸是中国首先发明的,又是中国与外国贸易中价值昂贵的出口产品,因此,丝绸作为货币是合乎逻辑的。但在小宗的交易中,丝绸当做货币使用却带来很大的不便,所以,周代(约公元前 1100 ~ 前 256 年)以前,贝壳仍然是人们交易中使用最广泛的货币。除了真正的贝壳以外,用骨头制作的贝壳仿制品也作为货币在市场上流通。

到了周朝后期,金属货币出现并开始流行。由于青铜的使用,使货币发生很大的变革。从公元前 6 世纪开始,人们就开始用青铜铸造货币。最早铸造的货币是铲子和小刀的形状,这就是人们说的铲币和刀币。这是中国最早的金属货币。金属货币也在不断发生变化,到了秦朝(公元前 221 ~ 前 206 年),就有了方孔圆形的铜钱。自秦以后,这种铜钱的式样成了历代王朝铸造金属钱币的标准模式。

西汉(公元前 206 ~ 公元 24 年)初期,国家安定,经济繁荣,人口增加很快,对货币的需要大大超过皇家货币的发行量。铸币所需要的铜在供应方面遇到越来越大的困难。面对这严峻的形势,西汉王朝曾于公元前 119 年试图用鹿皮作为货币使用,但没有取得成功。唐代,由于铸钱,铜的供应也出现过困难,唐王朝曾于 806 年使用过“飞钱”(即当时一种汇兑方式,可凭商号开的票券在异地取钱)。从货币发展的过程可以看出,金属货币是使用最广泛的一种货币。虽然也曾出现过铁币,但铜币的使用在宋代以前一直占统治地位。除了铜币之外,在唐朝,由于丝织业非常发达,铜币和丝绸在国家预算中同时作为货币使用。到了宋代,由于引进了棉花种植技术,丝绸产量下降,国家税收开始以银两计算,银子就上升到货币的地位,这在中国历史上是第一次以银代币。

公元 970 年,纸币开始发行。中国是世界上最早使用纸币的国家。在此之后的 400 多年里,纸币是使用最广泛的货币。公元 1375 年,明代的第一个皇帝朱元璋还颁布了货币法,使纸币合法化。但是随着盛产银、铜的云南被征服,皇家所需要的银、铜供应有了保障,在这种情况下,银子作为货币就又盛行起来,纸币反而逐渐消失了。

清代除了使用铜钱以外,还开始铸造银币。乾隆十七年(公元 1752 年)清王朝第一次铸造纯银币,当时仅在西康一带流通。光绪十七年(公元 1891 年),广东省购进了新的造币机器,铸造蟠龙银元,周围书写汉满两种文字,印有“光绪元宝广东省”字样,流通较广。1905 年,湖北省造币厂铸造大清一两银币。中华民国初期,继续铸造银币,有孙中山开国纪念币、黎元洪开国纪念币及袁世凯共和纪念币。几乎与铸造银元同时，1900年6月，广东省仿外国铜币式样，开始铸造新铜币，正面书“光绪元宝”，中有满文“广宝”二字，周围有“广东省”字样，这是中国铸造铜元的开始。

1935年，国民党政府实行法币政策，禁止银元流通，铜元也被禁止使用。但第二年，又发行新的铜辅币，分壹分、半分两种。

88. How Did Ancient Chinese Currency Develop and Evolve?

Chinese currency has a very interesting history. The earliest medium of exchange was cowrie shells. In analysing some Chinese characters, we can see that most of the characters that have a connection with trade or commercial activities are composed of the radical 贝 (shell). This shows that cowrie shells were used as a form of currency. As time moved on, jade and silk were also used as mediums. Since silk was indigenous to China and was the most valuable article for export, it was logical to use it as a form of currency. However, it was too clumsy to be used in small transactions hence cowrie shells were still the most widely-used form of money before the Zhou Dynasty (c. 1100—256 B.C.). And, in addition to real shells, bone imitations also came into circulation.

Metal currencies came into use in the late Zhou Dynasty. The employment of bronze brought great changes. Ever since the 6th century B.C., people had cast bronze in the shape of small knives and shovels, and used them as coins. This is the earliest metal money in China. Along with the evolutions, round copper cash with a square hole at the center was coined in the Qin Dynasty (221—206 B.C.) and became the standard form of metal currency thereafter.

With the establishment of the Han Dynasty (206 B.C.—24 A.D.), came peace, prosperity and great increase in population, making the problem of a sufficient supply of copper for coinage more and more difficult. In order to tackle this problem, in 119 B.C. an attempt was made to introduce deer skin as money, but it was unsuccessful. Again in 806 A.D. in the Tang Dynasty (618—907 A.D.), negotiable certificates were introduced, but were soon abolished. From the process of the development of Chinese currency, we can see that metal currency was most widely used, and copper cash had been always in a dominant position, despite of the appearance of iron cash. Owing to the development of silk production in the Tang Dynasty, the national budget was made up in terms of both copper coins and silk pieces. When the Song Dynasty (960—1279 A.D.) came into existence, the national income in silk considerably decreased probably due to the introduction of cotton which began to replace silk. Much of the tax which used to be collected in silk was now reckoned in silver, which for the first time in Chinese history came to be used as money.

In 970 A.D., paper money was issued. China is the first country to use paper currency. For the next four centuries and more paper became the most extensively-used currency. The Currency Law, promulgated by the first emperor Zhu Yuanzhang of the Ming Dynasty, legalized paper money in 1375 A.D., but, with the conquest of Yunnan, which produced silver and copper in considerable quantities, a larger supply of both metals was now available. Therefore, silver soon became the prevailing medium of exchange, while paper money gradually disappeared.

Apart from copper cash, silver cash was also coined in the Qing Dynasty (1644—1911 A.D.). Pure silver coins were first minted in the 17th year of the reign of Emperor Qianlong(1752) of the Qing Dynasty. They were in circulation merely in the Xikang area (presently west part of Sichuan Province and east part of Tibet). In 1891 during the reign of Emperor Guangxu of the Qing Dynasty, Guangdong Province bought new machinery and was inspired to coin silver dollars with a dragon on one side, around which the words "the Silver Dollar of Guangxu Made in Guangdong Province" in both Chinese and Manchurian languages were printed. They were in wide circulation at the time. In 1905, the *Daqing* silver coins of 1 tael was coined in Hubei Province. In the early days of the Republic of China, the coinage of silver dollars was continued, such as coins in Commemoration of the Republic of China for Dr. Sun Yat-sen (president), coins in commemoration of the Republic of China for Li Yuanhong (president of the *Beiyang* Government, and coins in commemoration of the Republic for Yuan Shikai (president). Almost at the same time, in June 1900, Guangdong started to coin new copper cash modelled in a foreign style. On the front side of the coin, the Chinese characters "Guangxu Yuanbao" and two Manchurian characters "Guang Bao" were printed, and around them were the words "Guangdong Province". This was the commencement of the coinage of copper cash in China.

In 1935, the Kuomintang government issued an order to prohibit the use of silver and copper coins. But one year later, they issued two new kinds of copper coins in the face value of 1 fen and half fen.

89. 为什么钱俗称“孔方兄”?

中国古代的铜钱中间都有一个方孔。早在晋朝时,一个名叫鲁褒的人写过一篇《钱神论》,抨击当时社会上崇拜货币、钱能通神的风气。其中写道:“亲爱如兄,字曰孔方,失之则贫穷,得之则富强。”从此,钱就一直被戏称为“孔方兄”,流传至今。

铜钱中有方孔,这是中国古代特有的货币文化现象。一般认为,中国古代金属铸币始于春秋战国(公元前 770 ~ 前 221 年)时期。当时的铜铸币大多是生产工具的模仿物。比如,当时齐鲁等国采用象征刀具的刀币;中原的一些诸侯国采用模仿铲状工具的铲币;晋国和秦国则流行模仿丝线的圜钱。公元前 221 年,秦始皇统一中国,废除六国货币,铸“半两”铜钱。这种钱外圆内方,叫方圆钱。它的形制后来为历代铜钱所采用,一直沿袭到清代末年,前后达 3000 多年。

为什么要把铜钱铸成方孔,不铸成圆孔,或者根本不要孔,像西方的铜币、银币一样呢?有人认为这是由于秦始皇相信方士的“天圆地方”之说而成。那么这种钱币有什么优越性呢?方孔钱便于修整,比其他铜币更容易生产;另外,方孔钱又易于保存,不易折断。中国古代铜币币值较低,交换贸易动辄成百上千,铜钱的方孔可供人们用绳索把钱串为一串,以一贯(1000 个)为单位交易。另外,铜钱上的方孔虽然一方面是出于制造工艺的需要,然而,它同时又符合了中国传统文化追求对称、均匀的审美要求。铜钱中的方孔正好将币面分成四个相同的部分,当铭文为两个字时,就形成轴对称的图形;当铭文为四个字时,就形成中心对称图形。

还值得一提的是钱币上的文字和书法。先秦的货币上都铸有本国的文字。到了秦代统一中国(公元前 221 年)以后,统一了文字,秦代的铸币上使用的是小篆。后来,铸币上的字多由著名书法家书写,字体除小篆之外,还有隶书、楷书、行书,个别的币上用草书。因此,古代金属铸币还为人们提供了古代政治、经济、历史等文化方面的宝贵资料。

89. Why Was Money Nicknamed *Kongfangxiong*?

All the copper cash in ancient China had a square (*fang*) hole (*kong*) at its center. As early as in the Jin Dynasty (265—420 A.D.), a man named Lu Bao wrote an article entitled *On the God of Money* to criticize the prevailing money worship of the time. There was a line in it: “It’s as dear as a brother (*xiong*), styled himself *kong-*

fang ; you will be poor when you lose it, and you will get rich when you get it." Ever since then, money had been nicknamed *kongfangxiong* , which is occasionally heard even tody.

The square hole at the center of the copper cash was a peculiar cultural phenomenon in ancient China. It is generally agreed that the Chinese came to know how to make metal coins since the Spring and Autumn and the Warring States periods (770—221 B.C.). At that time, most of the copper coins imitated the shape of working tools. For example, *daobi* adopted by the state of Qi and the State of Lu signified knives; and some states in the Central Plains used *chanbi* , which looked like shovel-shaped tools; *yuanbi* , which looked like silk thread, was popular in the states of Jin and Qin. In 221 B.C., the first emperor of the Qin Dynasty unified China and coined the *banliang* copper cash, doing away with the coins used in the six states at that time. This kind of coin was round in shape with a square hole at the center, and was called "Square-Round Coins". Its shape was adopted by later dynasties up till the end of the Qing Dynasty (1644—1911 A.D.), lasting more than 3000 years.

Why was there always a square hole at the center of the coin, but not a round hole, or just without a hole, like the copper and silver coins in the West? Some said that it came from the phylosophy at that time that believed "the sky is round and the earth is square". Then, what were the advantages of this kind of coins? They were convenient to be trimmed and therefore easier to be made than copper coins. Besides, they were easy to keep and were not easily broken. As the face value of the copper coins was very low, it would take tens of thousands to make a deal and the square hole made it possible to string them together to make a *guan* (a string of 1000), a unit for exchange. Furthermore, apart from the consideration of the technological requirements, it also conformed with the aesthetic standards of pursuing symmetry and balance. The square hole happened to divide the face of the coin into four equal parts, and it formed an axial symmetry when the inscriptions included two characters; and a central symmetry with four characters.

Another point worth mentioning was the characters and the styles of calligraphy on the coins. Before the Qin Dynasty, all the coins had local characters on them , and those after the unification of China and the standardization of the written characters used the calligraphy style of *xiaozhuan* (lesser seal script) on them. Later, the characters on the coins were written by famous calligraphers. Apart from *xiaozhuan*, there were also other calligraphy styles such as *lishu* (official script) *kaishu* (regular script), *xingshu* (running hand), and even *caoshu* (cursive script) occasionally. Therefore, the metal coins in ancient times also provide precious materials for the study of ancient politics, economics, and history of China.

90."买东西"一词是怎么来的?

人们常把上街买物品说成"买东西",而没有人说"买南北"。那么"买东西"一语是怎么来的呢?

据说,有一天宋代著名哲学家朱熹在街上碰见他的好朋友盛温如提着一个竹篮子,便问盛温如:"你去哪儿?"盛温如答道:"去买东西。""难道不能说买南北吗?"朱熹问了一句。盛温如解释说:"术数所托,假其相互生克之理以言古今因果。卜人休咎的金木水火土称为五行,与东西南北中相配,东方属木,西方属金,凡属金木之类可装在篮子里;南方属火,北方属水,水火之类在篮子里是装不得的,所以只能说买'东西'而不能说买'南北'。"

清代有一位叫龚炜的学者则认为:早在东汉时期,商贾大都集中在东京洛阳和西京长安,俗语说"买东"和"买西"即指到东京、西京购物,久而久之,"东西"就成了货物的代名词,"买东西"一词也就出现了。

90. How Did the Phrase *Mai Dongxi* Come into Use?

When people go shopping, they often say "*mai dongxi*", which literally means "to buy east and west", but nobody would say "*mai nanbei*" (to buy south and north). How did the phrase *mai dongxi* come into use?

It is said that one day, Zhu Xi, the famous philosopher in the Song Dynasty (960—1279 A.D.), met his old friend Sheng Wenru, who was carrying a bamboo basket in his hand. Zhu Xi asked him: "Where are you going?" Sheng answered: "To buy east and west". "Can't you say to buy south and north?" Zhu Xi asked. "Well," Sheng Wenru explained, "Let's apply the theory of fortune-telling about the interrelations and mutual influences of things to explain the law of causality in ancient times and nowadays. The five elements are metal, wood, water, fire and earth, which are combined with the five directions: east, west, south, north and the center. The east belongs to wood, and the west to metal. Wood and metal can be put in the basket. However, the south belongs to fire, and the north to water. But fire and water can never be put in the basket. That's why we can say to buy east and west, but not to buy south and north."

However, a scholar named Gong Wei in the Qing Dynasty (1644—1911 A.D.) had a different story. He said that in the Eastern Han Dynasty (25—220 A.D.), most merchants were concentrated in the east capital Luoyang (present Luoyang of Henan Province) and the west capital Chang'an (present Xi'an of Shaanxi Province). The common saying "to buy east" and "to buy west" actually meant to go to the east and west capitals to do shopping. With the passage of time, the term *dongxi* (east and west) became a synonym for commodities, and the phrase *mai dongxi* (to buy east and west) came into use ever since.

91. 为什么把医生叫"大夫"、"郎中"?

在中国北方人们习惯把医生称为"大夫",在南方(尤其在农村)人们则把医生称为"郎中",这种称呼可以追溯到1000多年以前的唐末五代(公元907~960年)时期。

唐末五代时期,朝政腐败,战乱频繁,统治阶级穷奢极欲,甚至把国家的官职拿来卖钱,致使官衔泛滥,吏治更加黑暗。当时,以官名相互称呼逐渐形成社会风气。比如叫读书人为"相公";称工匠为"待诏";卖茶人叫"茶博士";当铺老板叫"朝奉";有钱人叫"员外"、"宣敬"、"奉斋"。几乎社会上任何一个职业都可用一个相应的官职名称来称呼。

医生是上至皇帝下至贫民谁都离不开的人,受到人们的尊敬。因此人们就用官职中品级极高的"大夫"、"郎中"来称呼他们。但是,医生称"大夫"真正的起始,则要从宋代(公元960~1279年)开始。

在宋代,中国的医务制度和医学管理都有了相当的发展。当时负责管理医疗行政的官职很多,翰林医院的医官就分为7级,官职有22种之多,如和安大夫、成和大夫、成全大夫等。这样"大夫"就成了医生的正式称呼,并且一直沿称至今。

91. Why Are Doctors Called *Daifu* and *Langzhong*?

In north China, people habitually call doctors *daifu* while people in the south call them *langzhong* . The origin of these forms of address can be traced back to the late Tang Dynasty and Five Dynasties (907—960 A.D.) over a thousand years ago.

At that time, the government was corrupt, people suffered from frequent wars and the ruling class was so wallowed in luxury that they even used governmental posts as commodity to be sold for money. This abuse made the ruling even darker. At that time, to address each other by rank became a fashion. For example, scholars were called *xianggong* ; hand crafters were called *daizhao* ; tea sellers were called *chaboshi* ; pawnbrokers were called *chaofeng*; rich people were called *yuanwai* , *xuanjing* or *fengzhai* . People of almost all kinds of professions were addressed by a relevant rank.

No one could do without doctors, no matter whether he was as superior as the emperor or as humble as a common laborer. Paying great respect to them, people then used *daifu* and *langzhong* , the highest of the ranks, to call the doctors. However, the real beginning of *daifu* as a form of address for doctors started in the Song Dynasty (960—1279 A.D.).

In the Song Dynasty, both the medical system and administration of China underwent great development. Many officials took charge in medical administration. There were seven ranks and twenty-two kinds of officials in the Imperial Academy Hospital, e.g. *he'an daifu*, *chenghe daifu*, *chengquan daifu*, etc. Thus, *daifu* became the formal address for doctors and it is still used today.

92. 中国古董学的兴起和发展情况如何？

中国古董学的兴起始于宋代（公元960～1279年）初期，并在这之后的100多年里得到蓬勃的发展，奠定了中国文物古董学发展的坚实基础。18世纪和19世纪中国古董学的复兴，可以说是对宋代这一学术成就的继承和发展。

清代（公元1644～1911年）学者王国维在《宋代考古学》一书中概括了宋代学者在考古研究方面的显著成就。其中非常重要的成就，就是对古文物的收藏、归档记录和鉴别。他们取得的成绩是十分卓著的，在许多方面的研究水平直到现在还没有人超过。宋代考古研究的重要特点在于学者们在所有方面都进行了开创性的努力，许多有关历史、文化方面的文物学巨著都出于这个时期。如11世纪至12世纪出版的《考古图》、《博古图》成了古董收藏家们的必备书。书中有关文物的分类归档、复制都有着独特的体系。虽然现在人们对当时学者专家的文物测定和仿制的精确度进行核查，但他们的目的——对古文物进行准确的鉴定——却是十分明显的，他们所鉴定的大多数文物，其准确性也被现代的文物鉴赏家所确认。

由于宋代已发明了印刷术，有些东西的传播就非常迅速，古董文物学的传播也不例外。在宋代，收藏古董已是一种很时髦的风气。值得一提的是，尽管当时皇家的文物收藏量很大，并且所收藏的文物也最有名，但收藏文物这一风尚主要是私人兴起和发展的。当时文物收藏的范围主要是青铜器和玉器，但古币和碑文的收藏也是可观的。除了对古代文物的收集、复制和流通做了不懈的努力之外，宋代的古董收藏家对中国古董学有两大贡献，那就是对铭文、碑文的研究和对文物形制的考查及鉴定。在北宋初期大约100多年的时间里，他们创立了一门新的科学并且使新的技术进一步完善。即使在后来金兵南侵、北宋灭亡、宋室南迁的情况下，这一新的科学一直在继续发展，直到南宋末年。很多古董学的专著在南宋时期先后面世。正是由于古董学在北宋时期已经奠定了坚实的基础，所以在北宋之后几百年文物学不景气的时期，仍然有着很强的生命力。这种生命力为清代古董学的复兴起了极大的推动作用。阮元的青铜器铭文专著《积古斋钟鼎彝器款识》就是在古董学复兴时期问世的。清代末期在文物学史上的重要事件就是敦煌变文和甲骨文的发现，在这方面的研究也取得了相当大的成绩，其中早期最有名的研究学者就是罗振玉和王国维二人。

92. When Did the Antiquarian Studies of China Start? How Did It Develop?

Antiquarian studies in China started in the beginning of the Song Dynasty (960—1279 A.D.). They enjoyed a glorious period for more than one hundred years during which a solid foundation was laid for later development. The classical revival in the 18th and 19th centuries included a very strong current of antiquarian interest, which has been rightly considered as a direct descendant of the Song Dynasty.

In his book *Archaeology in the Song Dynasty*, Wang Guowei, a scholar of the Qing Dynasty, summarized the distinct achievements made by the archaeological scholars in the Song Dynasty in several different fields. The most important of all is the collecting, recording and identifying of antiquities. In all the fields, their merits rank very high. And some remain unsurpassed even today. The antiquarian study of the Song Dynasty was characterized by a great deal of initiating efforts. Many of the monumental works dated from this period. *Kaogu Tu* (*An Illustrated Book of Antiques*) and *Bogu Tu* (*An Illustrated Catelogue of Antiques*) published between the 11th and 12th centuries A.D. became the required collector's handbooks. A special system was created in the two books for recording and reproducing antiquities. It may not be possible to test the accuracy of their measurements and reproductions, but their aims at being accurate are more than obvious, and the ingenuity and correctness of their identifications have been confirmed by modern inspectors.

As printing was already invented at that time, new things were spread rapidly. So were antiquarian studies. The vogue of collecting was created and maintained chiefly by private individuals, in spite of the fact that the largest and the most well-known collection was the imperial one. The scope of collections included mainly bronzes and jades, as well as coins and some kinds of stone works, especially inscriptions. The archaeologists of the Song Dynasty made two great contributions towards the gradual building up of an antiquarian science in China, namely epigraphical study and identification of antiques, beside their persistent efforts in collecting, reproducing and circulating. In about a hundred years or so in the early period of the Northern Song Dynasty, they created a new science and perfected a new technique. This new science was ably continued even after the disastrous event of the *Jingkang* era when the Golden Tartars raided the capital city of Kaifeng and made it a ruin. In fact, it continued to the very end of the Southern Song Dynasty, and many notable monographs on antiquarian studies came out in the Southern Song Dynasty. Owing to this continued activity, the foundation of the new science was laid firmly, so even after a total slump of almost five hundred years after the Northern Song Dynasty, it still retained enough vitality to give new strength to the classical revival in the Qing Dynasty. Ruan Yuan's book *Jiguzhai Zhongding Yiqi Kuanshi* , one of the first treatises on the inscriptions on bronze wares, was written in this period. Two great events were also worth special mentioning. One is the discovery of the Dunhuang manuscripts and the other is the discovery of the oracle bone inscriptions, on which Luo Zhenyu and Wang Guowei were the most eminent scholars at the early stage.

93. 扇子的发明及演变过程如何?

最原始的扇子是从鸟的羽毛和树叶逐渐发展起来的。据记载,在中国商代(约公元前1600～约前1100年)就有了用山鸡翎毛制作的扇子。但后人一般都认为周武王(姬发,约公元前11世纪)是扇子的发明者。

早在公元前1106年,人们就把扇子应用到日常生活中了。不过,那时扇子是长柄的大扇,它的用处不是祛暑,而是用来扇跑马车奔驰时车轮带起来的尘土。到了公元前991年,用竹子、木料及象牙镶边的丝绸团扇已经出现。扇子用来纳凉,成为普通百姓普遍使用的用品,则是在汉代(公元前206～公元220年)。到了东晋(公元317～420年)时期,据说孝武帝(公元373～397年)曾下令禁止人们使用丝绸帛做扇子,后来的安帝于公元405年也下达过类似的命令。由此可见,当时扇子的数量是不小的,用丝绸制扇,当然会消耗掉大批的绸料。

团扇在中国出现最早,一直到唐宋(公元618～1279年)时期,团扇是扇子的主要模式。折扇出现较晚,是日本人发明的。这种扇子于公元11世纪经由朝鲜传入中国以后,在中国发展得很快。

扇子的种类很多,用的材料也各式各样。中国人制作的扇子主要有以下几种:竹子与纸做的;骨头与羽毛做的;象牙做的及雕漆与纸或丝绸做的。还有一种是用棕榈叶制成的芭蕉扇,因其价格低廉又非常实用,很受普通老百姓的喜爱,流传也很普遍。最珍贵的扇子要数用珍珠母做的扇子。

本世纪初,扇子的制作点主要集中在广州、杭州、南京、宁波等地。其中,广州以大量制作工艺扇而闻名,它制作的扇子不仅在国内销售,也出口海外。用老鹰的翎毛和其他鸟类羽毛做的扇子是出口的主要品种。杭州以生产折扇为主,年产量曾达到三百万把。当时的南京帛扇规模也很可观,据当时的统计数字看,制扇工人就达七万多人。另一制扇中心是宁波,以生产廉价的纸扇为主。由于宁波的纸扇特别便宜,把从日本进口的纸扇挤出了市场,占据了统治地位。

93. How Was Chinese Fan Invented? What Was the History of Fan?

The first fans were made of birds' feathers and tree leaves. It was recorded that a fan made of pheasants' feathers was made in the Shang Dynasty (c.1600—c.1100 B.C.) However, king Wu of the Zhou Dynasty (11th century B.C.) was reputed the inventor of Chinese fan.

In 1106 B.C., fans were used in daily life. However, the fans had a long shaft, and were not used to keep off the heat, but to keep off the dust raised by wheels of a cart. Round fans made of silk and framed with bamboo, wood and ivory appeared in 991 B.C. It was not until the Han Dynasty (206 B.C.—220 A.D.) that fans were used by common people to enjoy cool air in summer. It was said that in the Eastern Jin Dynasty (317—420 A.D.) Emperor Xiaowu once forbade people to make fans with silk. In 405 A.D., Emperor An also issued a similar prohibition. This proves that at that time fans were already in great quantity, and making fans had consumed too much silk material.

Round fans were first seen in China and remained the main shape of fans until the Tang and Song dynasties (618—1279 A.D.). Folding fans were invented by the Japanese. Introduced into China through Korea in the 11th century, they quickly gained popularity in China thereafter.

There are many kinds of fans made of different materials. The following are the major kinds made in China: fans made of bamboo and paper, bone and feather, ivory and carved lacquerware and paper or silk. Fans made of palm tree leaves are both economical and practical and are very popular among the people. And the most precious fans are those made of mother-of-pearls.

At the beginning of this century, Guangzhou, Hangzhou, Nanjing and Ningbo were the centers of fan manufacturing. Guangzhou was well known for its production of large quantities of ornamental fans. These fans were not only sold in domestic markets, but also exported to foreign countries. Fine fans made of eagles' feathers and other plumes were the major kinds for export. Hangzhou was famous for its folding fans. Its annual production once amounted to 3000000. And in Nanjing, silk fan industry once involved more than 70000 workers. Ningbo mainly produced low-cost paper fans. As paper fans produced in Ningbo had such a competitive price, Japanese paper fans were pushed out of the Chinese market.

94. 中国刺绣有哪些特点和种类？

刺绣是中国优秀的传统工艺，有着悠久的历史。刺绣是一种在织物上用各种线料织出种种图案的工艺。根据各地古墓出土的帛画和刺绣等实物可知，远在3000多年前的殷周时代，中国就已有华美的暗花绸和多彩刺绣。目前在河南发现的商代刺绣实物，是中国最早的刺绣工艺品。这种刺绣花纹为菱形纹和折角波浪纹，在花纹线条的边缘使用加绞拈的丝线，工艺达到了相当高的水平。西周（公元前1100～前771年）的刺绣印痕发现于陕西省宝鸡茹家庄的西周墓中。这种刺绣采用今天还在使用的辫子股绣的针法，运用了双线条，线条舒卷自如，针脚也相当均匀齐整，说明刺绣技巧是很熟练的。

这种丝织刺绣工艺品的生产，不仅对中国的社会起了很大的作用，而且在国际文化生活中也产生了很大的作用与影响。到了秦汉时期（公元前221～公元220年）刺绣已发展到了较高的水平，绣品也成为对外输出的主要商品。由于中国是丝绸的故乡，自古以来，富者以"闺房绣楼"为贞，贫者以"善织巧绣"为业。清代（公元1644～1911年），各地的民间绣品皆有传统的风味，形成了著名的四大名绣，即苏州的苏绣、湖南的湘绣、四川的蜀绣、广东的粤绣。此外还有北京的京绣、温州的瓯绣、上海的顾绣、苗族的苗绣等，产地不同，风格各异。刺绣的针法有错针绣、乱针绣、网绣、满地绣等。刺绣的花卉不闻犹香，飞禽栩栩如生，走兽神态逼真。

解放后，中国将油画、中国画、照片等艺术形式运用于刺绣，使之达到远看是画、近看是绣的绝妙效果。刺绣品的用途也进一步扩大，从戏剧服装到日常生活中的枕套、台布、屏风、壁挂及生活服装等。此外，刺绣品还是中国传统的外贸产品，经济价值很高。

中国刺绣的特色和艺术价值，直接体现在四大名绣上。

苏绣以针脚细密、色彩淡雅、绣品精细而著名，具有平、光、齐、匀、和、细、密等特点。题材以小动物为主。如《猫戏图》、《风穿花》、《鱼虾图》等。近年来出现的双面绣，两面有同有异。如猫的眼睛，两面颜色不一样，十分引人入胜，其刺绣技艺之高超，是刺绣中的精品。

湘绣以写实居多，色彩明快，以中国画为底，衬上相应的云雾山水、亭台楼阁、飞禽走兽，风格豪放。特点是绣虎、狮等，以独特的针法绣出的动物毛丝根根有力。人称湘绣"绣花能生香，绣鸟能闻声，绣虎能奔跑，绣人能传神"。

蜀绣构图简练，大都采用方格、花条等传统的民族图案，富有装饰性。色彩丰富鲜艳，针法严谨，虚实适宜，立体感强，平正光滑。所绣对象有花蝶、鲤鱼、熊猫等。

粤绣采用金银线盘金刺绣，绣线平整光亮。构图布局紧密，装饰性强，富有立体感。

绣面富丽堂皇、璀灿夺目，多用于戏装、婚礼服等。荔枝和孔雀是粤绣的传统题材。

94. What Are the Features and Categories of Chinese Embroidery?

Embroidery is an excellent traditional technology with a long history in China. It is a handicraft to embroider various designs with different kinds of threads and materials on fabric. The unearthed silk painting and embroidery prove that as early as more than 3000 years ago, there was already splendid silk with veiled design and of various colors. At present, the piece of embroidery of the Shang Dynasty found in Henan Province is the earliest embroidery handicraft in China. The rhombus, folding waves design with twisted thread at the edge show that the technology had reached a rather developed level. In a Western Zhou Tomb in Baoji, Shaanxi Province, a piece woven by the braid-strand method was found, which is still used today. The smooth lines and neat stitches showed the skill.

The production of embroidery products has not only promoted the productivity in China, but also influenced the international cultural life. In the Qin and Han dynasties (221 B.C.—220 A.D.), it had reached a fairly high level and had become an important mechandise for export. Being the homeland of silk, there was an old custom in China that the rich people took the "embroider boudoir" as their proof of loyalty and chastity while the poor people took the skill of embroidery and weaving as their profession. In the Qing Dynasty (1644—1911A.D.), the folk embroidery of different provinces all had their own characteristics and formed the four famous categories of embroidery, i.e. *suxiu* in Suzhou, *xiangxiu* in Hunan, *shuxiu* in Sichuan and *yuexiu* in Guangdong. Beside these, there were *jingxiu* in Beijing, *ouxiu* in Wenzhou, *guxiu* in shanghai, *miaoxiu* of the Miao nationality, etc. Each had its own distinct styles. The methods included crisscrossing, mixing, netting, scattering, etc. The flowers, birds and beasts on the embroidery were all as vivid as real living ones.

Since 1949, the art of oil painting, Chinese painting and photography have been applied to embroidery at such a terrific effect that they look like paintings from distance and embroidery at close range. The scope of usage also has expanded from theatrical costumes to pillow cases, table cloths, screens, wall hangings, clothes, etc. It is also a traditional exporting product, which is of high economic value.

The four famous categories of embroidery embody the characteristics and artistic value of Chinese embroidery.

Suxiu is famous for its neat stitches, elegant colors and fine quality. Smooth, bright, neat, even, fine and tight are its features. The subjects are mostly little animals like cats, fish and shrimps. The double-sided embroidery, with the two sides either identical or different, is of exquisite workmanship. For example, the cat's eyes are of different colors on the two sides, which is done by superb skill.

Xiangxiu has bright colors. With Chinese paintings as its background, clouds, mountains, rivers, pavilions, birds and animals are embroidered realistically. The techniques of *xiangxiu* is manifested fully especially in the embroidery of tigers and lions, with their hair embroidered in fine bold lines. There goes a saying: On *xiangxiu*, birds can sing, tigers can run, flowers are fragrant and people are lifelike.

Shuxiu is characterized by its simple structure, bright colors, well-knit stitches, smooth surface and traditional decorator designs like squares and stripes. Its subjects are mostly butterflies, carps, pandas, etc.

Yuexiu is done by embroidering with gold and silver threads, which are neat and bright. It has a tight layout, decorator designs and a gorgeous surface. *Yuexiu* is mostly used in theatrical costumes and wedding gowns. Lychee and peacocks are its traditional subjects.

95. 中国是茶叶的原产地吗？中国种茶、饮茶的历史如何？中国现有哪些名茶？

中国是茶叶的原产地，是种茶、制茶、饮茶最早的国家。据传说，三皇五帝之一的神农氏在尝百草中，曾遇到不少有毒的草木，喝茶之后才解了毒。两千多年前，中国只有蜀地（现在云南、四川）种茶，秦统一六国（公元前 221 年）后，茶树也从蜀地传到了其他地方。到唐朝（公元 618 ~ 907 年），长江流域已经广泛种植茶树了。

人们开始是把茶叶当做药来煎服的，味道很苦。后来在饮用中，逐渐发现茶除了有清热解毒的治疗作用以外，还有可口的清香味。因此从魏晋南北朝（公元 220 ~ 581 年）开始，人们逐渐把茶作为日常饮料。但是在宋朝（公元 960 ~ 1279 年）以前，人们在饮茶时还习惯加入姜、盐等调料。宋朝免去了调料，仍讲究用火煎茶。明朝（公元 1368 ~ 1644 年）开始用开水冲饮。

由于种茶和饮茶的历史很长，中国关于茶的著作也出现得很早。唐朝陆羽在公元 780 年撰写的《茶经》，是世界上最早的有关茶的专门著作。《茶经》不仅论述了茶的来历、烹茶和饮茶的方法，而且对烹茶的水以何处为好、烹茶的器具用什么最好等，都进行了论述。所以陆羽被后人尊为“茶圣”。

由于对茶叶加工方法的不同，中国所产茶的种类分为绿茶（不发酵茶）、红茶（发酵茶）、乌龙茶（半发酵茶）、白茶（用嫩茶叶焙干而成）和用绿茶加茉莉花窨制的花茶，还有紧压成型的紧压茶。

中国现有的十大名茶是：1. 龙井茶，产于浙江杭州，绿茶；2. 碧螺春，产于江苏吴县太湖之滨的山中，绿茶；3. 铁观音，产于福建安溪县，乌龙茶；4. 屯绿，产于安徽屯溪等县，绿茶；5. 白毫银针，产于福建松溪等县，白茶；6. 普洱茶，产于云南普洱县，红茶；7. 武夷岩茶，产于福建武夷山中，为乌龙茶中又一珍品；8. 祁红，产于安徽祁门县，红茶；9. 滇红，产于云南省，常被用做“功夫茶”；10. 茉莉花茶。

此外，中国一些少数民族有喝奶茶、酥油茶和乳扇茶的习惯。

1100 多年前，日本僧人把茶树籽带回国，茶即传入日本。17 世纪以后，茶又传入印度、印度尼西亚和欧、美各国，风行全世界，与咖啡、可可并称为世界三大饮料。

95. Is China the First Tea Producer? What Is the History of Planting and Drinking Tea in China? What Are the Well-known Chinese Teas?

China is not only the first tea producer, but also the first tea-planting and tea-processing country in the world where people drink tea as beverage. It was said that a Chinese ancestor was poisoned when he tasted different kinds of weeds and grass. However, as he drank some tea accidentally, he was ,beyond expectation, detoxified. Before the unification of China in 221 B.C., tea was grown only in the present Yunnan and Sichuan provinces. Afterwards, tea was introduced into other parts of China. During the Tang Dynasty (618—907 A.D.), tea trees were planted on a large scale in the Yangtze River valley.

At the very beginning, tea was stewed as a medicine and tasted quite bitter. Later on, people came to realize that apart from its medicinal function, tea also had a pleasing fragrant flavor. Hence, from the Northern and Southern Dynasties (220—581 A.D.) on, Chinese people gradually drink tea as a daily drink. But before the Song Dynasty(960—1279 A.D.), ginger, salt and some other flavourings were usually added in tea. During the Song Dynasty, though flavourings were no longer used, it was still stressed that tea should be stewed. It was not until the Ming Dynasty (1368—1644 A.D.) that the Chinese people began to make tea with nothing but boiling water.

In China, there were books on tea a long time ago because of its long history of tea planting and drinking. *Cha Jing* (*Book of Tea*), the first professional book on tea in the world, was written by Lu Yu in 780 A.D. The author introduced not only the quality and origin of tea and ways of tea brewing and drinking, but also the best water and ideal utensils. Therefore, he was respected as the tea saint.

In the light of the different ways of processing, Chinese tea can be classified as follows: green tea (unfermented), black tea (fermented), oolong tea (semi-fermented), white tea (baked sprouts), jasmine tea (green tea with jasmine flowers) and brick tea.

The ten kinds of well-known Chinese tea are :1. *Longjing* (the dragon well tea, a green tea produced in Hangzhou, Zhejiang Province); 2. *Biluochun* (a green tea produced in Wu County, Jiangsu Province); 3. *Tieguanyin* (a oolong tea produced in Anxi, Fujian Province); 4. *Tunlü* (a green tea produced in Tunxi, Anhui Province); 5. *Pekoe Yinzhen* (a white tea produced in Songxi, Fujian Province); 6. *Pu'er* tea (a black tea produced in Pu'er, Yunnan Province); 7. *Wuyiyan* tea (a oolong tea produced in Wuyi, Fujian Province); 8. Keemun black tea (a black tea produced in Qimen County, Anhui Province); 9. *Dianhong* (black congou tea produced in Yunnan Province with the nickname "*Kungfu* tea"); 10. jasmine tea.

Apart from these, milk tea, buttered tea, etc. can be seen in the drinks of some Chinese minorities.

Over one thousand years ago, tea was introduced into Japan when some Japanese monks took tea seeds home from China. From the 17th century on, tea gradually spread to India, Indonesia, and countries in Europe and America. Tea is so popular nowadays that it is one of the three major drinks (tea, coffee and cocoa) in the world.

96. 闻名于世的中国烹调历史是怎样的？中国有名的“八大菜系“各有什么特点”？何谓“山珍海味”？

烹调在中国历史文化遗产中，是很有特点的部分。“烹”字在古代是用火烧、煮食物的意思。据考古发现，在中国旧石器时代距今 170 万年的西侯度文化遗址中，已经有火烧过的动物骨、角。这是迄今所知人类最早用火的记录之一。最初人们只是用火直接烧烤食物，到距今约 3500 年前的商朝和其后的周朝，中国人的祖先用以烹制食物的铜器已经发展到十几种。“调”是调和诸味的意思。中国最早发现的调味品是盐。相传黄帝时期已经会制盐了。到周朝，已经用酱、醯(醋)、饴糖等调和味道了。经过历代人民积累经验，中国现有的菜肴品种有 10000 种之多。烹调方法有：烧、烤、炒、熘、炸、爆、炖、烩、熏、卤、煎、贴、煸等 40 多种。

由于中国幅员辽阔，各地物产、气候、风俗差异很大，形成了山东、江苏、安徽、湖南、浙江、广东、福建、四川八大菜系。八大菜系各有特点。山东菜的特点是：清香、鲜嫩、味纯；江苏菜选料严格，制作精细，讲究造型，酥烂可口；安徽菜重油、重色、重火功；湖南菜口味重酸辣、鲜香、软嫩；浙江菜讲究刀功，味道鲜脆软滑，保持原味；广东菜用料广泛，除了通常用的肉、禽类外，还用蛇、猴、猫等制成菜肴，菜的特点多以清淡、生脆、爽口、偏甜为主；福建菜以海产品为主要原料，注重甜酸咸香，色调美观，滋味清鲜；四川菜以麻辣、味厚著称，调味品众多，故有“一菜一格，百菜百味”之称。除此以外，近年来北京、东北各地以及新疆、云南等都有自己独特风味的菜肴。

“山珍海味”一般来说是指产于陆地和大海的美味食品。对于其中特别难得的美味佳品，自《周礼·天官》篇中记载了“珍用八物”后，历代对“八珍”的内容有不同的说法。现在通行的有上、中、下八珍之说。上八珍是：猩唇、驼峰、猴头、熊掌、燕窝、凫脯、鹿筋、黄唇胶；中八珍是：鱼翅、银耳、鲥鱼、广肚、果子狸、蛤什蟆、鱼唇、裙边；下八珍是：海参、龙须菜、大口蘑、川竹笋、赤鳞鱼、干贝、蛎黄、乌鱼蛋。

96. What Is the History of Chinese Cuisines? What Are the Characteristics of the Eight Well-known Schools of Chinese Cuisine? What Is *Shan Zhen Hai Wei* (Delicacies from the Land and the Sea)?

Pengtiao (cuisine) is an important part of Chinese culture. In ancient times the character *peng* with fire at its bottom meant roasting and boiling food. Out of the Xihoudu cultural relics of 1700000 years ago, animal bones and horns burnt by fire were discovered by archaeologists. These were one of the earliest evidence that fire was used by mankind. Food was put directly over the fire at the very beginning. About 3500 years ago in the Shang and Zhou dynasties, there were already over a dozen kinds of bronze cooking vessels. The character *tiao* meant to mix flavourings. Salt, the first condiment discovered in China, might have been made about 4000 years ago. Soy, vinegar, and malt sugar also came into use as early as about 3000 years ago. Up to now, there are as many as 10000 kinds of dishes and more than 40 ways of cooking, such as *shao* (braising), *kao* (roasting or baking), *chao* (stir-frying), *liu* (sauté with thick gravy), *zha* (deep-frying), *bao* (quick-frying with highly seasoned sauce over a high flame), *dun* (simmering in a covered pot), *xun* (smoking), *lu* (stewing in soy sauce), *jian* (frying in a little oil over a low flame), *tie* (baking in a little oil), *ta* (frying ingredients coated with egg and cornflour mixture in a little oil over a low flame), and so on.

Eight schools of cuisine gradually took shape in China because of her vast territory, varied local produces, and different climates and customs. Distinct features can be found among all these eight schools: delicate fragrance, freshness and pure flavour feature dishes of the Shandong cuisine; being particular with materials and meticulous makings feature Jiangsu cuisine; more oil, strong colour and high skill in using fire feature Anhui cuisine; sour, hot and soft taste features Hunan dishes; nice cutting, natural, soft and slippery taste feature Zhejiang dishes; varieties of materials including poultry, meat as well as snake, monkey and cat, and light, crisp and sweet taste feature Guangdong cuisine; sweet, sour and salty taste feature Fujian cuisine; and spicy, hot dishes with a wide range of flavourings feature Sichuan cuisine. In recent years, features of cuisine in Beijing, Xinjiang, Yunnan, the northeast and other parts of China have also produced a lot of special dishes of their own.

Shan zhen hai wei refers to delicacies from both the land and the sea. The composition of *ba zhen* (eight rare delicacies), though mentioned in one ancient book, has been the subject of argument for years. According to current saying, there are three sets of *ba zhen*: the top *ba zhen*, the middle *ba zhen* and the lower *ba zhen*, all including the most delicious and nourishing food that one could possibly think of.

97. 面条是如何演变产生的？

面条在中国已有两千多年的历史了。它的起源可追溯到东汉时期。东汉桓帝（刘志，公元147～167年）时，尚书崔寔在他所著《四民月令》一书中就提到“水溲饼”。据考证，“水溲饼”即是最早的水煮无馅面食，亦即中国面条的先驱。到公元3世纪的三国时代，出现了“汤饼”。汤饼类似后世的片儿汤。以后，“汤饼”泛指各种水煮无馅面食。南北朝（公元420～581年）时，出现了“水引面”，《齐民要术》记载了这种面食的制作方法。即先将面用水和好，然后用手将和好的面弄成筷子粗细的条，一尺一断，放入盘中用水浸，再把条弄薄如韭菜叶一般，用沸水煮熟，就是水引面。水引面看来已近似于现在人们吃的面条了。

唐代（公元618～907年），宫廷中每到冬天要造“汤饼”，夏天要做“冷淘”，“冷淘”就类似于现在的凉拌面。到了北宋（公元960～1127年），面条的花样增多，并且有了各种地方风味的面条，当时的面条已经是长条的了。据史书记载，南宋（公元1127～1279年）时期，面条已成了普通百姓家常吃的食品。元代（公元1271～1368年）、明代（公元1368～1644年）和清代（公元1644～1911年）的面条更是丰富多彩，品种繁多。不仅可以煮着吃，还可以煎、炒。据说，西方著名的“通心面”就是在元代马可·波罗从中国带回去的制面技术上加以改造而制成的。

经过1000多年的发展，中国面条的制作逐渐形成了擀、拉、抻、切和压及煮、炸、蒸等多种方法。现在人们吃的面条多为机器制作，但仍然可以吃到手工制的面条。

97. How Did Chinese Noodles Originate

Noodles in China have a history of more than 2000 years. Its origin can be dated back to the Eastern Han Dynasty (25—220 A.D.). During the reign of Emperor Huan (147—167 A.D.) of the Eastern Han Dynasty, one of the ministers, Cui Shi, mentioned *shuisoubing* in his book *Si Min Yue Ling* (*Monthly Ordinances for the Four Classes of People*), which was said to be the earliest boiled wheat food without fillings, the predecessor of the Chinese noodles. In the 3rd century A.D. of the Three Kingdoms Period, *tangbing* appeared, which resembles the "noodle flakes soup" of later times. Thereafter, *tangbing* was a name for various kinds of boiled wheat food without fillings. In the Northern and Southern Dynasties (420—581 A.D.), *shuiyin* noodles appeared. The way to cook it was recorded in the first book on Chinese agriculture

Qimin Yaoshu (*Important Arts for the People's Welfare*). Firstly, mix the flour with water to make the dough. Secondly, make the dough into chopstick-sized strips about 33cm long, and then soak them in water. Thirdly, make the strips as thin as the leaves of Chinese chives. And finally, boil them. *Shuiyin* noodles sound very similar to the noodles people have nowadays.

In the Tang Dynasty (618—907 A.D.), *tangbing* was cooked in winter and *lengtao* was cooked in summer for the imperial family. *Lengtao* was similar to today's cold noodles in sauce. In the Northern Song Dynasty (960—1127 A.D.), there was an increase in the variety and local flavor of noodles, and its shape was long stripes. In the Southern Song Dynasty (1127—1279 A.D.), noodles had become a common food for the ordinary people. There were even more varieties of noodles in the Yuan (1271—1368 A.D.), Ming (1368—1644 A.D.) and Qing (1644—1911A.D.) dynasties, boiled as well as fried. It is said that the well-known macaroni in the West was made on the basis of Chinese noodles which were introduced by Marco Polo in the Yuan Dynasty, and the way to cook it is a simple improvement based on the Chinese style.

Over the past one thousand years, different ways of making Chinese noodles have been evolved, e.g. rolling, pulling, cutting and extruding. There have also been different ways of cooking the noodles, such as boiling, frying and steaming. Most of the noodles people eat nowadays are made by machines, but hand-made noodles are still available.

98. 中国的传统武术是如何起源的？其中的太极拳有什么特点？

中国传统武术的起源，与古代人们渔猎生活及其后部落间的战争有很大关系。在与野兽搏斗中，人们逐渐培养了投掷石块、发射石镞和徒手格斗的技巧，后来就发展成器械和徒手两部分。相传在周朝（约公元前 1100 ~ 前 256 年）以前，人们在闲暇时头戴牛角、互相撞抵为戏，称为蚩尤戏。西周（公元前 1100 ~ 前 771 年）称为角力，秦朝（公元前 221 ~ 前 206 年）称为角抵。另外，有些人模仿动物活动姿态，伸展筋骨、活动血脉，称为“导引”。相传汉朝（公元前 206 ~ 公元 220 年）末年著名外科医生华佗在古代导引法的基础上，创编了“五禽戏”。通过仿效虎、鹿、熊、猿、鹤五种动物不同特点的活动，达到增长力气、活动关节、流通血脉的目的。以上是徒手武术和保健武术的起始。

从器械方面来看，中国在周朝以前就有了弓箭，其他武器还有矛、戈、戟等。商朝（公元前 1600 ~ 前 1100 年）开始有剑，到西周初步流行。

唐朝（公元 618 ~ 907 年）开始的武举制度，使习武的青年日渐增多。宋朝（公元 960 ~ 1279 年）以后，武术逐渐分为不同流派，各有成套的拳路和器械套路，如太极拳、太极剑、形意拳、八卦掌、通背拳、少林拳和少林棍等。

太极拳是中国众多拳术中的一种。关于这种拳的创始人有几种说法。其中一种说法是明朝（公元 1368 ~ 1644 年）武当道士张三丰。清朝乾隆（公元 1736 ~ 1796 年）年间，山西王宗岱以《易经》中太极阴阳之说阐述这套拳路的原理，并著《太极拳论》，太极拳由此定名。太极拳的流派比较多，影响较大的有：陈（王廷）式太极、杨（露禅）式太极、吴（鑑泉）式太极、武（高襄）式太极和孙（禄堂）式太极。但是以上各派基本手法和步法是一致的。太极拳动作柔和缓慢、贯串圆活，要求练时思想集中，呼吸和动作配合，做到深、长、匀、静。长期坚持练习可以在促进气血流通、改善内脏器机能方面收到功效，所以不仅在中国流行，不少外国人也乐于学习。

98. What Is the Origin of Traditional Chinese Martial Arts? What Are the Characteristics of *Taijiquan*?

The origin of traditional Chinese martial arts is closely connected with fishing and hunting of ancient people and their intertribal fights. Through hunting big game, ancient Chinese people gradually developed stone throwing, stone-arrowhead shooting, and bare-handed fighting skills. Later on, these skills developed into weapon fighting and bare-handed fighting. Legends say that before the Zhou Dynasty (c. 1100—256 B.C.), there had been a game called *chiyou* in which people butted each other with ox horns on their heads. Besides, some people stretched their limbs to activate the blood circulation in their bodies by imitating the gestures of animals. The noted doctor Hua Tuo of the Han Dynasty (206 B.C.—220 A.D.) invented a game called "five-bird-and-beast game" by imitating the gestures of the tiger, deer, bear, ape, and crane with a view to increasing strength, limbering up the joints, and activating the blood flow. This is regarded as the beginning of bare-handed martial arts and health-care martial arts.

Weapons such as bows, arrows, spears, knives and halberds had existed long before the Zhou Dynasty. Swords were created during the Shang Dynasty (1600—1100 B.C.) and became popular during the Western Zhou Dynasty.

During the Tang Dynasty (618—907 A.D.), the imperial examination system was introduced to select military personnel. Then, a growing number of young people engaged themselves in practising martial arts. After the Song Dynasty (960—1279 A.D.), different schools of martial arts appeared, each with a complete set of skills in Chinese boxing and weapon fighting. They include: *Taijiquan*, *Taiji* Sword, *Shaolinquan*, *Shaolin* Cudgel, etc.

Taijiquan is one of the Chinese boxings. As to its founder, there are different stories. Zhang Sanfeng, a Taoist in the Ming Dynasty (1368—1644 A.D.), is regarded as the founder in one of these stories. During the reign of Emperor Qianlong (1736—1796 A.D.) of the Qing Dynasty, in his book *Taijiquan Lun* (*On Taijiquan*), Wang Zongyue from Shanxi Province expounded the tenets of *Taijiquan* on the basis of the *Taiji* "*yin* and *yang*" (the positive and negative forces) theory from *Yi Jing* (*The Book of Changes*). Thereafter, *Taijiquan* was so named. Among the many schools of *Taijiquan*, the most influential include Chen Wangting's, Yang Luchan's, Wu Jianquan's, Wu Gaoxiang's and Sun Lutang's. However, the basic skills of the above schools are nearly the same. *Taijiquan* is a gentle, slow and complete exercise. In practising *Taijiquan*, one is required to concentrate his mind and adjust his breath to his gestures. Persistence in practising *Taijiquan* can facilitate the movement of the vital energy and the blood and improve the function of one's internal organs. Thus, *Taijiquan* is popular not only among the Chinese, but among foreigners as well.

99. 人们有时谈到“十八般武艺”，指的是什么？中国古代兵器是怎样发展的？

“十八般武艺样样精通”这句话是旧时用来形容一个人武艺高强，各种长短兵器都使用得很熟练的意思。也有说成“十八般兵器”的。

据说这一种说法最早出现在宋朝（公元960～1279年）。南宋华岳编的《翠微南征录》中，记载了“武艺一十有八，而弓为第一”。而其渊源，可能是在唐朝武则天（公元690～705年）设立武举制度，考试科目设有各种武艺，后来归纳成“十八般武艺”的。

对于哪些是“十八般武艺”，说法不完全一致。一种比较普遍的说法是：刀枪剑戟，斧钺钩叉，镋棍槊棒，鞭锏锤抓，拐子流星。中国古代的兵器当然不止十八种，这里只是列举了一些人们手中常用的兵器。

中国古代的兵器脱胎于新石器时代的工具。新石器时代的先民为了生活和狩猎的需要，制作了石斧、石刀等。随着部落兼并战斗出现，兵器也就发展起来了。中国早期出现的武器，以弓箭、戈、矛、刀、剑为主。弓和箭最早据说出现在传说中的黄帝时代。原始的弓箭制作比较粗糙，弓身用坚韧的树枝，弓弦用动物的皮、筋或植物纤维。商朝（约公元前1600～约前1100年）开始有多种铜箭镞。随后又发展成带有机括的弩。比起弓来，弩的射程远，命中率高，杀伤力也更强。商、周时期，戈、矛和剑也都开始使用了。《诗经·无衣》中便有“王于兴师，脩我戈矛。”“王于兴师，脩我矛戟。”的诗句。到春秋、战国时期（公元前770～前221年），兵器的种类和质量都有很大改进。湖北江陵在1965年出土的越王句践剑，虽然经过2000多年，仍然闪光锋利。当时攻城已经出现云梯，并且发展了马拉战车。屈原在《国殇》中对激烈的战争场面作了生动的描绘：“操吴戈兮被犀甲，车错毂兮短兵接。旌蔽日兮敌若云，矢交坠兮士争先。”意思是：手持锋利的吴戈，身穿犀牛皮甲。战车轮轴相错，短兵相接。旌旗遮住日光，敌人重重如乌云。箭矢纷纷落下，士兵个个奋勇向前。1974年发现的秦始皇陵兵马俑坑，更是大规模地展现了秦朝（公元前221～前206年）官兵全副武装、牵马奋战的雄姿。

99. What Are the *Shiba Ban Wuyi* (Skills in Wielding the Eighteen Kinds of Weapons) that Chinese People Often Talk about? How Did the Ancient Chinese Weapons Develop?

The saying *shiba ban wuyi* was used in ancient times to describe a person's skills in using each and every one of the eighteen kinds of weapons.

It was said that the saying first appeared in the Song Dynasty (960—1279 A.D.). In a book of the Song Dynasty, there was such a saying: "There are eighteen kinds of weapons. Among them, the bow is the most important one." However, the saying might have originated in the Tang Dynasty (618—907 A.D.) from the imperial examination for military personnel, in which the skills of using various kinds of weapons were tested. These skills were later on generalized into eighteen martial art skills.

As to what the eighteen kinds of weapons are, there are different stories. One of the widely accepted stories says that the eighteen kinds of weapons include knife, spear, sword, halberd, axe, battle-axe, hook, fork, *tang* (long-handled sharp fork), cudgel, lance, stick, whip, *jian* (long whip with a handle), hammer, cratch, crook, and shooting stars (long iron chain with two iron balls fixed on it). Surely, there were many more kinds of weapons in ancient China. The eighteen kinds of weapons as mentioned here were just the commonly-used ones.

The ancient weapons were developed out of tools in the Neolithic Age. Needs of living and hunting made the forefathers at that time create stone axes and stone knives. Later on, as intertribal annexation war occurred, weapons were developed. The early weapons in China were mainly bows and arrows, spears, dagger-axes, knives, and swords. It was said that bows and arrows first appeared in the age of the Yellow Emperor. The original bows and arrows were so crudely made that the main parts of the bow were made of branches of trees and the bowstrings were made of animal hide or tendon or even plant fibre. Various kinds of bronze arrowheads appeared during the Shang Dynasty (c.1600—1100 B.C.). Afterwards, device-operated crossbows were invented. Compared with bows, crossbows had a wider range, higher percentage of hits, and greater accuracy and power. During the Shang and Zhou dynasties, dagger-axes, spears, and swords also came into use. In *Shi Jing* (*The Book of Songs*), the following words can be seen: "The king is going to launch a war, please make dagger-axes and spears for me." "The king is going to launch a war, please make spears and halberds for me." Up to the Spring and Autumn and the Warring States periods (770—221 B.C.), the number of weapon types had increased and the quality improved. Gou Jian's sword unearthed in Jianglin, Hubei Province in 1965 still looks shiny and is fairly sharp and bright though it has been buried underground for more than 2000 years. Scaling ladders were used then in taking towns and fortresses, and later on, horse-drawn chariots were also used in wars. Qu Yuan, the most well-known patriotic poet in China who lived in that period, made a vivid description of fierce wars in his poem *Guo Shang* (*The Ode to the Fallen*). The terra-cotta warriors and figures of the first emperor of the Qin Dynasty discovered in 1974 show well-equipped officers and soldiers of the Qin Dynasty (221—206 B.C.) and their heroic postures.

100. 中国五岳的来历如何？泰山为什么独尊五岳？

“岳”在春秋时期(公元前770～前476年)前原是掌管大山的官吏职称。尧(传说中父系氏族社会后期部落联盟领袖)时分掌四方外事的部落首领就叫“岳”,后来把主管方岳的官吏与岳官驻地的大山名称统一起来,便出现了代表四方大山的“四岳”。春秋产生了“五行”之说,战国(公元前475～前221年)时颇为流行。由于阴阳学家邹衍、邹奭等人的大力宣扬,“五德始终论”越来越盛,“五岳”之说才应运而生。

“五岳”即东岳泰山、西岳华山、南岳衡山、中岳嵩山、北岳恒山。在五岳之中,泰山并不是最高,它次于恒山、华山,仅占第三位;在全国的大山中高度更是数不上。但它为什么成为赫赫于古今的“五岳之长”、“五岳独尊”呢?这得从泰山的地理环境和原始宗教谈起。

泰山崛起于华北大平原东侧的齐鲁古国,东临烟波浩淼的大海,西靠源远流长的黄河,南有汶、泗、淮三水,凌驾于齐鲁丘陵之上,相对高度达1300多米,与周围的平原、丘陵形成高低、大小的强烈对比,在视觉上显得格外高大。泰山群峰起伏,主峰突兀,山脉绵亘200余公里,基础宽大,形体集中。基础宽大便产生安稳感,所谓“稳如泰山”、“重如泰山”、“泰山压顶”等名言,正是上述自然特征在人们的精神上与心理上的反映。纵览东部沿海广大区域的地理形势,泰山居高临下,成为万里原野上的“东天一柱”。“中有岱岳”,即说明泰山居中,为天下的中心。这里气候温润、土地肥沃,成为古人类繁衍生息的中心地带及古文化的重要发源地。几千年来,这里一直是东方政治、经济、文化的中心。夏初(约公元前21世纪),禹分九州,其中冀、豫、青、兖、徐五州均在此;战国七雄时,这里有六国之都。泰山成了东方文明的代表,伟大庄重的象征。

东方是太阳出生的地方,古人即认为是万物交替、初春发生之地。按“五行”东方属于木,按“五常”为仁,按“四时”为春;在《周易》八卦中属震,在“二十八星宿”中为苍龙。“东(東)”字属会意字,此字从木,日在其中。“木”字在甲骨文中与“桑”字通用,故有“日出扶桑”之说。“仁”是天地大德;“春”是万物更生;“震”与“苍龙”则是帝王出生的腾飞之地。于是,泰山一变而为吉祥山、神灵之宅、紫气之源、万物之所。因此,泰山独尊五岳就不容置疑了。

100. What Are the Origins of *Wu Yue* (the Five Famous Mountains)? Why Is Mt. Tai Placed at the Head of *Wu Yue*?

Yue was originally a title for officials who took care of mountains in the Spring and Autumn Period (770—476 B.C.). During the reign of Emperor Yao, the tribal heads were called *yue*. Later on, *yue* became a unified term for both the officials who took charge of mountains and the mountains in the regions of their responsibility. Thus the term *Si Yue* came out to represent the big mountains in the four directions. The doctrine of the five elements (metal, wood, water, fire and earth) appeared in the Spring and Autumn Period and became prevalent in the Warring States Period (475—221 B.C.). Vigorously advocated by Zou Yan and Zou Shi, two *yin-yang* (the positive and negative forces) masters, the theory about the persistency of the five elements became more and more prevalent. Under this cicumstances, the term *Wu Yue* became popular and gradually replaced the term *Si Yue*.

Wu Yue refers to Mt. Tai (situated in the eastern part of China), Mt. Hua (situated in the western part of China), Mt. Heng (situated in the southern part of China), Mt. Song (situated in central China), and Mt. Heng (situated in the northern part of China). Mt. Tai is not the highest among the five mountains, instead, it is the third highest following Mt. Heng (situated in the northern part of China) and Mt. Hua. Its height is no comparison to that of other big mountains. Then, why has it been taken as the head of *Wu Yue* in China for such a long time? The answer lies in its geographical location and the primitive religion in China.

Mt. Tai is situated in the old state of Qi and the state of Lu on the North China Plain, with the sea to its east, the Yellow River to its west and some other rivers to its south. Standing high above the hills in the area, with a height of more than 1300 meters, Mt. Tai contrasts sharply with the plain and hills around it. Visually, it looks extremely high and great. Since its ranges run more than 200 kilometers and it has a very wide base, Mt. Tai looks very solid and steady. Idioms like *wen ru Taishan* (as stable as Mt. Tai), *zhong ru Taishan* (as heavy as Mt. Tai), and *Taishan ya ding* (bear down on one with the weight of Mt. Tai) represent a reflection of the basic features of Mt. Tai on Chinese people, both spiritual and psychological. In view of the geography of the coast of east China, Mt. Tai, standing high above others, looks like a pillar under the eastern sky. The idiom *zhong you Daiyue* means that Mt. Tai is located in the central of the world. With its mild climate and rich soil, this area was the home for the ancients and an important origin of ancient culture. For millennia, this area has been the center for the oriental politics, economics, and culture. At the beginning of the Xia Dynasty (21st centary B.C.), China was divided into nine states. Among them, five were located in this region. During the Warring States Period, there were six capitals of those states here. Mt. Tai has become the representative of oriental civilization and a symbol of greatness and graveness.

The east is the place where the sun rises. The ancient people at that time believed that the east was the place where all creatures were born. According to the theory of the five elements, the east should be wood; according to the five virtues, the east is *ren* (benevolence); according to the four seasons, the east is spring; in *Yi Jing* (*The Book of Changes*), the east is *zhen* (thunder) of the eight diagrams; in the 28 constellations, the east is the dragon in the sky; and the Chinese character 東 (east) is an ideograph which is composed of 木 (wood) with 日 (sun) in it. *Ren* is the way of the universe; spring is the origin of all creatures; *zhen* and the dragon in the sky represent the places where the emperors were born and grew up. Therefore, Mt. Tai became a lucky and sacred mountain. No wonder it is respected as the head of *Wu Yue*.

附录
Appendix

中国历史年代简表
A Brief Chinese Chronology

夏 Xia Dynasty			c.2100 ~ c.1600 B.C.
商 Shang Dynasty			c.1600 ~ c.1100 B.C.
周 Zhou Dynasty	西周 Western Zhou Dynasty		c.1100 ~ 771 B.C.
	东周 Eastern Zhou Dynasty		770 ~ 256 B.C.
	春秋 Spring and Autumn Period		770 ~ 476 B.C.
	战国 Warring States		475 ~ 221 B.C.
秦 Qin Dynasty			221 ~ 206 B.C.
汉 Han Dynasty	西汉 Western Han		206 B.C. ~ 24 A.D.
	东汉 Eastern Han		25 ~ 220 A.D.
三国 Three kingdoms	魏 Wei		220 ~ 265
	蜀汉 Shu Han		221 ~ 263
	吴 Wu		222 ~ 280
西晋 Western Jin Dynasty			265 ~ 316
东晋 Eastern Jin Dynasty			317 ~ 420
南北朝 Northern and Southern Dynasties	南朝 Southern Dynasties	宋 Song	420 ~ 479
		齐 Qi	479 ~ 502
		梁 Liang	502 ~ 557
		陈 Chen	557 ~ 589
	北朝 Northern Dynasties	北魏 Northern Wei	386 ~ 534
		东魏 Eastern Wei	534 ~ 550
		北齐 Northern Qi	50 ~ 577
		西魏 Western Wei	535 ~ 556
		北周 Northern Zhou	557 ~ 581
隋 Sui Dynasty			581 ~ 618
唐 Tang Dynasty			618 ~ 907
五代 Five Dynasties	后梁 Later Liang		907 ~ 923
	后唐 Later Tang		923 ~ 936
	后晋 Later Jin		936 ~ 946
	后汉 Later Han		947 ~ 950
	后周 Later Zhou		951 ~ 960
宋 Song Dynasty	北宋 Northern Song Dynasty		960 ~ 1127
	南宋 Southern Song Dynasty		1127 ~ 1279
辽 Liao Dynasty			916 ~ 1125
金 Jin Dynasty			1115 ~ 1234
元 Yuan Dynasty			1271 ~ 1368
明 Ming Dynasty			1368 ~ 1644
清 Qing Dynasty			1644 ~ 1911
中华民国 Republic of China			1912 ~ 1949
中华人民共和国 People's Republic of China			1949 ~

图书在版编目（CIP）数据

中国文化释疑：汉英对照/金乃逯主编．

－北京：北京语言文化大学出版社，1999.7 印。

ISBN 7－5619－0726－5

Ⅰ．中…

Ⅱ．金…

Ⅲ．文化－中国－对照读物－汉、英

Ⅳ．H319.4：G

中国版本图书馆 CIP 数据核字（1999）第 09615 号

责任印制：乔学军

出版发行：北京语言文化大学出版社

（北京海淀区学院路 15 号　邮政编码 100083）

印　　刷：北京北林印刷厂

经　　销：全国新华书店

版　　次：1999 年 7 月第 1 版　1999 年 7 月第 1 次印刷

开　　本：787 毫米×1092 毫米　1/20　印张：14.8　彩页：2

字　　数：300 千字　印数：0001－4 000

书　　号：ISBN 7－5619－0726－5/G·9934

定　　价：30.00 元